Computer-Based Data Analysis

Nelson-Hall Series in Psychology

Consulting Editor: Stephen Worchel
Texas A&M University

Computer-Based Data Analysis

Using SPSS^x in the Social and Behavioral Sciences

David Rowland
Valparaiso University

Daniel Arkkelin
Valparaiso University

Larry Crisler
Millikin University

Nelson-Hall Publishers/Chicago

Project Editor: Dorothy Anderson
Copy Editor: Ro Sila
Cover Painting: *Black Cantilever* by Judith Nahill

Library of Congress Cataloging-in-Publication Data

Rowland, David (David L.)
  Computer-based data analysis: using SPSS^x in the social and
behavioral sciences / David Rowland, Daniel Arkkelin, Larry Crisler.
    p. cm.
  Includes bibliographical references and index.
  ISBN 0-8304-1181-X
  1. SPSS X (Computer program) 2. Social sciences—Statistical
methods—Computer programs. I. Arkkelin, Daniel. II. Crisler,
Larry. III. Title.
  HA32.R68 1991
  300'.01'5195—dc20   90-38020
                                                          CIP

Manufactured in the United States of America

10 9 8 7 6 5 4 3 2

The paper used in this book meets the minimum requirements of American National Standard for Information Sciences—Permanence of Paper for Printed Library Materials, ANSI Z39.48-1984.

Contents

Preface

There is no doubt that computer statistical packages provide scientists and technicians with a relatively easy way of dealing with complex data analyses, and that the use of computer-based data analysis has increased dramatically in recent years. For these reasons, the understanding and use of statistical packages at the undergraduate level is becoming an increasingly common goal in courses on statistics and experimental methods. We have found that presently available introductions to statistical packages lack one of two important features: either they provide little or no background on computers, computing, and data analysis for the beginning student, or they lack the step-by-step explanations necessary for actually implementing a particular package and interpreting the resulting output of statistical procedures. We believe that this book fills these gaps by providing an easily accessible introduction to SPSS^x in the context of a hypothetical research project, in addition to providing exercises that give the student "hands-on" experience with analyzing the data from this project.

The text begins with an explanation of how computers operate and how they can be used to solve problems in the social sciences, health sciences, and business. A discussion follows which is devoted to developing an understanding of programmed statistical packages in general, and SPSS^x in particular. With this background, students are then introduced to a hypothetical research project on leadership effectiveness and sex-role stereotypes. This project was carefully designed to incorporate variables of interest to students in psychology, sociology and business. The variables selected also permitted illustration of a wide range of statistical procedures with SPSS^x on the same data set. We present the "data" from this study and provide the detailed instructions for creating a computer data file and accessing SPSS^x. (As with any manual of this type which deals with a variety of computer systems, the instructor should have a working knowledge of the computer operating system to be used—this information is normally required to operate SPSS^x on any system.)

We begin the data processing with several procedures that enable simple frequency distributions and the creation of new variables from existing ones. The remaining chapters introduce the student to a wide range of SPSS^x routines. Emphasis is placed on the conceptual understanding and interpretation of each statistic. Here also, step-by-step instructions and examples are provided with each new procedure introduced. They are all done in the context of the same leadership project data file to encourage continuity and a sense of an unfolding of the "results" of the project. Sample SPSS^x printouts and accompanying explanations are provided with each chapter, and each concludes with exercises for the student to complete involving an analysis similar to that presented in the chapter, but on a different set of variables in the data file. The exercises in chapters 10 through 14 generally assume a higher level of computer competence than those given early on. Optional sections within several chapters introduce more advanced level procedures. Two supplemental appendices provide information on coding the data for entry into the computer and on constructing scales from items on a questionnaire. We believe that this book is appropriate for both students with no previous experience with computers as well as non-beginners. In short, this book provides a "user-friendly" introduction to SPSS^x in the context of an interesting research project, and gives students practice with the basic tools needed to conduct computer-based statistical analyses.

The book is designed to be useful as either a supplement to statistics and research methods texts in such areas as the social and natural sciences, health sciences, and business and education, or as a stand-alone text in applications-oriented courses such as laboratories or practicum experiences. The material in the chapters introducing statistical procedures is self-contained and complete, but it is important that all students read Chapters 1, 2, 3, 4, 5, and 7 as these cover material necessary to the general understanding of SPSS^x, the data file, the variables in the data file, and the general procedure for data analysis. Beyond this restriction, however, the instructor is free to use any other chapters in any order s/he desires. For those instructors who might choose not to have students complete the exercises relevant to the sex-role and leadership project, each chapter also includes separate, self-contained, optional exercises. These exercises include small data sets to which the statistical procedures presented in that chapter can be applied. These exercises increase the flexibility of the text, and also could be used to reinforce learning of the statistical procedures when assigned in conjunction with the exercises relevant to the leadership project.

Finally, while most parts of the manual are largely self-directed and self-explanatory, there are times when it would be helpful for students to receive additional hands-on or classroom guidance from the instructor. This is particularly true when students need to make the transition from instructions in the manual to a procedure on their local computer system. We have found that scheduling two or three computer lab sessions can reduce students' anxieties greatly and facilitate their learning accordingly. For example, a hands-on session dealing with the local operating system and the procedure for creating and editing files has resulted in a quick understanding of the basics. A short review of the research project (Chapter 5) and each of the variables in the project makes interpretation of the results in subsequent chapters both easier and more meaningful. After these introductory sessions, however, we have found that students can successfully complete the remaining chapters with minimal guidance.

The authors would like to thank Ronald Warncke for his interest in this manual and Stephen Ferrara and Dorothy Anderson of Nelson-Hall for seeing it to completion. Special thanks are due to Douglas Kleckner for assistance in creating and testing the data file and to all the students in our statistics and research methods classes who have given us useful feedback on the book.

1 Computers: A Brief Introduction

In this chapter we discuss:

- some basics about the computer
- differences between software and hardware
- input and output devices
- files and directories

1.1 Why Use Computers?

In general, computers offer several advantages over the more traditional methods of information-processing (e.g., the human brain, calculators, etc.), and although computers cannot actually think, they can be extremely useful in relieving us from certain types of mental activities. For one, computers work at superhuman speeds—in computing, work time is measured in thousandths of seconds or less. Many jobs that require several hours of computer time may require days, even months, of "human" time. In fact, some tasks, because of their complexity and length, simply could not be performed without the help of the computer. Second, computers do not make mistakes. So-called computer errors are usually nothing more than human errors that are attributed to the computer. The computer is merely doing what it has been programmed to do, rather than what it *should* have been programmed to do. (Mechanical problems tend to be quickly apparent, just as when the battery is losing power in your calculator.) Finally, the computer never tires of tedious or repetitive tasks. Ever

This chapter has been coauthored by Gregory Hume, M.S., Computer Science, Valparaiso University.

have to balance several months of checkwriting in your checkbook? As you know, even these relatively simple tasks can end up being rather arduous, especially if your balance and the bank's balance don't match. Could you imagine how tedious the bank's job would be if its staff had to perform all the calculations for the checking accounts by hand, or with adding-machines!

Electronically, computers are sophisticated pieces of machinery. But the computer is basically just a tool, very much like a table saw is a tool. A person may need to understand the makeup of the tool in order to use it effectively, and some training may be required if the person really wants to master its use. Both a table saw and a computer can be misused, and both can be left unused in favor of more primitive, although less intimidating, tools. Both are also just one of several tools typically used to complete a project—a carpenter also may use tape measures, drills, and planes, while a social scientist may use the additional tools of psychological tests, surveys, recording devices, and counters.

1.2   A Word about "Computer Phobia"

Computers often intimidate people who have never used them. A beginner may be fearful of "breaking" the computer, making errors, ruining important files, or may just be totally confused. If you're a beginner, you will encounter many frustrating situations, but if you hang in there, someday you will look back on these situations with amusement. Even if you have advanced this far in your academic career without ever having used a computer, you can still benefit now by learning about computer usage. In this manual, for example, you will learn to use a statistical software package (we'll define that later), and the skills you learn here can be carried over to many other applications. All you need is some instruction, computer facilities, and determination.

If you're apprehensive at first, you're normal. When you first climbed onto a bicycle seat or sat behind the wheel of a car, your heart probably started to beat a little faster. But now, driving has become second nature and you could probably not fall off a bike if you tried! As you begin to use the computer, remember that you will not understand everything all at once. When you are confused, ask a question. Your questions usually will have simple answers. Your instructor and computer operator are obvious sources of help, and many of your classmates who have had some computing experience also will be glad to help (you'll find that some like to demonstrate how much they know!). Your questions will most likely be those of a typical beginner, so don't worry about sounding "stupid."

1.3   What Does a Computer Do?

We already stated that a computer is a tool. What does this tool work on? Is a computer really analogous to a table saw? Let's take a minute to examine this analogy a little more closely. The craftsman uses the table saw to cut wood; he or she starts with a plain, rectangular piece and cuts it to some specified size and shape. The final product is still wood, but it may now begin to resemble something quite different. For example, it may look like the side of a cabinet. Thus, the table saw transformed a "raw" piece of wood into a "processed" object, and this object may now be used with other processed objects to produce a finished product.

A computer performs a very similar function, but on a different kind of material. A computer starts with the raw material of *data* and produces a transformed product in the form of *information*. This is a very simplistic view, as computers can perform a wide range of functions. However, the processing of data into information represents the traditional role of computers, and this is exactly what you will be doing with the computer when you learn to use a statistical software package.

Before we begin to describe this process, some definitions need to be made. As you will see, there is an overwhelming amount of jargon associated with the use of computers, but to work with computers effectively, it's necessary to learn some of the terminology. We will explain some of the more important terms in this first chapter.

1.3a   Data

Data is a collection of unprocessed symbols. For our purposes, these symbols typically consist of a series of numbers representing scores or values on some variable. Data is "raw" in the same sense that a piece of wood is raw. Because it is unprocessed, raw data does not usually have immediate meaning. Consider the very simple example of the isolated list of numbers in column *a* of Table 1.1. With no organization, headings, or explanations, these data have no immediate meaning, nor will they have meaning until something further is done with the numbers.

1.3b   Information

Now consider the numbers in column *b* of Table 1.1. Now that headings have been added, the numbers organized, and the average computed, the numbers take on meaning. We now have **information**. Data was processed (not necessarily with a computer) in that it was given a context, a label, and a summary, and the result is information.

Table 1.1   The Difference Between Data (*a*) and Information (*b*)

a	b This week's high temperatures
61	Mon 71
71	Tue 73
68	Wed 68
65	Thu 61
65	Fri 65
	—
	Ave 67.6

The data in column *a* of Table 1.1 is an example of **input** and the information in column *b* of Table 1.1 is an example of **output**. Using a computer to transform data into information is called **data processing**. Simply illustrated:

INPUT ⟶ PROCESSING ⟶ OUTPUT

or

Data ⟶ Computer ⟶ Information

1.4   So How Does the Computer Operate? Bits and Bytes

Computers send and receive information by the transmission of electronic signals. These signals are either "on" or "off" signals and are represented by the numbers 1 and 0 (1 for on, 0 for off). Any one signal is called a **bit**.

The collection of bits used to represent a "character" (e.g., a letter of the alphabet) is called a **byte**. For most computers today, the number of bits in a byte is eight. When the user strikes the uppercase "A" on the keyboard, a series of eight bits is sent to a part of the computer (for now we'll call it the processor) where it can be represented by the byte 01000001. The processor decodes this signal according to a computer code. Most computers use the **ASCII** code, an acronym for American Standard Code for Information Interchange.

As just mentioned, a bit represents one of two possible numbers, either zero or one. A byte, a collection of zeros and ones, is actually a number in the binary number system. To illustrate, the binary number (or byte) 01000001 is equal to the more commonly designated decimal number, 65. Uppercase "A" is the 65th character on the ASCII code so the processor will interpret the above byte as an uppercase "A". The processor then sends the same signal back to the terminal's screen that has just been received from the keyboard. This is called an **echo**. So when you press an "A" on the keyboard, it is converted to bits, but those bits are further processed so that the letter you typed appears on the screen as you enter information.

The above information is sometimes of little immediate use to the user of software packages. It is, however, to your advantage to have some knowledge about the inner workings of a computer just as it is to your advantage to know something about the inner workings of a car. A person can drive a car without any knowledge of the engine, but that person could well spend time and money at the mechanic's shop for unnecessary or trivial repairs. For those who wish to learn more about the technical aspects of computing, most colleges offer a variety of computer literacy courses.

1.5   Why Do Computers Come in So Many Sizes and Shapes?

Computers have traditionally been classified into one of three categories. These are **mainframe** computers, **minicomputers**, and **microcomputers** (sometimes referred to as personal computers, or "PC's"). These classifications have been made according to how fast the computer operates, how much internal memory a computer has, how many people can use the computer at once, the physical size of the computer, and various other factors. There are two problems with this classification scheme. First, computing technology has evolved to the point where it is difficult to precisely categorize a computer by traditional measures. For example, traditionally, mainframe computers could have several users at once whereas microcomputers could have only one; minicomputers were too large to move about whereas microcomputers were very portable. Now, however, we find microcomputers that several individuals can use simultaneously, and minicomputers that are quite portable.

The second problem with traditional classifications is that they are not very useful to the typical user. Most users do not need to know the difference between a mainframe and minicomputer. However, it is important for the user to know the difference between a multi-user and single-user computer, and for that reason, we will classify computers into one of these two categories.

Multi-user computers are machines that many people can use at the same time. The most obvious feature of a multi-user computer is that a user must obtain authorization to use it. A multi-user computer requires a user to **"log on"** to the computer, which requires a user identification name and a password. Many large statistical software packages, such as the one that we will discuss in this manual, are set up on multi-user systems. If you will be using a multi-user computer, your instructor will guide you through the procedure of logging on.

A **single-user** computer, a machine that only one person can use at any one time, does not generally require a log on process. There is an equivalent procedure called **booting up**. Software packages that are available on multi-user systems may sometimes be scaled down in size for use on a single-user system. If you are going to use a single-user machine, your instructor will guide you through the process of booting up.

1.6   What Is Computer Hardware?

The **computer** is an electronic device used to execute specific instructions. Computer **hardware** refers to any physical component of the computer or components connected to the computer. This includes the frame, the boards, and all the wires, nuts, and bolts. With this definition in mind, we will now look at some of the components of the computer and their relation to the overall process of computing.

1.6a   Input and Output Devices

An **input device** provides a mechanism for data to be entered into the computer. The most common input device is the **terminal**, which consists of two parts: a **keyboard**, much like a typewriter keyboard, and a **screen**, much like a television screen. This screen is called a **CRT**, an acronym for cathode ray tube. As you will see, in order to input data, there will be a considerable amount of typing involved, and those of you who are not proficient typists may initially feel frustrated and at a real disadvantage. But this is only a slight handicap as it does not take much time to become fairly proficient at two-finger typing. Furthermore, unlike the typewriter, there is a delete key to help fix the many typing mistakes that you're bound to make (the "delete" key will be one of the first keys you'll want to look for when you sit down at the terminal for your first time).

The information that results from the data processing is sent back to the user through an **output device**. The terminal, as well as being an input device, also serves, through the CRT, as a common output device; the other commonly used output device is the **printer**, which produces a copy of the results on paper (called "hard copy").

A typical computing situation might start with a user having access to data, for example, a list of IQ scores. The user communicates with the computer by issuing commands through an input device such as a terminal. By using such commands, the data could be entered at the terminal and

Figure 1.1: User-Computer Interaction for Data Processing

stored in the computer's memory. Then the user might instruct the computer to process the data (perhaps computing a mean IQ through use of a statistical software package) and send the information to an output device where the user can view the results of the processing. Notice that data processing starts and ends with you, the user, at the terminal. Figure 1.1 illustrates several typical steps in data processing along with some of the hardware components that are involved in these steps. As shown, the user enters input data and instructions at the terminal, the computer then processes the data and sends the output information to either the CRT screen at the terminal or a printer, where the user can view the output.

1.6b   The CPU and Internal Memory

While there are other input devices, output devices, and hardware components to a computer, our focus will now turn to what might be called the heart (or brain) of a computer: the **CPU** and **internal memory** (see Figure 1.2).

CPU stands for Central Processing Unit. The CPU is divided into two parts, the ALU and the control unit. The **ALU**, or Arithmetic and Logic Unit, performs all the arithmetic operations of the computer. *Logical* and *relational* operations are also performed by the ALU. Logical operators involve the use of "and," "or," and "not." These operators work much in the same way as one would use these words in normal conversation. The relational operators are "equal," "greater than," "less than," and their converses "not equal," "less than or equal," and "greater than or equal." Together, these arithmetic and logical and relational operations are the only ones that a computer performs. As you come to use computers more, you will agree that they are indeed very simple-minded in what they can do.

The above operations need to be carried out in a controlled and systematic way. This function belongs to the **control unit**, the second component of the CPU. The control unit decodes computer instructions in sequence and delegates the work to the ALU and other hardware components of the computer. The CPU, meaning both the ALU and control unit together, is generally placed on one **chip**. A chip is a piece of silicon that contains literally thousands of electronic circuits. The CPU chip is often called a **processor**. Thus, the CPU is the computer hardware that coordinates and executes processing the raw input data to yield the output information.

Internal memory is that portion of the computer where data are stored. It consists of two parts, ROM and RAM. **ROM** stands for "read only memory," so-named because what is stored in ROM cannot be changed, it can only be "read." On many computers all of the instructions of the operating system are stored in ROM since the operating system of a computer may be updated or changed only very infrequently.

RAM stands for "random access memory." The contents of this portion of memory change constantly during the use of a computer. For example, data that are undergoing analysis are entered into RAM so that various operations can be performed on the data. When the analysis is completed, the memory is erased and becomes available for the next job. Not only data, but entire computer programs may be temporarily stored in RAM as they are being executed.

Figure 1.2: Components of a Typical General Purpose Computer

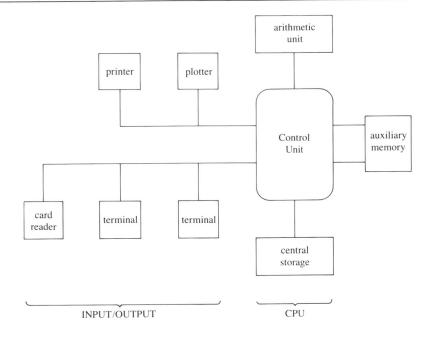

In order to conceptualize how the above hardware components work, consider the numbers that we viewed in Table 1.1. Through the operating system's job control language (we'll define this under "software"), the user instructs that a particular computer program be run. The control unit, in conjunction with ROM, reads a computer program into RAM. The control unit, in conjunction with the computer program instructions which are now in RAM, then directs that the data in Table 1.1, column *a*, be input into RAM. The control unit instructs that the data be transferred back and forth between RAM and the ALU where various operations are performed. Finally, the control unit, in conjunction with the program instructions in RAM and the operating system instructions in ROM, sends the data from RAM to an output device. The result, column *b*, is in the form of usable information.

1.6c Secondary Storage

Any computer has a finite amount of internal memory. Since this memory is designated for use during processing (i.e., when the computer is actually doing something) there is a need for a secondary memory, or storage of information, that is not undergoing immediate processing. The media used most often for this type of storage are disks and tapes. Disks and tapes are often referred to as **secondary** or **auxiliary storage** devices.

1.6c.1 Disks and Disk Drives: Disks come in many different sizes but all disks share some basic characteristics. Disks are round and have circular tracks which make them somewhat analogous to a record album. A **read/write head** on the disk drive, which is somewhat like a stylus on a turntable, transfers data to and from the computer. A major difference between disks and albums is that disks have **sectors**, pie-shaped areas on the disk (see Figure 1.3).

When data are to be accessed, a disk rotates so that the proper sector is under the read/write head. The read/write head moves one-dimensionally in and out to the proper track for scanning. Together, the read/write head and the mechanism to rotate the disk are called the **disk drive**. Multi-user computers (see Section 1.5) generally have a device that contains several disks and read/write heads mounted one on top of another. These devices are called **disk packs**, and they function in the same basic manner as single disks.

With multi-user machines, the user does not generally come into contact with a disk; responsibility for disk operations is typically assumed by computer center personnel. Single-user computers employ disks and drives, but these computers require the user to be responsible for some of the disk operations. A single-user computer generally has one or more

Figure 1.3: Computer Disk Showing a Sector and Track

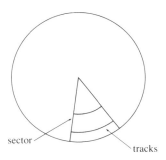

disk drives into which the user inserts a floppy disk. **Floppy disks** are inexpensive, small, portable disks used to store software and data. It is not uncommon for some single-user computers to have a scaled down version of a disk pack called a **hard disk**. Hard disks are much more expensive than floppy disks but offer a greater amount of storage and faster access time.

1.6c.2   Tapes and Drives: Multi-user machines usually use magnetic tape (similar to that found on cassette tapes) as an additional secondary storage device. Tapes operate sequentially, much in the same manner that a music cassette tape operates. In order to access a location on tape, the tape must be wound to that correct location. Accessing data on a tape is called **sequential access** as opposed to the **direct access** of a disk. A tape read/write head is used to transfer data to and from the computer and is housed in a unit called a **tape drive**.

The cumbersome procedure of sequential access makes tape a poor secondary storage device for normal use. Tape is, however, inexpensive and can store large amounts of data, so it is an ideal medium for back-up storage. Tapes are used to transfer large amounts of data from one computer to another, to store a disk's data as insurance against disk damage, and to store data for long periods of time. Large statistical software packages (such as the one we will use) are frequently transferred from the distributor to the computer site on tapes; the content of the tapes is then loaded onto a hard disk for use on multi-user systems. Single-user computers generally do not use tape, but rather rely on floppy disks to perform back-up functions.

You should be aware that disks and tapes require proper handling and care. Because floppy disks and tapes both use magnetized spots to store data, they should not be in close proximity to magnets or electronic devices which generate magnetic fields (e.g., some video monitors, airport metal detectors, etc.).

1.7   How Do You Make the Computer Do What You Want?

Now that we know something about the hardware of the computer, let's talk about how we make the computer process data to produce information. Obviously, we need a way to communicate with the computer, to make it do what we want it to. This basic process is accomplished with the use of software. **Software** is a program or collection of programs used to perform a function. A **program** is a set of specific instructions for the computer to execute. A **software package** refers to the software program, along with other materials such as manuals.

1.7a   Software and Its Use

Software is what makes the computer run, and without it the computer is a useless tool. For our purposes, understanding software and how to use it is really more important than knowing a lot about the technical aspects of computer hardware. However you decide to use the computer, it is the software that enables you to do so. If you want to use the computer to keep track of various business accounts, you need software that allows you to do that. If you want to use the computer for word processing, or data analysis, or producing graphs, you need software that can be used for each different application. Obviously, then, one's knowledge and choice of software is critical to meeting the needs and goals of the user.

Software, of course, can be engineered poorly; and the quality of the software affects the quality of the results in your particular application. As a user of software, you want software that is easy to learn and that protects you from the potentially disastrous results of making "stupid mistakes." But a word of clarification—everyone makes mistakes when using computers: good software helps minimize the likelihood of such mistakes.

1.7b   The Operating System

The first piece of software you must become familiar with is called the **operating system**. The operating system is the main software component of the computer. It is typically stored in ROM, and this is the system in which you are operating when you first "log on" or "boot up" the computer. The operating system has many functions, but the most important from our perspective is that it is the *communication link* between you and the computer. When you want the computer to do something, you use the language provided by the operating system. This language is called the **job control language (JCL)**. The commands that comprise this language (which are typically recognizable words or phrases in the English language) enable you to execute a variety of functions, including creating, accessing, deleting, printing, and reviewing your files. When you want to input data to a computer, you instruct the computer, through the operating system's job control language, to execute a specific program which allows you to enter the data.

Different computers may have different operating systems, and each operating system has a different job control language. Although these job control languages are similar, they do differ from one computer to the next. So you will eventually have to learn the language that is specific to your computer system. But once again, take heart. Once you have learned to use one operating system, you will find it easier to learn others. Your instructor or computer center can provide you with some basics about the operating system and the job control language you will use. In other words, the computer skills you acquire here will be transferable to future situations.

1.8 How Do You Keep Track of Your Information in a Computer? Files and Directories

Even if you have never used a computer, you have an intuitive notion of what a file is. For example, you may think of papers that are put in a file folder and then stored in a file cabinet. Computer files store information, very much like paper files do. Although the definition may vary slightly according to the different perspectives of computer users, a **computer file** is basically a collection of characters stored together. If you have used a word processor, you have already created files to store texts, such as term papers and letters. Our most common use of files will be to store input data, programs (which will then be executed and analyzed), and to read output to a file consisting of the results of the processing.

The contents of files are generally stored on disks (secondary storage). One of the major responsibilities of an operating system is to manage files by interacting with both the user and disks. Some of the disk responsibilities of the operating system include the maintenance of file names, of file dates, of locations of files on disks, and so on.

1.8a *Editors and Word Processors: What's the Difference?*

There are primarily two ways that a user can create a file: using a word processor and using an editor. A **word processor** is a software package designed to be responsible for the entry of text. A typical word processor also will "format" text, that is, adjust margins, center headings, allow for different styles of type, set bold and regular type, underline, and so on. Under most circumstances, however, you do not use a word processor to prepare files for data analysis, since you, the user, want to be responsible for the bulk of the formatting in this situation. For example, data for input files often need to be in a format of one item per line or a specified number of items per line. Because a word processor is not designed to accommodate these types of requirements, most files for data analysis will be created using an "editor."

An **editor**, also a software package, is generally less powerful than a word processor, but this has its advantages. Specifically, it is usually quite easy to learn the small number of basic editor functions and commands. In addition, the execution speed of an editor is usually very fast. Besides being able to create a file with the editor software, you can perform a variety of "editing" functions such as modifying, deleting, rearranging and adding lines of text to a file. Your instructor or computer center will help you understand the editor (or word processor, if that should be the case) that you will use to create files for data analysis.

1.8b   Filenames and Extensions (Optional)

The operating system always identifies a file by a name. This, of course, suggests to the astute observer that every file must therefore have a name. This name might be provided by the user, the operating system, or the software. The name of a file should always give the user a clue as to the purpose and contents of the file. It should also be easy to recognize and remember. Once a filename has been established, it must be typed in *exactly* as created in order to retrieve the file.

Most operating systems allow for an extension to a filename in order to help the user remember what files are for what purposes. A **file extension** is that part of a filename that is listed after the period. On many computer systems, the text or name before the period is automatically generated by the particular account and username that is assigned to the user; the text or name following the period is the title of the file established by the user. Consider the following examples:

```
prjtx.hlp
prjtx.in1
prjtx.in2
prjtx.out
```

A glance at these filenames might remind the user that these files are for project X and there is a help file, two input files and an output file. A consistent scheme for managing files will help you be productive in the same way that an organized tool box helps a carpenter be productive.

1.8c Directories and Subdirectories (Optional)

Operating systems generally provide subdirectories as an aid to file organization. A **directory** is, from the user's point of view, a place to store related files, much like a file cabinet contains related files. Computer users often generate hundreds of files and need to store them in separate subdirectories, as opposed to having all files stored in a single directory. A **subdirectory** is like a file drawer in the cabinet, that is, it is a directory that is logically related to the directory in which it resides. Individual files are stored in the subdirectory just as file folders are stored in a cabinet. Depending on the type of computer that you're using, you may or may not have the option of organizing files with subdirectories.

To provide some orientation to subdirectories, consider Table 1.2, which represents a typical interaction with the operating system. Note that the line numbers on the left are for reference purposes only. In addition, lower case type represents input/commands entered by the user, while upper case type is information/responses generated by the computer.

Table 1.2   Sample Interaction Between a User and the Operating System

1	C:\ dir	
2		
3	PROJECTX	<DIR>
4	PROJECTY	<DIR>
5	PROJECTZ	<DIR>
6		
7	C:\ cd projectx	
8		
9	C:\PROJECTX\ dir	
10		
11	NYFILES	<DIR>
12	CODE	<DIR>
13	RESULTS	<DIR>
14		
15	C:\PROJECTX\ cd nyfiles	
16		
17	C:\PROJECTX\NYFILES\ dir	
18		
19	COUNTY.NY	
20	STATE.NY	
21	CITY.NY	

Line 1 shows a typical computer prompt: "C:\". Prompts come in many different forms, including common ones such as \, *,), #. A **prompt** is a signal that the user should issue a command.

The command "dir" entered by the user is a job control language command which tells the operating system to display the contents of the current directory. We see from the computer response (lines 3–5) that there are three subdirectories, as designated by the "<DIR>" after each entry. The names of the subdirectories will remind the user of projects X, Y, and Z.

Line 7 shows a command "cd" (again entered by the user) that will connect the user to the PROJECTX subdirectory. Line 9 is another request for a directory listing of the PROJECTX subdirectory, and lines 11–13 list the subdirectories of PROJECTX. After connecting to the NYFILES subdirectory (line 15), a directory listing (line 17) shows three files (lines 19–21). The names of the files (county, state, city) along with their file extensions (NY, for New York) should help the user remember the general contents of the files.

Notice that the above prompts from the computer changed depending on the subdirectory to which the user was currently connected. This capability is typical of most operating systems, which provide different prompts depending on the subdirectory or subsystem in which the user is operating. The user can recall which subdirectory or system to which s/he is connected with just a glance at the screen. It takes some time to learn how to use the various tools provided by the operating system, but the investment of your time will enable you to have the computer do more complicated tasks for you. Also, experienced users usually are happy to assist the beginner with these tasks, so don't be afraid to ask someone for help.

1.9 Let's Take a Break . . .

If you've worked with computers before, much of what has been presented here has been review. But if you've never been exposed to computers before, you're undoubtedly feeling overwhelmed by all the new information and terminology provided in this first chapter. Two points that you should keep in mind: it takes time to learn about the many different aspects of computing; and as you gain practical experience at the computer terminal, you will have a better framework for the ideas and information that we have been discussing.

In the meantime, it's important to have some basic understanding of computers and how they work. Review some of the terms in bold type in this chapter, and see if you can recognize and define terms from the comprehensive list that is provided in the exercise below. You will also find it useful to reread this chapter after your first session at the computer terminal.

Exercises

1. Take some time to make certain you understand the terms listed below. If you need to, refer back to the section of the chapter where the concept is discussed.

Term	Reference	Term	Reference
ALU	1.6b	INPUT	1.3b
ASCII	1.4	INPUT DEVICE	1.6a
BIT and BYTE	1.4	INTERNAL MEMORY	1.6b
BOOTING UP	1.5	JOB CONTROL LANGUAGE	1.7b
CHIP	1.6b	LOG ON	1.5
CONTROL UNIT	1.6b	MULTI-USER	1.5
CPU	1.6b	OPERATING SYSTEM	1.7b
CRT	1.6a	OUTPUT	1.3b
DATA	1.3a	OUTPUT DEVICE	1.6a
DIRECT ACCESS	1.6c.2	PROCESSOR	1.6b
DIRECTORY	1.8c	PROGRAM	1.7
DISK PACKS	1.6c.1	PROMPT	1.8c
EDITOR	1.8a	RAM	1.6b
ECHO	1.4	READ/WRITE HEAD	1.6c.1
FILE	1.8	ROM	1.6b
FILE EXTENSION	1.8b	SEQUENTIAL ACCESS	1.6c.2
FLOPPY DISKS	1.6c.1	SINGLE-USER	1.5
HARD DISK	1.6c.1	SOFTWARE	1.7
HARDWARE	1.6	TAPE DRIVE	1.6c.2
INFORMATION	1.	TERMINAL	1.6a

2 Statistical Software Packages and Other Computer Applications in the Sciences and Business

In this chapter, we will discuss:

- why we use statistical software packages
- characteristics of statistical software packages
- a variety of other applications for the computer in science and business
- accessing your computer system (Box 2.1)

2.1 Introduction

Business, education, and nearly all fields of science have come to rely heavily on the computer. As the cost of computers continues to decrease and their accessibility continues to increase, this dependence will certainly continue to grow. Computer technology has invaded nearly every phase of research and experimentation in the social and health sciences; and within business, the use of computers in such areas as marketing research, consumer behavior, and trend analysis and forecasting has now become routine.

One of the first and primary uses of the computer for social scientists has been that of data analysis. Clearly, it is this single aspect of computing that has enabled social scientists to grasp the truly complex nature of human behavior and social organizations. It is not surprising, then, that as students of statistics, our focus will be on the computer's ability to manage, process, and analyze data. Nevertheless, as you will eventually discover (and as is discussed in the second part of this chapter), social and health scientists have come to involve the computer in nearly every phase of their research, from the literature search, to the implementation of the experiment, to the writing of the manuscript on a word processor. In this chapter we will begin with a discussion of statistical software packages for data analysis, and then provide a brief overview of the variety of computer applications that exist within the social sciences, health sciences, and business.

2.2 Statistical Software Packages for Data Analysis

With the advent of the first statistical package for data analysis in the mid-sixties, the task of telling the computer what to do and how to do it became greatly simplified for the individual interested in data management. In essence, a statistical software package consists of a series of pre-written and pre-tested programs which perform a number of specified operations on data. Many statistical software packages are currently available. Since these packages are merely large software programs, they are purchased separately from the computer and separately from each other. They are then stored on tape or disk as part of the secondary or auxiliary memory of the main computer; or if you're using a single-user (microcomputer) system, they may be booted up each time you need to use the software. The cost of or "annual subscription" to these packages may range anywhere from several hundred to several thousand dollars. Each statistical package has its own set of unique capabilities and commands. However, there are common elements to the logic behind almost all statistical packages, so as you learn one system, you'll also find it easier to work with other systems.

2.3 Why Use a Statistical Software Package?

There are several reasons why someone interested in data analysis might choose to use a "customized" software package to analyze data rather than to write a program from scratch using a programming language such as FORTRAN or BASIC. For one, in order to write a suitable program in FORTRAN, BASIC, or another programming language, the user must become proficient in a relatively sophisticated system of communication, a task which may take some time and effort to accomplish. In contrast, languages of statistical software packages are rather easy to learn. Not only does the terminology in the programmed package make intuitive sense to individuals with only minimal computer experience, but the procedure for executing various operations is generally less complex. Compare the following two programs, both of which instruct the computer to calculate the mean for a group of scores:

Using FORTRAN		Using a Statistical Software Package	
	REAL VAR (20)	DATA LIST	AGE 1-2
	SUM = 0	CONDESCRIPTIVE	AGE
	DO 10 I=1,20	STATISTICS	ALL
10	READ (5,1) VAR(I)	READ INPUT DATA	
1	FORMAT ( )	FINISH	
	DO 20 I=1,20		
20	SUM = SUM + VAR(I)		
	AVE = SUM/20		
	WRITE (6,2) AVE		
2	FORMAT (F7.3)		
	STOP		
	END		

As you can readily see, by using the software package (right column), one can obtain the same results with fewer commands. Even more attractive is the fact that in the case illustrated above, the statistical software package calculates not only the mean, but also the median, standard deviation, standard error, range, mode, and other less commonly used descriptive statistics. Of course, the software package places restrictions on the kinds of operations the user can perform—the user is limited to those statistical operations that have been written into the package. But because many such packages have been designed for use over a variety of disciplines including social sciences, natural and health sciences, and business, it is possible to perform nearly all possible analyses with access to only one or two major software packages.

2.4   Overview and Characteristics of Statistical Software Packages

The number and types of statistical software packages that are available continue to grow each year. Initially, these packages could run only on large mainframe computers such as those in the academic computing centers in colleges and universities. Now there are many which can be run on smaller desktop computers due mainly to the great advances that have been made in the memory capability of these smaller computers. Some of the more common packages for data analysis in use today are:

Name	Description and Use
SPSS	Statistical Package for the Social Sciences
BMDP	Biomedical Computer Programs
SAS	Statistical Analysis System
OSIRIS	Organized Set of Integrated Routines for Investigations with Statistics
P-STAT	Princeton Standardized Statistical Routines
MiniTab	Software Package from Penn State

These and other statistical software packages share many common features. For example, most can transform data, create data files, perform correlations, analysis of variance, and numerous other statistical tests. But not all packages can perform all operations, and so there may be times when the student of statistics finds it necessary to use a package with which s/he is not familiar. A situation like this may arise when the user wants to apply nonparametric statistics such as the Spearman rank order correlation, a test that is used to correlate data that are ordinally scaled. Whereas one package may not be capable of performing this correlation, another might have that capability. But as we've mentioned, once you have learned the logic and rules of one statistical software package, it is usually quite easy to switch to another package.

2.5   Why Have We Chosen to Work with SPSS?

In this manual, we have chosen to limit our presentation to a single program package, SPSS (Statistical Package for the Social Sciences). SPSS was chosen because of its popularity within both academic and business circles, making it the most widely used package of its type. Nearly all colleges and universities have SPSS capability; not nearly as many have SAS, BMDP, OSIRIS, or one of the others. Furthermore, SPSS is a versatile package that allows many different types of analyses, data transformations, and forms of output.

The SPSS software package is continually being updated and improved; and so with each major revision comes a new version of the package. The particular version that is used and referenced in this manual is referred to as SPSS^x. Thus, in order to use this manual for data analysis, your computer center or instructor must have access to the SPSS^x software package.

In the meantime, you should make certain you know what's involved in logging on to your computer system. If you don't, take time to read Box 2.1 and complete the exercises listed at the end of this chapter

2.6   Research Applications for the Computer Within the Social Sciences, Health Sciences, and Business

Aside from statistical analysis, how else do social scientists make use of computers? Computers, of course, have widespread application in many technical fields such as engineering and medicine, but our interest lies mainly in the research advantages that are made possible by computers. It is possible to conceptualize research as following a particular course of events. For example, first there is preparation for the study—this may

BOX 2.1   Accessing Your Computer System

Sometimes the hardest part of learning to use the computer is sitting down at the terminal for the first time and overcoming the feeling of being totally helpless and confused. Obviously, you're not alone—everyone went through this phase when first beginning to use the computer. If you've already used the computer system at your institution, then you're that much ahead. If not, now's a good time to find out how easy it really is! Here's what's involved.

A. Before going to the computer center on campus, you must acquire an account. Accounts may be obtained through your instructor who will assign you a "username" and "password" or, in some cases, may ask you to select them. The "username" identifies you to the computer and distinguishes you from other users. Your "password" is for your protection and should be known only to yourself and the instructor. This password prevents others from gaining access to the system (and your files!).

B. Logging on and off the system. Most of the time the terminal you choose will be ready to accept your log on procedure (if you have difficulty, consult the personnel at your computer center). Upon settling in front of a terminal, first push the RETURN key (your computer may have a different but comparable key, such as an ENTER key, that performs the same function); the screen will then ask you for your "username." Enter it as you would on a typewriter, and when you finish, push RETURN again.

Now you are asked for your "password." Enter it, and again push RETURN. In some cases, your password may not appear on the screen as you enter it. This is for your own security, and while it does not print visually, the system will record the password and welcome you to the computer with a short message. A "prompt" symbol will appear at the left margin, indicating that the computer now stands ready to accept your job control language commands. Prompt symbols vary with different computers; some use a right bracket "]" or parens ")", others use a dollar sign "$" or asterisk "*" (make a note as to what symbol your system uses). To log off the system when you are finished with your work, enter the appropriate exit command in response to the prompt symbol. The exit command may be obtained from your instructor—usually they are commands such as BYE, EXIT, END, FINISH, LOGOFF, etc.

involve such steps as finding and reviewing the relevant literature (journal articles) on the topic as well as defining hypotheses and designing methodology and procedures. Second, the procedure must be executed. In some instances, for example in an experiment, an independent variable is manipulated, extraneous variables are controlled, dependent variables are measured, and the data are collected. Third, the data from the study are analyzed, conclusions are drawn, and the study is written up for the purpose of communicating the information to the scientific community. In the following sections, we will illustrate how the computer can assist in some of these phases of the research process. In addition, we will briefly discuss other uses of the computer which have proven valuable to the behavioral and social sciences but which are not necessarily linked to research applications. It is not our intention to discuss all the possible ways in which computers may be used in these fields. Rather, we hope to provide a sampling of applications that might give you a better idea of how the computer can be put to work within the social, behavioral, and health sciences.

2.7   Preparing for a Research Study

One of the first steps in conducting any study is to locate other research that may be relevant to the rationale and understanding of the project that the researcher is about to undertake. This process, often referred to as a **literature search**, can be a very time-consuming process. Many a student and faculty alike can attest to the frustration of having to spend hours in the library buried in *Psychological Abstracts, Sociological Abstracts, Social Science Index* or some other source of information, searching for a reference that may not even exist. In a growing number of colleges and universities, it is now possible to request a computer search of the relevant scientific literature, a service that provides all the references related to a particular topic over a selected number of years. Usually these requests are submitted through the college library and may cost a small fee.

It is the responsibility of the individual requesting the search to provide several keywords under which the references may be indexed. For example, if you are interested in locating all the studies published over the past three years that have dealt with the effects of diet on hyperactivity in children, then you might provide the following keywords: hyperactivity, hyperkinesis, diet, nutrition, children. This information, along with other relevant parameters, is then entered through a terminal that is connected via phone lines to a computer having a large data base of sources specifically in the area of, say, psychology and medicine. The computer would then be directed to search for, locate, and print out the full references of all the studies that have been indexed under the keywords that have been provided. It might be noted that when an individual requests a computer search, the request is usually channeled through a third person, namely a reference librarian or terminal operator at the library. Thus, the individual is actually asking for a computer-based service and does not necessarily interact with the computer directly.

2.8   Carrying Out the Study

Many aspects of the implementation of a study can be placed under computer control, and typically, the more mechanized the procedure, the more it lends itself to computer control. Thus, an experiment conducted in a laboratory with animals may be almost totally computerized—from the presentation of stimuli, to the measurement and recording of behaviors, to the on-line collection and storage of data. On the other hand, a sociological study dealing with the description of a particular religious cult may benefit only minimally from the application of computer technology to the actual process of data collection.

Where computers are usable for the implementation of experimental procedures, they tend to be either mini- or microcomputers that are programmed (using a higher level language such as BASIC) to carry out several very specific functions that are important to the particular type of research being conducted. Two ways in which these types of computers have been used to assist in experimental procedure are discussed below.

2.8a Stimulus Presentation

The automation of stimulus presentation has enabled the experimenter to attain exact control over such procedures as the timing, sequencing, and patterning of stimulus material. Computer controlled stimulus presentation has proven beneficial in studies dealing with perception, learning, memory, and cognition where stimuli conforming to certain specifications must be presented exactly, rapidly, and under very controlled conditions. In the study of depth perception, for example, computers are used to generate patterns consisting of dots arranged in a particular fashion, an effect that would be virtually impossible to create without the use of a computer. Even when stimulus presentation does not require such precision, the computer can facilitate matters greatly. Suppose you want to find out how consumers react to a number of different corporate logos (a logo is a symbol or emblem used to identify a corporation, e.g., golden arches). You could easily program the computer to generate different logos that would be presented at a video terminal. Questions designed to measure an individual's reaction might follow each presentation, and the subject's responses at the terminal might be collected and stored on a disk for later analysis.

2.8b Measurement of Responses

In some instances, as the one described just above, the responses of the subject can be automatically recorded and stored in the computer. However, sometimes the raw data require further transformation and analysis before they can be readily comprehended by the researcher. For instance, in sleep research, an experimenter might be interested in recording the EEG (electroencephalogram, a measure of the overall electrical activity of the brain; see Figure 2.1) of a human subject having insomnia. The experimenter might like to determine the number of hours spent in deep sleep over a twenty-four-hour period; once this has been done, she would like to train the subject in relaxation techniques and determine whether

Figure 2.1: Typical EEG Recording for a Human Subject

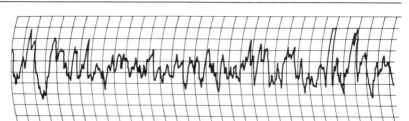

there is an increase in the amount of time spent in deep sleep. Printed records of EEG recordings, however, tend to be rather voluminous (perhaps as many as three hundred pages of recordings for a twelve-hour period), and the hand scoring of these records to specify the amount of time spent in each of the different stages of sleep would be a tedious and time-consuming task. On the other hand, if the EEG recording is fed directly into a computer, it can be analyzed immediately, and the researcher can gain an idea of the amount of time spent in each stage of sleep, the average length of each stage, when each occurred, and so on. In the end, an analysis that might have taken days to complete is finished in a matter of minutes or seconds.

2.9   Other General Uses for the Computer in Science and Business

1. **Computer simulation**, in the social sciences, refers to the analysis of behavior patterns by constructing models that simulate these behaviors with the help of the computer. These computer-generated models have been used to solve problems, to develop theories, and to describe processes that lead to behavior. In essence, they enable one to create a simplified mini-world where behavioral phenomena can be examined. By introducing new variables or using different assumptions in the system, the scientist can attempt to answer questions about the system and apply solutions to real world situations.

Computer simulations are applicable to many different fields of study, and so they have proved useful within both science and business as well. In the social sciences, for example, programs exist that can simulate world population growth, the organization of social groups, and survey sampling; they can predict under what conditions the adoption of innovative techniques will take place within a society, they can be applied to international relations and diplomacy, and they can be used to generate the hypothetical behavior of a rat in an operant conditioning paradigm. In business, simulations have been applied to many different areas—for example, they can provide practice in planning and decision-making within a typical business environment, they can be used for improving negotiating skills, and they can assist in forecasting market behavior and consumer trends, thereby providing advice on buying decisions.

A particular application of computer simulation is seen in **expert systems**. An expert system is computer software that simulates the activities of an expert in a particular field. This activity can range from providing information and/or advice to actually performing the functions of an expert without any intervention from a human expert. In the case of the former, the advantage is that the advice is usually provided with great speed. In the case of the latter, an expert does not have to be on site.

There are usually several components to an expert system, the most important being the knowledge base. If we view expert systems in terms of traditional data processing, the knowledge base is the data. There are generally two components to a knowledge base: facts and heuristics. Facts are identifiable, objective and absolute; they constitute "public" knowledge. Heuristics, on the other hand, are harder to identify and tend to be somewhat subjective. Heuristics, described as general rules of thumb, are the tangential skills an expert acquires over many years and are often referred to as "private" knowledge. These heuristics are difficult to transfer to non-experts, so a person called a "knowledge engineer" is responsible for extracting knowledge from an expert(s) and designing a scheme to represent that knowledge.

Expert systems to date have had some successes and have some limitations. Expert systems whose domains are narrow in scope and whose knowledge bases have been primarily "facts" (as opposed to heuristics) have been the most successful ones. Such computer-based fields as artificial intelligence, speech recognition, vision and robotics, and natural language processing will enhance the capabilities of expert systems in the future.

2. **Word processing** has, of course, become an important time-saving function of the computer for researchers as it allows the writing, editing, and revising of reports directly on the computer. Let's suppose that you are writing a scientific report. It is possible to compose the rough draft at the terminal keyboard with a copy appearing on the video screen. You could store a copy of the rough draft on the computer, obtain a printout of the draft, and take it to your instructor for comments. After receiving some constructive criticism, you return to the terminal, recall your file from the storage unit (disk, tape, etc.) to the screen, and begin the process of revision. You can add or delete words or phrases, shuffle sentences, rearrange paragraphs, and make other changes with a minimal amount of effort. In addition, the computer will make adjustments in

margins and spacing, check your spelling, and upon request, print out the new copy. An end to erasing, scratching out, typing, and messy copy!

3. **Electronic Spreadsheet** software was one of the first widely used application software packages for microcomputers. Electronic spreadsheets are used in business, natural science, social science, engineering and other fields. This software allows the user to store and organize data, to analyze data from several different perspectives, and to generate easy-to-read reports.

The basic structure of a spreadsheet is a matrix, a table consisting of rows and columns. Values are placed in the intersections of rows and columns, called cells. The most common type of entry in a spreadsheet is a number, but formulas and text (e.g., labels or names) may be entered as well. Typical uses of formulas are to calculate sums and averages of rows and columns, whereas labels are typically used to identify rows and columns. Table 2.1 shows a simple spreadsheet.

Cells are referenced by column (down), then row (across). In cell 0,0 we find the label 'Name'. This label identifies the first column, just as the other labels in row 0 identify other columns. The values in column 0, rows 2–6, are labels that identify each row. The values in columns 2 and 3, rows 2–6, are numbers. These numbers are the raw data we wish to manipulate. The values we see in column 5, rows 2–6, appear to be numbers. They were, in fact, entered into the spreadsheet as formulas to calculate the average of numbers found on the corresponding rows. Thus, if one score was modified, the corresponding average for that row would immediately change.

4. A **data base** consists of a repository of an organization's data and the software used to access that data. In order to explain data bases it would be useful to examine how data were typically accessed before data base software was used. For example, a manager in some organization might request that a computer program be written to generate a particular report. Unfortunately, when the manager had need for a different kind of

Table 2.1   A Typical Spreadsheet Matrix

	0	**1**	**2**	**3**	**4**	**5**
0	**Name**		**Test 1**	**Test 2**		**Average**
1						
2	Adams		78	71		74.5
3	Ballard		83	79		81.0
4	Carson		79	85		82.0
5	Edwards		94	93		93.5
6	Mullins		62	70		66.0

report, a second computer program had to be written, and so for each new report, a new program had to be generated.

Frequently, a separate department in the same organization might be creating its own computer programs with separate data files. This process of generating many separate computer programs with separate data files makes it nearly impossible for an organization to maintain its records and data in an efficient manner. Often the same data would be stored several times in different files, and updates would require that all data files be modified. To minimize the redundancy in storing data, data bases and data base software were developed. These developments have allowed all data to be stored in one place and accessed by the one piece of software, rather than through many separate computer programs.

Data base software is designed to allow the user to make "ad-hoc queries." In other words, the user is able to request different types and forms of information in order to answer particular questions, yet a separate computer program does not have to be written just because there is a new type of request. The user generally has to learn a "query" language, or a small collection of commands, in order to communicate with the software. Data base software often has facilities to also create reports that include textual information, tabular information, charts and graphs.

In actuality, computerized literature searches, as described in Section 2.7, make use of data bases and data base software. The data bases consist of bibliographic information for one or several disciplines (e.g., *Psychological Abstracts, Social Science Index,* etc.) and the data are accessed by using several different commands that specify the topic of interest and the amount of information to be provided to the user (e.g., article references, complete abstracts, and so on). The *General Social Survey* is another data base that is commonly used within the social sciences. This data base consists of the results of a large survey which deals specifically with the attitudes of Americans on a variety of social issues. These results have been made available on computer tape for use and analysis by social scientists.

2.10   In Conclusion . . .

The above discussion of computer applications is far from being exhaustive, yet it should provide you with an idea of the many ways in which computers might assist you within your field of study. The purpose of this manual is, of course, limited in scope to the manipulation and analysis of data using the computer. In simple terms, this means that we will learn to use the computer to perform statistical tests that ordinarily might be carried out by hand or with the aid of a calculator. You may be surprised to learn how easy it is to use the computer for this purpose—it's merely a matter of learning some basic rules, becoming accustomed to computer jargon and, perhaps more importantly, overcoming the anxiety that often comes with having to deal with a machine that you don't understand very well.

In the next chapter we will introduce you to SPSS^x, the specific data analysis package that we use in this manual. Only then will we be ready to begin the process of creating data files and analyzing data.

Exercises

1. Obtain your username and password from your instructor, and find out what procedure is used for logging on.
2. Find out how to log off the computer when you have finished the computer session.
3. Study the sample computer keyboard illustrated in Figure 2.2. Note that the central part of the keyboard is similar to that found on a typewriter. Often there is a numeric pad to the right of the keyboard and perhaps a row or two of "special function" keys along the top. Sometimes special functions may be carried out by using a special "control" key in conjunction with another key on your board. For

Figure 2.2: Sample Keyboard for a Computer Terminal

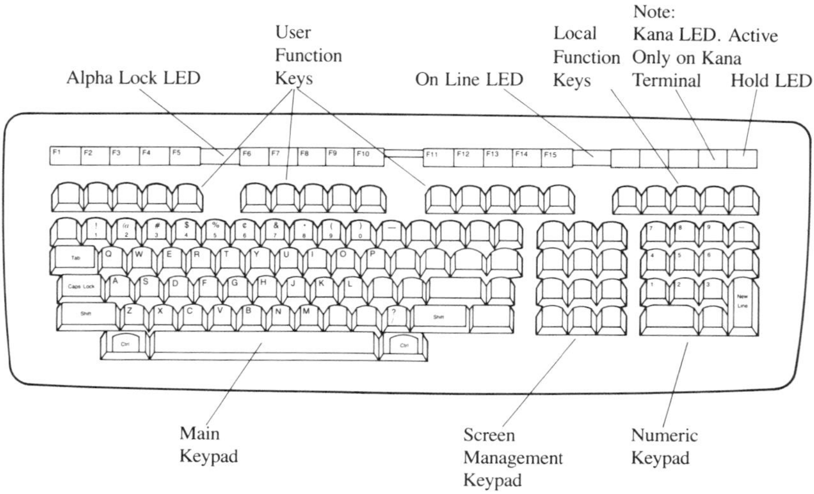

Source: Data General Corp.

example, on some systems, when the control key and the "s" key are depressed simultaneously, the information or output on the screen will stop scrolling. Your computer center or instructor may have a handout that explains some of these special functions on your system. In general, most of your work will be done with the main keys that correspond to typewriter keys. However, knowing how to use the special function keys will often assist you in the process of creating and editing your files.

Now try logging on and logging off the computer (refer to Box 2.1 if you need help). In general, you will be prompted for both your username and password, and you will have to depress the "RETURN" key (or comparable key) after each command or whenever you want to enter a new statement into the computer. For example:

```
Username:   enter username (press RETURN)
Password:   enter password (press RETURN)
            Log off with appropriate command (RETURN)
```

Some computer centers require that you change your password after the first time you log on. If this is the case with your computer system, this might be a good opportunity to change your password.

```
Username:   enter username (press RETURN)
Password:   password (press RETURN)
            Log off with appropriate command (RETURN)
```

Some computer centers require that you change your password after the first time you log on. If this is the case with your computer system, this might be a good opportunity to change your password.

3 SPSS^x and Your Computer System

In this chapter, we discuss:

- the SPSS^x data analysis package
- the difference between Operating System (OS) and EDIT modes
- SPSS^x command statements and data records
- guidelines for preparing SPSS^x statements

3.1 An Introduction to SPSS^x

Although SPSS has been around for over twenty years, SPSS^x was not introduced until 1983. The capability of SPSS^x, as is the case with most software packages of this type, is truly astounding. The package enables you to obtain statistics ranging from simple descriptive numbers to complex analyses of multivariate matrices. You can plot the data in histograms, scattergrams, and other ways; you can combine files, split files, and sort files; you can modify existing variables and create new ones. In short, you can do just about anything you'd ever want to with a set of data using this software package.

A number of specific SPSS^x procedures are presented in the chapters that follow. These are procedures that are relevant to the kinds of statistical analyses covered in an introductory level statistics course or research methods course typically found in the social and health sciences, natural sciences, or business. As such the procedures treated herein are most applicable to data analysis within these areas of study.

Yet we will touch on just a fraction of the many things that SPSS^x can do. Our aim is to help you become familiar with a single statistical software package so that you can learn the logic inherent in these programs. We will introduce you to many of the common statistics taught at an introductory level undergraduate statistics course. We hope this limited introduction to a few of the basic SPSS^x programs will lead you to see the usefulness of these types of packages—how they can help you better understand your data, how they can enable you to test hypotheses that were once too difficult to test statistically, and how they can save you incredible amounts of time as well as reduce the likelihood of making errors in the data analysis.

3.2   Using SPSS^x at the Computer Terminal

SPSS^x operates through "batch processing." In practical terms, this simply means running an SPSS^x program occurs in two steps: first you assemble a number of statements into a file, and then you submit the file of statements to the SPSS^x software for analysis.
Let's spell out each of these steps in a little more detail.

1. You must first create the file by entering the data and preparing a number of SPSS^x statements. These statements, along with the data, constitute an SPSS^x "program" or "control file." Preparing these SPSS^x statements is much like using a typewriter to type out the list of SPSS^x commands that you want to submit to the computer for processing. This stage of the SPSS^x is typically done on the "editor" of your computer system.

2. After you have prepared the file consisting of SPSS^x statements and data, this file is submitted (as a "batch" or as a single unit) to the SPSS^x software program for execution. Execution of the program, that is, the data analysis or processing, is typically done via a special command in the operating system (OS). The results of the analysis by SPSS^x (e.g., tables, various statistics, etc.) are stored in an "output" file, separate and distinct from the "SPSS^x control file" that was submitted for processing. The contents of this output file may be displayed at your terminal, or if you prefer, sent directly to the printer for hard copy output.

3.3   The Difference Between the OS and EDIT Modes

Before we proceed any further, it would be wise to distinguish between the job control language and functions of the **operating system** (from here on referred to as the "**OS** mode"), and the language and functions of the **editor** (referred to as the **EDIT** mode or editor). All computers are different and, therefore, the procedure for preparing SPSS^x statements and submitting a program to SPSS[x] will vary slightly depending on the specific requirements of your system. For most users, both the OS mode and the EDIT mode will be used in constructing and running SPSS[x] programs.

3.3a The OS Mode

When you first log onto the computer, you will be in the OS mode. In this mode you use the job control language of the operating system to perform a variety of "housekeeping" functions on the computer, that is, basically functions that allow you to obtain information about your account, your files, etc., so that you can keep your account in good shape. For example, you can "list" all the files in your account, you can "delete" files, you can "type" the contents of files (i.e., view the contents on your screen), you can "print" files, you can "access" software packages such as SPSS, and you can log off the computer in this mode. In general, *in the OS mode you will be dealing primarily with activities that involve entire files;* thus you'll print a file, delete a file, view the directory of your files, and so on. As you will see, you will have to learn several important job control language commands in the OS mode that enable you to carry out these kinds of operations. You will also learn several commands while in the OS mode that will give you access to other software programs in the computer, including such software as the "editor" and SPSS[x].

3.3b The EDIT Mode

One OS command that you learn will enable you to access the EDIT mode (or the editor). The EDIT mode is actually just another set of software that enables you to carry out a variety of editing functions. When you are in the edit mode, you can create new files (including SPSS[x] files), and write and modify programs. As you work at the terminal to create SPSS[x] files, most of your time will be spent in the edit mode, since it is in this mode that you will set up your data file, enter SPSS[x] statements, and prepare your SPSS[x] file for execution. In general, *in the edit mode, you will be dealing with the contents of a particular file*; thus you will start a new file, add to it, rearrange it, modify it, delete portions of it, etc. Again, in order to use the editor effectively, you will have to learn a number of simple commands that enable you to modify, delete, rearrange, and insert various statements.

3.3c SPSS[x], the OS Mode, and the EDIT Mode

To reiterate, when you first log onto the computer system, you will be in the OS mode. You will then enter the EDIT mode to prepare your SPSS[x] statements. Once you've created your file on the editor, you will exit from the editor (this requires a particular command), thereby placing you back in the OS mode. You will then execute the SPSS[x] program with a special command from the OS mode (these steps are illustrated in Figure 3.1)

Remember, SPSS[x] is a software package that becomes available to you only after you call it up from secondary storage—it is not something you access just by turning on the computer—so you will have to learn to use a command that is specific to the computer system at your site. For example, the VAX 11/780, a system manufactured by Digital Equipment Corporation, uses the command "$SPSS", followed by the name of the control file, to access and execute SPSS[x], whereas the Data General MV8000 uses "SPSSX" followed by input (control file) and output file-names. Either your instructor or an operator at your computer center will know the exact commands that you will need to gain access to SPSS[x].

What you need to realize is that there are two basic modes in which you'll be working, OS and EDIT. Each serves a slightly different purpose, and each uses a different set of commands to carry out functions. You will prepare your program of SPSS[x] statements in the EDIT mode, you will submit the program for execution from the OS mode.

Figure 3.1: Steps in Running an SPSS[x] Program

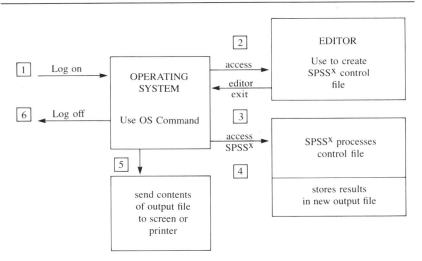

1. Log on the computer (OS mode)
2. Access EDIT mode to create SPSS[x] control file
3. Exit from EDITOR back to OS mode
4. Execute program by submitting to SPSS[x] software; new output file created
5. View contents of output file on screen or produce hardcopy on printer
6. Log off the computer

To summarize, you will progress through the following steps as you create and execute an SPSS^x program:

1. log on the computer, which will put you in the OS mode;
2. access the EDIT mode (editor) using a special command;
3. create or modify your SPSS^x file;
4. exit from the editor back to the OS mode;
5. execute the program for analysis by accessing SPSS^x with a special command while in the OS mode.

3.3d   Prompts and Cursors

When you first log on the computer, you will be greeted with a prompt. A **prompt** is a signal that the user should issue a command. Prompts may take many different forms, with some of the more common prompts including *, \, >,), #. The specific prompt that the computer issues generally depends upon the particular software in which you are currently operating. For example, the operating system (OS) may use the ">" prompt; however, once you enter the software for the EDITOR, the prompt may change to "*". As a result, you can typically identify which software system you are in simply by glancing at the prompt. Remember that the commands that are appropriate for one system or mode may not function or be appropriate for another. You will need to keep in mind (or on a sheet of paper nearby; see Section 3.7 Exercise 5) the commands/ language that are functional in each specific software mode (OS or EDIT).

A **cursor**, on the other hand, may be thought of as a special type of prompt which indicates the point at which text entry is occurring. The cursor is usually indicated with a block, arrow, flashing signal, or some other obvious indicator. As you enter text (i.e., statements, phrases, sentences, paragraphs, etc.) in a file, the cursor moves with each character as it is being entered. As you will learn, the terminal keyboard enables you to move the cursor freely to any part of the text that you would like. When you are working in the EDIT mode, you will spend most of your time entering and editing the text (mainly data and SPSS^x commands) by typing at the point of the cursor and moving the cursor around to parts of the text that need changing or revising.

3.4   Some Preliminaries about SPSS^x Input

It's important to remember that SPSS^x can read only information and statements that conform to its expected format. Thus, there are two aspects about learning SPSS^x statements: (1) learning the content (words and phrases) of the various statements which tell the computer what to do; and (2) learning the proper form or "syntax" (including the order, spacing, punctuation, etc.) of the statement. While the two aspects are in many instances tied together, there are several general rules about format and procedures that need to be established early on.

3.4a The SPSS* file: Command Statements and Data

At one time, all SPSS statements were entered on 80 column IBM cards (the kind that were used when input took the form of punched cards). Each card contained a single statement or command, and therefore, the list of SPSS statements could be thought of as comprising a stack of "cards," where each card represented a different SPSS statement.

Since nearly all SPSS* users now have switched to on-line terminals, the term "card" is no longer appropriate and has been replaced with the term "record." Thus, an SPSS* program consisting of eight different lines on the terminal would have eight "records," with each record consisting of a single line. The term "record" then is used to denote a single line of input to an SPSS* file. Yet, while "record" applies to any single line of SPSS* input, it is often helpful to make the distinction between records consisting of *SPSS* statements* (or commands) and *those consisting of data*. For example, the following record which contains recognizable words can be considered an SPSS* statement or command:

ADD FILE

On the other hand, this next record consists solely of data and would be considered a data record:

4 2 32 16 96

So while "record" refers to any line of SPSS* input, we can categorize any record in our file as either a SPSS* **statement** or **data** record.

3.4b The 80 Column Rule

Any record, whether an SPSS* statement or data record, cannot exceed 80 "columns" or characters for most computer systems (80 columns represents the width of an old punched card, and is usually slightly wider than the typical screen on a video terminal). You should be aware of the fact that some systems have a slightly smaller column width which you can use when creating an SPSS* file.

3.5   SPSS[x] *Statements* Have Control and Specification Fields

All SPSS[x] statements consist of two parts: a **control** field and a **specifica-tion** field. The control field may occupy *up to* the first fifteen columns of a line of input. The control field contains a word or set of words (e.g., DATA LIST, FREQUENCIES, RECODE, etc.) that instructs SPSS[x] to perform a certain function. The spelling and spacing of these words must be identical to the samples provided in this manual or to those given in the SPSS[x] manuals. The specification field follows the control field and must always be separated from it by at least one blank space. Thus, it's possible that the specification portion of the statement may occupy the latter part of the first 15-space segment if the control field does not occupy all 15 spaces (refer to Figure 3.2 for an example).

In the specification field, the user can provide detailed instructions that are appropriate to the needs of a specific situation. For example, the user may want an analysis performed on two particular variables chosen from a larger set of variables, or s/he may select particular descriptive statistics over others, etc. Such selections are made in the specification field of the record.

If the instructions within the specification field exceed the space allowed on a single record (i.e., 80 columns), then the instructions may be continued on the next record (or line), *but they must be indented at least one space* (see Figure 3.2, Example 3). Thus, it is important to remember that if the control and specification fields of an SPSS[x] statement amount to more than 80 columns, the statement must be spread over two records, with at least one space in the first column of the second record. Of course, you must also remember that subsequent SPSS[x] statements must begin in column one of a record so that they will not be interpreted as a continuation of the previous statement.

3.6   Some Final Technical Points

1. Naming variables. When you analyze data, the data will always repre-sent values of some variable that have been measured; for example, if you collected information on the ages of sixty subjects, you have data on the variable "age." Obviously then, it will be necessary to name all our variables so that we have a way of referring to them so they can be analyzed, modified, or manipulated by the computer. Although you can name your variables nearly anything you want, it's best to provide names that describe the variable. Thus, the variable name EDUC might be used to refer to the variable for years of education, SEX might refer to the sex of the subject, and so on. The rules for naming variables are simple, but they must be followed carefully:

- Rule 1: the length of the name of the variable may range from one to eight characters; the first character must be a letter.
- Rule 2: names may consist of letters and numbers, but no other characters (e.g., hyphens, commas, etc., are not allowed).
- Rule 3: no spaces are permitted within the variable name.

2. Keywords. Some words are used to convey general operations or particular relationships among variables, and therefore, these words

Figure 3.2: Control and Specification Field Examples

In the following example, the term FREQUENCIES comprises the control field, while the term VARIABLES= followed by the list of variables V1 to V4 appears in the specification field. Note that the two fields must be separated by at least one blank, but can be separated by more than one blank if desired. Both examples below are correct.

Example 1: The control field occupies fifteen spaces (the last four are blanks), and the specification field begins in Column 16.

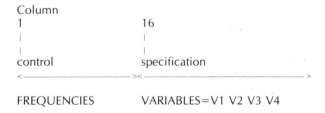

```
Column
1                       16
|                        |
|                        |
control                 specification
<-------------------------><------------------------------------->

FREQUENCIES            VARIABLES=V1 V2 V3 V4
```

Example 2: The control field occupies eleven columns, the specification field begins in the thirteenth column. This method is generally more efficient than the one above since the user does not have to insert several blanks within each record.

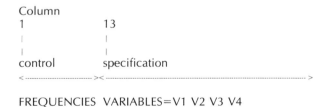

```
Column
1                13
|                 |
|                 |
control          specification
<----------------><----------------------------------------->

FREQUENCIES  VARIABLES=V1 V2 V3 V4
```

Example 3: The specification field is extended to a second record to accommodate the long list of variables. Note that the second record is indented at least one space.

```
FREQUENCIES VARIABLES=V1 V2 V3 V4 5V 6V V7
        V8 V9 V10
```

have special meaning in the SPSS^x system. These so-called keywords must be typed exactly as they appear (may not contain spaces), and must appear on one line. The most common of these keywords are TO, BY, and WITH. In order to avoid coincidental use of a keyword as a variable name, the complete list of keywords is presented here: ABS, ALL, AND, ATAN, BY, CASWGT, COS, EQ, EXP, GE, GT, LE, LG10, LN, MOD10, NE, NOT, OR, RND, SEQNUM, SIN, SQRT, TO, TRUNC, WITH.

3. Common delimiters. Within the *specification* field of the statement, you may separate names, keywords, etc., to make them more readable by using "common delimiters." The two common delimiters are the comma and the space, characters that may be used interchangeably. Essentially this means that you may insert commas or spaces wherever you desire as long as you are within the specification field.

Exercises

1. Each SPSS^x line of input is referred to as a record. The two types of records are ⟶c̶o̶m̶m̶e̶n̶t̶ and ̶d̶a̶t̶a̶   .

2. The maximum number of characters that can appear on a single record is ̶8̶0̶. Up to the first 15 spaces of an SPSS^x statement are occupied by the ̶c̶o̶n̶t̶r̶o̶l̶ field, while the remaining spaces consist of the ̶s̶p̶e̶c̶i̶f̶i̶c̶a̶t̶i̶o̶n̶ field. If the control field occupies fewer than 15 spaces, the specification field may occupy spaces within the first 15 columns as long as the two fields are separated by a ̶s̶p̶a̶c̶e̶.

3. List the three rules that must be followed in naming variables. Why should you not use the word ALL as one of your variable names?
̶p̶3̶7̶

4. Based on what you know about naming variables and about common delimiters, which of the following records are *not* correct? In the examples below, the control field consists of the words NONPAR CORR, a statement that requests that a nonparametric correlation be performed. In the specification field are three variables corresponding to age, heart rate, and blood pressure.

   a. NONPAR CORR   AGE with HEART-RATE, BP
   b. NONPAR CORR   AGE with HR BP
   c. NONPAR CORR   AGE# with HR, BP
   d. NON PAR CORR   #AGE with HR, BP
   e. NONPAR CORR   AGE with HR, BP

5. List the appropriate commands in both the OS mode and EDIT mode that will perform the following functions. These commands are

specific to your particular computer system and software and they
may be obtained from your instructor or your computer center.

OS MODE

list the files in your account _____

delete a file _____

type the file contents onto screen _____

send the file to the printer _____

enter the EDIT mode _____

access SPSS^x _____

log off the computer _____

other _____

EDIT MODE

create a file _____

add to a file _____

delete a particular line in the file _____

modify a line in the file _____

replace a line in the file _____

insert a line in the file _____

display a particular line in the file _____

save a file _____

exit to the OS mode _____

other _____

You will also find that your knowledge of and proficiency on the keyboard
will come in handy at some point; find out from your instructor how you can
use the keyboard to:

scroll forward _____

scroll backward _____

stop scrolling _____

continue scrolling _____

move the cursor _____

delete and/or backspace _____

4 A First Encounter with SPSS^x

In this chapter, we discuss:

- the way in which a typical SPSS^x run is set up
- how to create an SPSS^x data file
- the purpose and components of the DATA LIST statement

4.1 A Typical SPSS^x Run

The specific SPSS^x records (statements and data records) and the sequence of these records are usually quite similar from one run to another. There will always be a DATA LIST statement at the beginning of the run. This statement is used to describe the names of the variables in your data file to SPSS^x as well as where each variable is located on the data records. We will discuss how to write the DATA LIST statement in Section 4.3. As you might have surmised, even if you are doing several different types of data analysis on the same set of data, as long as your data file does not change, the DATA LIST statement will remain the same.

Second, several optional statements may be included after the DATA LIST statement. These statements may be used to provide more extensive or readable labels for the variables (or for the values of the variables) that have been named in the DATA LIST statement. For example, with the variable SEX, the user might prefer the labels "male" and "female" on the printout rather than "1" for male and "2" for female. Other optional statements may be included at this point to compute new variables, re-code existing ones, or carry out other preliminary transformations of the data file.

Third, the particular action to be taken on the data must be specified. This is accomplished with a "procedure" or routine statement, the name of which changes depending on what analysis or action you want performed. For example, one type of statement is used to obtain descriptive statistics on single variables (CONDESCRIPTIVE) while another is used to correlate two variables using the Pearson correlation procedure (PEARSON CORR).

Fourth, requests for certain statistics and types of output may be required. Particular specifications within the procedure record may accomplish this for some types of analyses; for others, the STATISTICS and OPTIONS statements are used.

Finally, the data file, consisting of all the data records, is included. The data file is enclosed by BEGIN DATA and END DATA statements.

In Box 4.1 is a list of records as they might typically appear within an SPSS^x run. Only the control field (i.e., the part of the command that may occupy up to the first fifteen columns) is given for each record, since this is the only part of the record that always remains the same. The specification field (which, as you recall, follows the control field and is separated from it by at least one space) changes depending on the variables that you are analyzing, the statistics that you are requesting, and so on. Those records marked "optional" in Box 4.1 do not have to be included in the run for it to be successful, but they may be helpful in providing supplemental information and specifying format and statistical analyses.

4.2   Learning How to Create a Data File in SPSS^x

Before you can begin the process of analyzing data, you must first create a file consisting of the data that you wish to analyze. This "data file" consists of all the data records that will actually become part of the larger SPSS^x file (this larger file includes SPSS^x statements or commands as well as data records). In the example of a typical SPSS^x run (Box 4.1), the data file lies between Record 10 and 10+n+1. The data for each subject or case is entered on a separate record, and therefore there must be at least one data record for each subject or case in your study. In some cases, there may be more than one data record per subject. For our purposes, there will be only one record for each subject, so if there are twenty-five subjects in the study, there will be twenty-five records in the data file. If the data for an individual subject or case does not fit onto a single eighty column record, then the data for that subject is extended onto a second record. In this situation, there would be two records for each subject, or a total of fifty records for the twenty-five subjects. There is no reasonable limit on the number of data records that might be required for a single subject, but remember, you must have *at least one record for each subject* or case in your data file. You might note that when you have more than one data record for each subject, all the data records for a single subject

BOX 4.1 SPSS^x Records Included in a Typical Run

1	DATA LIST	gives number of records, variable names and locations
2	VARIABLE LABELS (optional)	provides more extensive or meaningful labels to variables and values so readout is easier to interpret
3	VALUE LABELS (optional)	
4	MISSING VALUES	provides for special treatment of items for which no valid response has been obtained
5	COMPUTE (optional)	used to modify variables or create new variables from existing ones
6	RECODE (optional)	
7	procedure or routine	requests particular data analysis
8	OPTIONS (required for some)	specifies type and form of output, including the specific statistics such as mean, range, variance, etc.
9	STATISTICS (required for some)	
10	BEGIN DATA	this is the point at which the actual data appear within the file; these records comprise the data file
10+n	here you enter the data, at least one record for each case or subject; n refers to the number of data records	
10+n+1	END DATA	
10+n+2	additional procedures or routines may be added here	

appear consecutively in the data file. For example, the two data records for the first subject would be followed by the two data records for the second subject, and so on.

The way in which your data appear in the data file is determined by the DATA LIST statement, so for all practical purposes, the DATA LIST statement and the data file are created together. Assume, for example, that you have data on three variables (height, weight, and blood pressure) that you wish to enter into a data file. Which variable you enter first on the data record, how many spaces are allocated to that variable, and in which columns the data from that variable will appear are all determined by the information that is given in the DATA LIST statement.

In addition, the data file is always preceded by the command BEGIN DATA and after all data has been entered is followed immediately by the command END DATA.

In the next section, you will learn how to set up the DATA LIST statement so you can go about the process of creating a data file.

4.3   The DATA LIST Statement

As with any SPSS^x statement, the DATA LIST statement consists of a control field and a specification field. The words "DATA LIST" make up the control field, and this portion of the statement must always appear exactly as it is given above. Assume that the first letter of the DATA LIST statement, namely the "D" in DATA, always appears in column 1 of the record.

The appearance of the specification field changes depending on the requirements of the data file. For our purposes, the specification field of the DATA LIST record will be used to tell SPSS^x three things:

1. the number of records for each case (or subject) in the data file;
2. the names of the variables in the data file;
3. the column location and number of decimals for each variable in the data file.

4.3a   The Number of Records

The number of records for each case is specified with RECORDS= and is followed by the actual number of data records per case (or subject) in the particular data file set up. If the data for each case or subject is contained all on one eighty column record, the DATA LIST statement would appear as:

DATA LIST   RECORDS=1

If the data for each subject is contained on two separate records, the DATA LIST statement would appear as:

DATA LIST   RECORDS=2

4.3b   The Names of the Variables

The names of the variables that will be read from the first record follow the RECORD= specification; these variable names are separated from RECORDS= by a slash (/) and the record number. Suppose that three variables, height (HT), weight (WT), and diastolic blood pressure (BP), are to be read from the first record for each subject. The DATA LIST statement might read

DATA LIST   RECORDS=1
   /1 HT 2-3 WT 5-7 BP 9-11

indicating that the data for all three variables for any given subject will appear on the first record. For the moment, ignore the numbers that follow the assigned variable names in the above statement; we'll tackle those in a moment. But note that in the above example, some of the information was placed on a second record (i.e., a new line on a terminal). This was done only to improve the readability of the statement. In the above example, because we are continuing the DATA LIST statement on another record, we must begin this next record with an indentation of at least one space (see Section 3.5). If we had wanted, the assignment of variable names could have followed all on the same line, as is illustrated in the following:

DATA LIST   RECORDS=1 /1 HT 2-3   WT 5-7   BP 9-11

Both statements shown above convey the same information, and both are correct.

Now let's suppose a slightly more complex situation. There are two records for each case or subject, and on the second record, a fourth variable "hours of vigorous exercise each week" (EXERCISE) is to be read. Our DATA LIST statement might now appear:

DATA LIST   RECORDS=2
    /1 HT 2-3   WT 5-7   BP 9-11
    /2 EXERCISE 2-4

The above example indicates that there will be two records for each case, that the variables HT, WT, and BP will be found on the first record, and that the variable EXERCISE will be found on the second record. You might note that in the above example, we easily could have squeezed all the variables and their locations on a single line or record. However, there may be times when it is advisable to use several lines or records for each subject even when it is not necessary, for example, to improve the readability of the data file when we print it out.

4.3c   The Location of Each Variable

The location of each variable in the data file is indicated by the number or numbers that follow the assigned variable name. In the preceding example, the data for HT will be found in Columns 2–3 of the first data record for the subject. The data for WT will be found in Columns 5–7, and the data for diastolic blood pressure (BP) will be found in Columns 9–11. The "hours of vigorous exercise each week" or EXERCISE will be found on the second record in Columns 2–4. Obviously, you will want to reserve enough spaces for each of your variable values. For weight that is measured to the nearest pound, three columns would suffice since the maximum weights of adult humans will be no more than three-digit numbers. So the number of columns reserved for each variable depends on the maximum number of digits of the data representing that variable.

The actual columns within the eighty column record that are chosen, however, are somewhat arbitrary. We could have chosen to place HT in Columns 4–5 and WT in Columns 6–8, and so on. In the above example, we chose to separate data from each other with spaces, primarily for the sake of readability.

4.3d   The Number of Decimal Places

The number of decimal places for any variable is placed in parentheses following the column designation for that variable. If weight were measured to the nearest tenth of a pound (i.e., one decimal place), then the number "1" would appear in parentheses following the column designation for WT:

    DATA LIST   RECORDS=2   /1 HT   2-3 WT 5-8(1)   BP 9-11

Note that in the above statement we had to expand the number of columns reserved for WT to 4 (i.e., col. 5–8) in order to accommodate the additional digit in the weight (e.g., a weight of 122 might be refined to 122.6). Note also, however, that as long as we specify a decimal place in the DATA LIST statement, we do not need to reserve a space on the data record for the actual decimal point. You need to be aware of the fact that if the data contain decimal places, and *if you specify the number of decimal places in the DATA LIST statement, you do not include the decimal point as you enter the data to create your data file.* If, on the other hand, you do not specify the number of decimal places in the DATA LIST statement, then you must include decimal points as you enter the data (assuming there are decimal places in the data), and you must have an extra column designated in the DATA LIST statement in order to accommodate the decimal point.

One further point needs to be made about how data are to be entered into the appropriate columns of the data records. If you have reserved three spaces for a variable (e.g., WT 5-7), but the actual data on this variable for one of the subjects requires only two of those spaces (e.g., one subject weighs only 87 pounds), that two-digit number is placed in the last two columns indicated by the DATA LIST statement (i.e., in columns 6 and 7). The end result is that all the values for the weights of the subjects on the data records will be right-justified (they will all end in the same column, 7). Conversely, not all values for a given variable will necessarily begin in the first column specified, in this case column 5. In general, then, blank spaces on data records in columns where data can appear are read as zeros.

The following data, which represent the ages and IQs of four fourth-grade children, are right-justified and appear as they would on four consecutive data records.

9	106
10	118
9	97
9	109

4.4 An Example of a DATA LIST Statement and Data File

The DATA LIST statement tells SPSS^x how the data in the data file are to be read. The computer does not actually read and store the data until the BEGIN DATA record is processed.

Let's suppose you want to create a data file having four variables: age, sex, marital status, and annual auto insurance premium. You have a small sample, only 6 subjects (or cases). You plan to include the data for all four variables for each subject on a single record, and you assign the names AGE, SEX, MARSTAT, and AUTOINS to the variables.

The actual data are as follows:

SUBJECT	AGE	SEX	MARSTAT	AUTOINS
1	25	Male	Married	$ 372.22
2	38	Female	Married	$ 301.90
3	18	Male	Single	$ 577.43
4	27	Female	Single	$ 346.65
5	53	Male	Divorced	$ 292.18
6	26	Male	Married	$ 437.86

AGE is measured in years, so you need two columns for this variable. SEX (1 = male and 2 = female) and MARSTAT (1 = single; 2 = married; 3 = divorced) are categorical variables, so you require only one column for each of these variables. And AUTOINS is recorded to the nearest cent, so you allow five spaces for this variable, two of which will be to the right of the decimal place. The DATA LIST statement and data file might be set up in the following way (again, assume that the first letter of DATA LIST begins in column 1 of the record):

```
DATA LIST   RECORDS=1
    /1 AGE 1-2   SEX 4   MARSTAT 6   AUTOINS 8-12(2)
BEGIN DATA
```

```
25  1  2  37222
38  2  2  30190
18  1  1  57743
27  2  1  34665
53  1  3  29218
26  1  2  43786
END DATA
```

Our file would consist of ten records, three of which are SPSS^x statements (although one, DATA LIST, is extended to a second line) and six of which are data records. Had there been two records of data for each subject, those two records would appear consecutively in the data file; in other words, the first two records for the first subject would be placed in succession, followed by the two records for the second subject, followed by the third subject, and so on. The data for any given variable appear in the column(s) specified in the DATA LIST statement. Also, as mentioned previously, the data file is preceded by BEGIN DATA and succeeded by END DATA. Note that the above SPSS^x file represents only the data file and its related statements; no data analyses have been requested on the data in the above file. Such analyses would be executed by placing procedure records between the DATA LIST statement and the BEGIN DATA statement. Any additional analyses would be specified in additional procedure records that would be placed after the END DATA record.

4.5   A Final Note Before Proceeding

SPSS^x is not very tolerant of mistakes, whether they are spelling errors, misplaced spaces or punctuation, or records out of sequence. If a mistake in format is detected, the program may be terminated without completion, and the number and location of the errors will be indicated. These errors must then be corrected by the user, and the program must be run again. As you can see, mistakes can cost money (in terms of CPU time) and valuable time for the user, particularly if the turn-around time is long. There are several steps that can be taken to decrease the likelihood of errors and to save time.

1. When you create or enter programs in a file, follow the sample format programs in each section as closely as possible. These programs have already been tested on the computer. Words in uppercase type (CAPITAL LETTERS) in the sample programs indicate the actual words and characters that you will enter into the computer. Words in lowercase type provide additional information and instructions and will not be entered per se, but will tell you how to order information.

2. Most errors are the result of misspelling, improper spacing, and so on. Double check all your records, including data records, before submitting your program for a run.
3. Not all the records that are included in the sample programs are required to run the program. Some records are included to provide certain statistics, to make the output more readable, and so on. As you will see, careful selection of OPTIONS and STATISTICS records can be very time-saving. In the sample programs, we have suggested some of the more appropriate options and statistics, but you may want to investigate these further at some point in the future.

4.6   If You Want to Know More Than What's Given in This Manual . . .

Only a fraction of the possible things you can do with SPSS^x are presented in the following pages. We have limited our discussion in this manual to the types of analyses that are typically carried out in a basic statistics or research methods course. If you should ever want to know more about SPSS^x or about the way in which other software packages operate, you'll want to consult the manuals published by those companies that distribute the software packages. For example, a more extensive treatment of the SPSS^x software system can be found in the *SPSS^x User's Guide*.

Exercises

1. What is the function of the DATA LIST statement?
2. Set up a DATA LIST statement that tells SPSS^x to read:
   a. three variables, V1, V2, and V3, from the first record;
   b. three variables, V4, V5, and V6, from the second record.

   Assume that V1, V2, and V5 each require two columns; V3 and V6 require three columns, but V3 has one decimal place while V6 has two decimal places. V4 requires four columns. Use the space below (after exercise 3) with the designated columns for setting up the DATA LIST statement as you would enter it at the terminal.

3. Use the data from the four subjects given below (you need not enter the subject number), along with the DATA LIST and BEGIN DATA and END DATA statements, to finish compiling the SPSS^x file. Again use the column markers below to assist you in planning how the information will be placed in the correct columns.

Subject	V1	V2	V3	V4	V5	V6
1	22	95	13.5	1110	67	3.34
2	18	77	6.3	800	88	3.11
3	18	81	11.0	320	89	2.90
4	21	90	12.3	154	82	3.60

Work space:

4. Once you have the above file worked out, check with your instructor to see that it has been done correctly. Now create the above file on your computer system using the editor (EDIT mode). Be sure to correct all errors, then save the file. Obtain a printout of your file by using the appropriate Operating System (OS) command.

5 Selecting Variables and Creating a Data File

In this chapter, we discuss:

- the rationale for a study on leadership effectiveness
- variables to be entered into the data file
- coding schemes for scores on these variables
- organization of scores in the data file
- the DATA LIST statement of variable names and locations

5.1 Creating a Data File

Before we begin analyzing data using SPSS[x] subroutines, it is first necessary to create a data file which will serve as the basis for the analyses. In this chapter we will discuss file creation. In creating a data file, we must (1) decide which variables to include, (2) have measurements of these variables (i.e., "scores") from subjects, (3) organize these scores for input to the computer, and (4) enter the scores into a data file to be stored in the computer's memory. This data file could then be accessed at a later time, and SPSS[x] subroutines could be used to conduct statistical analyses.

Were we to carry out an actual research project, some of the steps described above could be both involved and time consuming (especially steps 1 and 2, which require reviewing the literature, designing the research project, and carrying it out). We will save time by designing a hypothetical "experiment" for which we will generate "data" that might be considered typical for the study that will be described. Thus, at the end of this chapter we will present you with a hypothetical set of data generated from this "experiment" which you will be able to enter into the computer, thereby creating a data file.

You will then be able to access this newly created data file in order to conduct various statistical analyses via SPSS^x subroutines. These subroutines will be introduced in the remaining chapters of this manual, and you will be asked to apply them to the analysis and interpretation of the "results" of your hypothetical experiment. In the following we will first discuss the rationale behind this "experiment," defining the variables to be studied, describing the measurement of these variables, and explaining the meaning of the scores that would result from this measurement. We will then explain how you would organize these scores for input into your data file, and conclude with instructions for creating this file.

As we progress through the above steps, we will suggest how the results of this study might turn out, but we will stop short of a full explanation. Thus, even after reading our description and creating your data file, you may still feel confused about how the data relate to the supposed purpose of this "experiment." But that's all right, as many researchers feel the same way after actually having completed a study! That is what statistical analyses are for—helping the researcher understand the data—and part of the excitement of research comes from the gradual unfolding of the results of the experiment through data analysis. You will find that SPSS^x is a powerful tool that can assist you in this process of discovery.

5.2   Selecting the Variables to Be Included in the File: A Hypothetical Experiment Involving Sex Roles, Leadership Style, and Leadership Effectiveness

Suppose that you are a social scientist who has been hired by a large corporation ("E-Z Manufacturing, Inc.") to conduct a study of leadership effectiveness. The upper level management of this organization is particularly interested in obtaining information that would be relevant to their planned affirmative action program of promoting women to management positions. While they are enthusiastic about this program, there is some apprehension due to the fact that these positions traditionally have been exclusively occupied by men. They have asked you to draw upon previous research in this area to conduct your study in their organization. They hope that your research will help them determine what types of individuals (both men and women) are most likely to be effective leaders at E-Z Manufacturing.

Upon reviewing the literature, you determine that there are two broad areas of research that are relevant to your task of identifying variables that

lead to effective leadership: (1) GENDER AND SEX ROLE STEREO-
TYPES and (2) LEADERSHIP STYLE. Specifically, you are interested
in finding out how these variables might be related to good leadership skills
as determined by (3) PERFORMANCE EFFECTIVENESS in situations
requiring leadership.

The first topic above, gender and sex roles, concerns the extent to
which various men and women internalize societal expectations about
masculinity and femininity in their self concepts. The relevance of this
research to your planned project lies in the fact that masculine traits have
traditionally been associated with leadership positions at E-Z Manufacturing. Furthermore, both gender and sex role stereotypes have been found
to be related to "leadership style" which, in turn, seems to be related to
performance effectiveness in leadership situations. Finally, a fourth area
of research has shown significant relationships between leadership style
and both the (4) AGE and EDUCATIONAL BACKGROUND of a
leader—variables that are also related to sex role stereotypes. You further
determine that there is potential overlap in the specific variables that have
been studied in these four areas of research, and that it might be useful to
investigate all of these variables at E-Z Manufacturing. Before you can
begin to see the overlaps and utility of studying these variables, it is first
necessary to gain an understanding of the meaning of each factor. We
turn next to a consideration of the definitions and measurement of these
variables.

5.2a Sex Role Stereotypes

Sandra Bem (1972) and others have conducted numerous investigations
indicating that the male and female roles in society are typically perceived
in rather different and stereotypic ways. For example, men are generally
thought to be assertive, independent, aggressive, and unemotional, while
women are seen as sympathetic, compassionate, nurturing, and emotional.
Of course, these are stereotypes of men and women, and it is possible for
a woman to be assertive and a man to be compassionate. However,
studies have shown that most men and women perceive themselves in
stereotypical ways. That is, a "SEX-TYPED" man would have a self-
concept consisting of primarily "masculine" characteristics, and a sex-
typed woman would perceive primarily "feminine" traits in herself. Despite the fact that most people think of themselves (and others) in stereotyped ways, Bem has identified a second category of men and women that
she terms "ANDROGYNOUS" in their sex role self-concepts. Androgynous men and women are individuals who perceive themselves to be both
masculine and feminine. Thus, an androgynous man would see himself

as both "assertive" and "sympathetic," and an androgynous woman would see herself as both "independent" and "compassionate."

Bem has devised a personality questionnaire to assess the degree to which an individual is sex typed vs. androgynous in his/her self-concept: the BEM SEX ROLE INVENTORY, or "BSRI." Assume that you decided to employ this questionnaire to measure the first variable of your study, "Sex Role Self-Concept," and that you administered the BSRI to all the employees at E-Z Manufacturing. You simply call this first variable "BSRI." High positive scores indicate FEMININE SEX TYPING in the self-concept, and low negative scores indicate MASCULINE SEX TYPING, with scores near zero indicating ANDROGYNOUS self-concept. Listed below are the critical "cut off" scores on the BSRI that Bem has determined classify a person as sex typed or androgynous:

Variable 1: BSRI
  a. MASCULINE SEX TYPED: These are individuals who use mainly stereotypically masculine adjectives in describing themselves (resulting in BSRI scores = -2.1 and lower)
  b. FEMININE SEX TYPED: These are individuals who use mainly stereotypically feminine adjectives in describing themselves (resulting in BSRI scores = $+2.1$ and higher)
  c. ANDROGYNOUS SEX ROLE: These are individuals who use both masculine and feminine adjectives in describing themselves (resulting in BSRI scores between -2.00 and $+2.00$).

To review, assume that the first variable that you measured is Sex Role Self-Concept, and that you obtained scores on the BSRI for a group of men and women in this organization. The scores you obtained will be entered in your data file as the first variable, and we will call this variable "BSRI."

5.2b Gender

It may have occurred to you that the employees' GENDER is an important variable to consider in obtaining and recording BSRI scores. That is, we cannot simply assume that a high positive BSRI score necessarily means that the individual is a woman. Indeed, it is possible for a man to score in the feminine sex-typed direction and for a woman to score in the masculine sex-typed direction. Such individuals, referred to as "cross-sex typed," would not be of interest in this particular experiment, so you decide to exclude these types of individuals from your study. Of greater relevance, since it is possible for both men and women to be androgynous, you would want to record a person's gender in order to keep track of which androgynous individuals at E-Z Manufacturing are men and which are women, especially since upper management is interested in applying your results to their affirmative action program of promoting women to management positions.

In order to keep track of which employees in your study are men and women, we will need to create a second variable, called "GENDER." This is accomplished easily enough by asking each employee to circle a "1" at the top of the BSRI if he is a man, and a "2" if she is a woman. Thus, assume that the second variable you measure is gender and that you code all men as "1" and all women as "2" in scoring this variable, as indicated below.

Variable 2: GENDER
a. MEN (score = 1)
b. WOMEN (score = 2)

Now that we have defined and described the scores on the first two variables to be entered into your data file, we turn to the second major area of research that you determined was relevant to E-Z Manufacturing's affirmative action program of promoting women to management positions: leadership style. In the following we will discuss the research relating to this variable, and will describe the measures that you used to assess leadership style in this corporation.

5.2c Leadership Style

The research on leadership effectiveness has indicated that people differ in their preferred "LEADERSHIP STYLE." The two main categories of leadership style are "RELATIONS" orientation and "TASK" orientation regarding leadership (Feidler, Chemers, and Mahar, 1976). Relations-oriented leaders gain satisfaction from interpersonal relationships, while task-oriented leaders gain satisfaction from task accomplishment. Relations-oriented leaders attempt to maintain high productivity by promoting good interpersonal relationships among subordinates, whereas task-oriented leaders attempt to maintain productivity by arranging working conditions such that the "human element" interferes to a minimal degree.

Research shows that each of these leadership styles is likely to be effective in some situations, but ineffective in other situations. For example, some leadership situations (e.g., leading a communication skills workshop for salespersons) call for "RELATIONS-ORIENTED" leadership behaviors, such as putting people at ease and attentive listening. Situations calling for these types of behaviors might be well suited for a relations-oriented leader, while a task-oriented leader might be ineffective in these situations. Other situations (e.g., initiating a new computer system in the company) call for "TASK-ORIENTED" leadership behaviors, such as directing the installation of the hardware and establishing usage guidelines. This kind of situation would be well suited for a task-oriented leader, while a relations-oriented leader might not perform well in this situation.

While the above discussion might seem to suggest that all managers are *either* solely "relations" or "task" oriented in their leadership styles, more recent research (Blake & Mouton, 1980) suggests that these are independent dimensions of leadership, and that it is possible for a person to be *both* strongly relations and task oriented in his/her leadership style. Further, on a day-to-day basis, it is unlikely that a manager will always be in situations calling for *only* relations- or task-oriented behaviors. Thus, overall leadership performance effectiveness might depend on an individual's ability to be *either* task or relations oriented, according to the demands of the situation. This suggests that the most effective manager is one who is able to adapt his/her leadership style to the situation, and that people who are both strongly task and relations oriented in their leadership style might be the most effective managers over the long run.

Blake and Mouton (1980) have developed a questionnaire, known as the "Managerial Grid," which permits the researcher to obtain scores from subjects on both task and relations leadership styles. Without going into the details of this questionnaire, we will simply say that it allows for the possibility of a subject obtaining a high score on both the TASK and RELATIONS scales. For that matter, a person could score low on both scales. However, since upper-level management is not interested in promoting people who are neither task nor relations oriented, assume that you exclude these people from your study, just as you excluded "cross-sex typed" people. Thus, assume that you decided to administer this measure to the employees at E-Z Manufacturing. The result is that you will have scores on two more variables for your study: RELATIONS ORIENTATION and TASK ORIENTATION in leadership style. Listed below is the range of scores for these two variables, which we will simply call "RELATION" and "TASK."

Variable 3: RELATION
Relations-orientation: Scores range from "1," indicating low relations-orientation, to "9," indicating a high relations-orientation.

Variable 4: TASK
Task-orientation: Scores range from "1," indicating a low task-orientation, to "9," indicating a high task-orientation.

5.2d   Performance Effectiveness

To review, you now have scores on four variables from employees at E-Z Manufacturing for entry into your data file: (1) BSRI, (2) GENDER, (3) RELATION, and (4) TASK. Next you need to obtain measures of PERFORMANCE EFFECTIVENESS from each employee. This could be a rather complicated process, but to simplify things, let us assume that you have asked each employee's supervisor to examine his/her performance within a variety of leadership situations during a six month period. The supervisors are asked to give an overall rating (from 1 to 9) of the employees' performance at the end of six months, yielding your fifth variable, Performance Effectiveness, which we will call PERFORM. Listed below are the scores that could be obtained on this measure.

Variable 5: PERFORM
Performance effectiveness: scores range from "1" (indicating "not at all effective") to "9" (indicating "extremely effective").

5.2e   Relevant Demographic Variables: AGE and EDUCATION

As was mentioned previously, AGE and EDUCATION are associated with sex role stereotypes, as well as with leadership style. For example, it may be that as age increases, so does sex role stereotyping; while as number of years of education increases, so does androgyny. It is therefore likely that both these variables should be taken into consideration in implementing the affirmative action program at E-Z Manufacturing. You therefore collect data on the age and education of the employees, and you call these variables AGE and EDUC, respectively.

Variable 6: AGE
Age of subjects: measured in years, these range from 20 to 64 at E-Z Manufacturing.

Variable 7: EDUC
Education of subjects: measured in years, these range from 11 to 19 for the employees at this corporation.

Table 5.1 summarizes the variables and ranges of scores obtained from employees that will comprise your data file. The file itself will consist of the scores each employee receives on each variable.

5.3   From Raw Data to a Data File

Assume that you have had your underlings collect data on each of these variables from all employees at E-Z Manufacturing. Since this corporation

Table 5.1   Summary of Variables and Possible Scores Obtained on Those Variables

Variable	Scores
BSRI	(-2.1 and lower = Masculine Sex Typed) (-2.0 to $+2.0$ = Androgynous) ($+2.1$ and higher = Feminine Sex Typed)
GENDER	(1 = Men) (2 = Women)
RELATION	(1 = Low Relations Orientation to 9 = High Relations Orientation)
TASK	(1 = Low Task Orientation to 9 = High Task Orientation)
PERFORM	(1 = Not at All Effective to 9 = Extremely Effective)
AGE	Range from 20 to 64 years
EDUC	Range from 11 to 19 years

employs several hundred people, you decide to limit your study to only certain individuals. For example, as mentioned earlier, you discard data from any employees who are "cross-sex typed" or who score low on both task and relations orientation. You further decide to limit your study by selecting only a sample of the remaining employees that would yield scores for fifteen masculine sex-typed men, fifteen feminine sex-typed women, fifteen androgynous men and fifteen androgynous women, *for a total of sixty subjects*.

Despite the above restrictions, you would still obtain a great deal of data on several variables from sixty employees in this corporation. The next step would be to arrange the data into a file, which you could access for SPSS[x] analyses. (For more detailed information about how to go from a survey instrument to creating a computer data file, refer to Appendix A, "Coding the Survey Questionnaire.") The previous chapter explained how to construct an SPSS[x] data file. The last section of this current chapter presents raw data for this hypothetical experiment—your assignment for this chapter will be to create a data file of these scores. Once this file has been created, you will be ready to analyze the data using SPSS[x] subroutines. The subsequent chapters in this manual will be devoted to teaching you how to "get to know" your data, to modify the data file and to conduct the various possible analyses that this study would permit. You will also learn how to interpret your hypothetical results so that you can report them to this corporation.

5.4 Organizing the Data

The data for your "experiment" are presented in Table 5.2. Note the scores
have already been organized to some degree in accordance with the order
of the variables and the restrictions placed on selecting your sample. That
is, the data are listed such that Subjects 1–15 are masculine sex-typed
men, Subjects 16–30 are feminine sex-typed women, Subjects 31–45 are
androgynous men and Subjects 46–60 are androgynous women.

In creating your data file, it is important to pay attention to the
"columns" of the data "record" for each subject. That is, in order to

Table 5.2   Hypothetical Data from Study on Sex Roles, Leadership Style, and
Performance Effectiveness

SUBJECT	BSRI	GENDER	RELATION	TASK	PERFORM	AGE	EDUC
01	−6.3	1	1	9	7	61	12
02	−5.4	1	2	8	6	64	11
03	−5.0	1	3	7	5	24	15
04	−4.8	1	8	4	6	31	13
05	−6.2	1	3	9	7	59	12
06	−5.8	1	2	8	1	42	12
07	−3.1	1	6	6	4	64	12
08	−5.2	1	7	3	5	64	12
09	−3.8	1	3	8	2	58	13
10	−4.9	1	6	2	1	60	12
11	−2.1	1	7	3	6	47	12
12	−2.2	1	6	7	4	28	12
13	−3.1	1	6	8	5	58	16
14	−2.5	1	4	9	4	28	12
15	−3.5	1	6	6	3	53	12
16	6.8	2	4	6	4	48	14
17	4.8	2	6	4	6	61	13
18	6.5	2	8	4	4	42	17
19	4.9	2	8	4	3	24	16
20	5.3	2	9	4	1	36	15
21	4.2	2	7	3	7	60	17
22	5.3	2	6	4	6	37	19
23	6.8	2	4	7	5	31	14
24	7.0	2	9	3	6	31	15
25	5.6	2	7	7	5	22	15
26	3.6	2	7	3	3	40	16
27	4.3	2	6	6	4	44	14
28	5.8	2	7	6	7	46	12
29	6.9	2	4	7	6	24	15
30	5.1	2	7	3	5	29	14

Continued

instruct the computer to analyze the data, it is necessary that the scores from our seven variables all appear in the same column for each subject. Thus, when you create your file, make sure that you organize the data for each subject according to the system outlined in Table 5.3. Note that we have assigned a subject number to each employee to be entered in your data file. The purpose of this is to make it easier to correct data entry errors that might occur when you enter your data into the computer. Also note that a blank space is included between scores on each variable in order to improve readability and to permit easy eye inspection of the data. Finally, note that the BSRI scores will not be entered with a decimal point; in order to enter data in this manner, the format for decimal places must be included in the DATA LIST statement, as described in the previous chapter.

Table 5.2   *(Continued)*

SUBJECT	BSRI	GENDER	RELATION	TASK	PERFORM	AGE	EDUC
31	−1.3	1	6	9	8	21	16
32	1.8	1	9	6	5	20	13
33	−1.8	1	6	8	7	34	14
34	1.2	1	7	7	9	28	14
35	−2.0	1	4	8	4	29	16
36	1.8	1	9	8	8	39	14
37	−1.9	1	9	3	5	38	15
38	.8	1	4	6	7	46	17
39	−2.0	1	9	8	6	21	12
40	1.8	1	8	7	5	25	13
41	− .6	1	6	7	4	53	12
42	1.8	1	8	4	3	29	12
43	−1.9	1	4	8	9	25	12
44	−2.0	1	7	7	7	53	18
45	−1.3	1	8	9	8	54	12
46	−1.2	2	8	9	8	50	12
47	1.9	2	4	7	4	37	16
48	− .6	2	9	7	7	29	12
49	1.9	2	6	6	3	60	12
50	− .8	2	7	3	6	56	12
51	.6	2	8	8	7	59	12
52	1.5	2	9	4	6	46	12
53	−2.0	2	6	7	7	57	12
54	1.9	2	4	8	6	34	16
55	−1.2	2	7	9	9	28	12
56	1.7	2	9	6	6	36	15
57	−1.9	2	6	8	8	23	13
58	1.5	2	9	8	8	27	14
59	−2.0	2	6	4	7	62	16
60	1.3	2	9	7	7	53	12

Table 5.3   Format for Organizing Data for Entry in SPSS^x Data File

Column	Variable Name	Values
1–2	SUBJ (for subject number)	01 to 60
4–6	BSRI (this allows 1 column for + or − sign)	−6.3 to +7.0
8	GENDER	1 or 2
10	RELATION	1 to 9
12	TASK	1 to 9
14	PERFORM	1 to 9
16–17	AGE (in years)	20 to 64
19–20	EDUC (in years)	11 to 19

Thus, the data records for the first three subjects would look like the following:

COLUMN OF RECORD:	1–2	4–6	8	10	12	14	16–17	19–20
RECORD 1	01	−63	1	1	9	7	61	12
RECORD 2	02	−54	1	2	8	6	64	11
RECORD 3	03	−50	1	3	7	5	24	15

The SPSS^x DATA LIST statement for your data file could be set up to specify one record, with all the variables for each subject located on that one record. Below is one example of how your DATA LIST statement could appear:

DATA LIST   RECORDS = 1 /1   SUBJ 1–2   BSRI 4–6(1)   GENDER 8
RELATION 10   TASK 12   PERFORM 14   AGE 16–17   EDUC 19–
20

Exercises

You are now ready to create a data file by entering the scores in Table 5.2 into a computer file via a terminal. This is a simple and somewhat tedious process, but it is important to be careful to avoid errors in creating the file. If errors occur in SPSS^x statements, the computer may not execute the job; if errors occur in the data file (incorrect values or data not appearing in the appropriate columns), the results of your statistical analyses will be incorrect.

1. Set up the DATA LIST statement for the file appearing in Table 5.2. Use the example given in this chapter as a model (you may want to alter it slightly if you prefer a different format, but remember that the

Table 5.4   Sample Printout of Data File

```
DATA LIST RECORDS=1
 /1 SUBJ     1-2 BSRI 4-6(1) GENDER 8 RELATION 10 TASK 12
  PERFORM 14  AGE 16-17 EDUC 19-20
BEGIN DATA
01 -63 1 1 9 7 61 12
02 -54 1 2 8 6 64 11
03 -50 1 3 7 5 24 15
04 -48 1 8 4 6 31 13
05 -62 1 3 9 7 59 12
06 -58 1 2 8 1 42 12
07 -31 1 6 6 4 64 12
08 -52 1 7 3 5 64 12
09 -38 1 3 8 2 58 13
10 -49 1 6 2 1 60 12
11 -21 1 7 3 6 47 12
12 -22 1 6 7 4 28 12
13 -31 1 6 8 5 58 16
14 -25 1 4 9 4 28 12
15 -35 1 6 6 3 53 12
16  68 2 4 6 4 48 14
17  48 2 6 4 6 61 13
18  65 2 8 4 4 42 17
19  49 2 8 4 3 24 16
20  53 2 9 4 1 36 15
21  42 2 7 3 7 60 17
22  53 2 6 4 6 37 19
23  68 2 4 7 5 31 14
24  70 2 9 3 6 31 15
25  56 2 7 7 5 22 15
26  36 2 7 3 3 40 16
27  43 2 6 6 4 44 14
28  58 2 7 6 7 46 12
29  69 2 4 7 6 24 15
30  51 2 7 3 5 29 14
31 -13 1 6 9 8 21 16
32  18 1 9 6 5 20 13
33 -18 1 6 8 7 34 14
34  12 1 7 7 9 28 14
35 -20 1 4 8 4 29 16
36  18 1 9 8 8 39 14
37 -19 1 9 3 5 38 15
38  08 1 4 6 7 46 17
39 -20 1 9 8 6 21 12
40  18 1 8 7 5 25 13
41 -06 1 6 7 4 53 12
42  18 1 8 4 3 29 12
43 -19 1 4 8 9 25 12
44 -20 1 7 7 7 53 18
45 -13 1 8 9 8 54 12
46 -12 2 8 9 8 50 12
47  19 2 4 7 4 37 16
48 -06 2 9 7 7 29 12
49  19 2 6 6 3 60 12
50 -08 2 7 3 6 56 12
51  06 2 8 8 7 59 12
52  15 2 9 4 6 46 12
53 -20 2 6 7 7 57 12
54  19 2 4 8 6 34 16
55 -12 2 7 9 9 28 12
56  17 2 9 6 6 36 15
57 -19 2 6 8 8 23 13
58  15 2 9 8 8 27 14
59 -20 2 6 4 7 62 16
60  13 2 9 7 7 53 12
END DATA
```

data file must conform to whatever format is specified in DATA LIST).
2. Create a file consisting of the data in Table 5.2. Do not enter decimal points if you specify a decimal format in the DATA LIST statement.
3. Precede your data file with the BEGIN DATA record, follow it with the END DATA record. Your SPSS[x] file should take the following sequence:

```
DATA LIST   RECORDS=1 /1 . . . (etc.)
BEGIN DATA
```

60 data records (one for each subject)

```
END DATA
```

4. Obtain a printout of the entire SPSS[x] file by using the appropriate OS commands. Your printout should look like that provided in Table 5.4.

6 Getting to Know Your Data: Obtaining a Frequency Distribution for Each Variable

In this chapter, we discuss:

- obtaining frequencies with SPSS[x]
- SPSS[x] FREQUENCIES command statement
- VARIABLES and FORMAT subcommand statements
- interpretation and discussion of FREQUENCIES output

6.1 Data Organization and Interpretation

Now that you have created your data file, you probably realize that there is an enormous amount of information available to you, but that clear relationships are not easily seen through "interocular inspection" (i.e., "eyeballing the data"). What to do? Here is where you can begin to experience the power of the computer in helping to summarize and organize data into a manageable form. Through the use of the computer in this chapter, not only will you get an idea of how SPSS[x] can help you understand your data, you will also gain insight into how the computer can be used to generate information that you may not have originally planned to obtain from your study.

6.2 The FREQUENCIES Procedure: Determining "What's Out There"

The first step in your analyses of the data should begin with finding out how many scores there are at each value of the variables you have measured. For example, for the data file created in the previous chapter, you might be interested in knowing how much variation there is in PERFORMANCE scores from employees at E-Z Manufacturing. In other words, you may want to determine how many of the subjects in your sample received a score of "9" (indicating extreme effectiveness), compared to the number of people receiving a score of "1" (low effectiveness). You might also be interested in how many people received high or low scores on the TASK and RELATION scales. SPSS^x provides a simple procedure (FREQUENCIES) for obtaining this information. The FREQUENCIES procedure provides a frequency tabulation of the number of times each score occurs on a variable (both actual frequencies and percentages) for all subjects on each variable specified in the command statement. It also provides the "cumulative" percentages of the scores of all subjects on each variable (e.g., a column is provided indicating what percentage of subjects received either a score of "1" or "2" on PERFORMance, and this percentage would be listed on a line next to the "2"; the next line down would indicate the percentage of subjects with "1," "2," or "3," and so on).

The FREQUENCIES command consists of both a control field and a specification field. The control field consists of the word FREQUENCIES; any text (or subcommands) beyond this comprises the specification field. The FREQUENCIES command required to obtain frequency distributions on all variables in your data file is listed below.

FREQUENCIES VARIABLES = ALL

6.2a   *The VARIABLES= Subcommand*

By using the VARIABLES= subcommand (followed in this case by ALL), the above statement will generate frequencies of scores on all variables in your study. However, it is possible to obtain a frequency count on only a subset of variables. For example, if you only wanted to examine frequencies of scores on the variables PERFORM, RELATION, and TASK, the command would look like the following:

 FREQUENCIES VARIABLES = PERFORM, RELATION, TASK

It is, of course, possible to do a lot more with the FREQUENCIES procedure, including obtaining descriptive statistics on each variable as well as pictorial representations of the data in the form of bar charts or histograms. Since our present purpose is simply to obtain frequency distributions of scores, we will not concern ourselves here with these additional capabilities. These statistics will be described in greater detail in Chapter 8. If you're interested in learning even more about the FREQUENCIES procedure, refer to the SPSS^x User's Guide.

6.2b   The FORMAT Subcommand

Before you generate a printout of the FREQUENCIES analysis, a few words need to be said about the format of the printout. If you consider the number of different scores that exist for each of your seven variables, you will realize that the resulting frequency distributions will be short for some variables, but rather extensive for other variables. For example, GENDER has only two possible values ("1" or "2"), and therefore the frequency table will simply indicate the number and percentages of "1's" and "2's." However, since the values of AGE range from twenty to sixty-four, there could be as many as forty-five different values listed in this one table. When there are so many possible values to be included within a single table, one runs the risk of creating tables that are split between pages, and which consequently are very difficult to read.

Another subcommand (FORMAT=) is available for use with the FREQUENCIES statement which instructs the computer to organize the printout such that tables are not split over two pages. Since subcommands are always separated from each other within a statement by a slash (/), this second subcommand would follow after a slash and would take the form FORMAT=ONEPAGE.

```
FREQUENCIES VARIABLES = PERFORM, RELATION, TASK
   /FORMAT=ONEPAGE
```

Adding the FORMAT subcommand not only improves the readability of the printout, but it also conserves computer time and paper.

6.3   A Sample SPSS^x Run Using the FREQUENCIES Procedure

The FREQUENCIES command is inserted in your data file by using the EDIT mode of the computer after the DATA LIST and before the BEGIN DATA statement. The sequence of records would be:

```
DATA LIST   RECORDS=1 . . . . . etc.
FREQUENCIES VARIABLES = . . . etc.
   /FORMAT=ONEPAGE
BEGIN DATA

data records

END DATA
```

6.4   Running the SPSS^x Program: The Output File

As part of the exercises included in this chapter, you will be required to run your first SPSS^x program. Thus, after you have inserted the

FREQUENCIES statement in the position shown above and assembled your SPSS[x] file, you will be ready to execute the program by calling up the SPSS[x] package and submitting your job for processing. The results of the SPSS[x] run are stored in an output file. This file is typically given a file name, either by the user or automatically by the computer. The output file (which contains the results of any operations or statistics on the data) can be accessed (using the appropriate OS mode commands) for display on the screen or for obtaining a hard copy printout from the printer.

Although the output from an SPSS[x] run may vary slightly from one computer to another, all runs will by default contain the following preliminary information:

1. A list of SPSS[x] statements included in your data file. The raw data from the data file will not be listed.
2. A table that summarizes your variables, including the variable name, record number, columns, width, and decimal places.

6.5 Explanation of Output from a FREQUENCIES Run

In addition to containing the above information, the output from a FREQUENCIES run will include a frequency table for each variable indicated in the FREQUENCIES statement. In this table are included (1) the frequency of occurrence of each score in the distribution; (2) the percentage of scores within the distribution that have a particular value; (3) the "valid" percentage of scores that have a particular value (this is relevant when there are missing observations or data points); and (4) cumulative percentages for scores within the distribution.

At the bottom of each table appear the total frequencies, percentages, and valid percentages for the variable. The number of valid and missing cases is also presented.

An example of the output for two variables (TASK and RELATION) obtained from a FREQUENCIES run is shown in Table 6.1. The preliminary information regarding SPSS[x] statements and variable definitions, listed in the previous section (6.4), is also shown. While the FREQUENCIES command specifies frequency tables for seven variables, we have included only two of the tables in this table. Obviously, the actual printout would contain frequency tables for all variables listed in the FREQUENCIES command.

Exercises

1. Insert the FREQUENCIES command listed below into your data file right before the BEGIN DATA statement. Include the FORMAT

Table 6.1   Sample Output from FREQUENCIES

```
1  0        DATA LIST RECORDS=1
2  0           /1 SUBJ   1-2 BSRI 4-6(1) GENDER 8 RELATION 10 TASK 12 PERFORM 14
3  0           AGE 16-17 EDUC 19-20
```

THE ABOVE DATA LIST STATEMENT WILL READ   1 RECORDS FROM FILE INLINE

VARIABLE	REC	START	END	FORMAT	WIDTH	DEC
SUBJECT	1	1	2	F	2	0
BSRI	1	4	6	F	3	1
GENDER	1	8	8	F	1	0
RELATION	1	10	10	F	1	0
TASK	1	12	12	F	1	0
PERFORM	1	14	14	F	1	0
AGE	1	16	17	F	2	0
EDUC	1	19	21	F	3	0

END OF DATALIST TABLE.

```
4  0        FREQUENCIES VARIABLES=BSRI GENDER RELATION TASK PERFORM AGE EDUC
5  0           /FORMAT=ONEPAGE
```

RELATION

VALUE LABEL	VALUE	FREQUENCY	PERCENT	VALID PERCENT	CUM PERCENT
	1	1	1.7	1.7	1.7
	2	2	3.3	3.3	5.0
	3	3	5.0	5.0	10.0
	4	9	15.0	15.0	25.0
	6	15	25.0	25.0	50.0
	7	11	18.3	18.3	68.3
	8	8	13.3	13.3	81.7
	9	11	18.3	18.3	100.0
	TOTAL	60	100.0	100.0	

VALID CASES   60   MISSING CASES   0

TASK

VALUE LABEL	VALUE	FREQUENCY	PERCENT	VALID PERCENT	CUM PERCENT
	2	1	1.7	1.7	1.7
	3	8	13.3	13.3	15.0
	4	9	15.0	15.0	30.0
	6	9	15.0	15.0	45.0
	7	13	21.7	21.7	66.7
	8	13	21.7	21.7	88.3
	9	7	11.7	11.7	100.0
	TOTAL	60	100.0	100.0	

VALID CASES   60   MISSING CASES   0

subcommand so that the output tables are not split between pages. Run this SPSS[x] program, and obtain a printout of frequency distributions for the variables BSRI, GENDER, RELATION, TASK, PERFORM, AGE, and EDUC.

FREQUENCIES VARIABLES=BSRI, GENDER, RELATION, TASK,
PERFORM, AGE, EDUC /FORMAT=ONEPAGE

Note that you will not only need to insert this command in your SPSS[x] file, but you will also need to execute the program by calling up SPSS[x]. If you are using an on-line terminal, this is accomplished by using a command while in the OS mode which allows you access to the SPSS[x] software program (refer to Chapter 3, Sections 3.3 and 3.7).

2. Now obtain a printout of your output file. After you obtain the printout, study it carefully (it should look similar to the one shown in Table 6.1) to help you get an idea of the distributions of scores for each of the variables requested. Is it possible to tell from the printout where the scores of most employees at E-Z Manufacturing fall on PERFORM (performance effectiveness)? Do many employees show a high task orientation? A low relations orientation? Are BSRI scores clumped around any particular point, or do they seem to be fairly evenly distributed across the range of scores? What might you consider "typical" age and education levels for the employees, or do you find it difficult to identify "typical" ages and years of education? In answering these questions, write a brief paragraph discussing the results of this first analysis of your study at E-Z Manufacturing.

3. (Optional) Below are listed the scores of a class of twenty statistics students on a ten-point quiz. Construct an SPSS[x] data file and DATA LIST statement (call the variable QUIZ1) and then use the FREQUENCIES command to obtain a printout of a table of frequencies for each score. Examine this table and write a description of these students' performance on this quiz (Assume 9 = A; 8 = B; 7 = C; 6 = D; less than 6 = F):

9, 8, 9, 5, 6, 6, 7, 9, 8, 9, 8, 5, 5, 5, 9, 8, 5, 6, 6, 7

7 Transforming Data and Creating New Variables with the "RECODE" and "IF" Procedures

In this chapter, we discuss:

- transforming a continuous variable into a categorical variable
- the SPSS^x RECODE command statement
- using scores on two variables to create a new variable
- the SPSS^x IF command statement
- the SPSS^x LIST VARIABLES command statement

7.1 Data Transformation: Making Sense of "What's Out There"

While your first analysis using FREQUENCIES may have helped you get a preliminary "feel" for your data, you may have found that it was not particularly helpful in providing clear insights into what relationships exist among your variables (e.g., what can you tell upper management about who should be promoted to managerial positions at E-Z Manufacturing. You may be concerned that you might not gain your consulting fee after all.) Not to worry! You have only begun the process of "massaging" your data so that they make sense to both you and your employers at E-Z Manufacturing. SPSS^x offers many more subroutines to help you make sense of your data by "transforming" scores on continuous variables that have many levels (such as the 1 to 9 scale for performance effectiveness) into simpler scores representing categorical variables (such as "highly effective" and "not at all effective"). These newly created variables can then be used in further statistical procedures to help you make sense of your data.

7.2 Transforming a Continuous Variable to a Categorical Variable: BSRI Scores into SEXROLE Categories

You may recall that we have already suggested that one way of organizing your data would be to group employees' scores on the BSRI (which is a continuous variable) into categories such as "sex typed" and "androgynous" (you may have noticed that the subjects are already grouped in your data file in this manner). BSRI scores range (in our data file) from -6.3 to $+7.0$, yet we've indicated that BSRI scores of less than -2.1 represent a masculine sex type, scores greater than $+2.1$ represent a feminine sex type, and scores in-between represent an androgynous type. However, you cannot really analyze differences between sex-typed and androgynous individuals unless common numbers are assigned to all people within each of these discrete categories. Just as we assigned the number "1" to all men and the number "2" to all women, we could also develop a coding system for distinguishing among sex-typed and androgynous individuals. Thus, one way to organize the data would be to transform BSRI scores of your subjects into a categorical variable to be called "SEXROLE." This new variable SEXROLE will be "created" by transforming BSRI scores of your subjects into a categorical variable which would have only three values:

"1" = Masculine Sex Typed   (scores ≤ -2.1)
"2" = Feminine Sex Typed   (scores $\geq +2.1$)
"3" = Androgynous   (scores from -2.0 to $+2.0$)

In the following we will discuss the SPSS^x procedure for accomplishing this transformation of BSRI into SEXROLE.

7.3 Using the RECODE Command

SPSS^x has several procedures that permit data transformation (e.g., "COMPUTE," "RECODE," and "IF" statements). The RECODE statement provides an easy way of transforming scores from a continuous variable to a categorical variable. In doing so, the original variable is retained in the file, but a new variable is created by the computer to accommodate the newly generated categorical data. To transform BSRI scores to the categorical variable described above using the RECODE command, you would include the statement listed below in your data file:

RECODE   BSRI (LO THRU −2.1=1) (2.1 THRU HI=2)
(−2.0 THRU 2.0=3) INTO SEXROLE

7.3a   Format for the RECODE Statement

The word RECODE makes up the control field for the above record. In the specification field we first name the variable that is to be transformed (BSRI in this case). The "input" value(s) (the values to be recoded) as well as the "output" value (the new value) are placed in parentheses and joined by an "equal" sign. In the simplest case, for example, if BSRI scores of −3.0 (the input value) were to be recoded to "1," (the output value), the RECODE statement would appear

RECODE   BSRI (−3.0=1)

7.3b   Using the Keywords THRU, LO, and HI

When a range of scores is to be recoded to a single category (e.g., all scores between −2.0 and +2.0 will be recoded to "3"), then the keyword THRU may be used to connect the endpoints of the range. Thus, rather than listing all the scores between −2.0 and +2.0 that are to be recoded as 3, we can abbreviate the statement by incorporating the keyword THRU into the RECODE statement in the following way:

RECODE   BSRI (−2.0 THRU +2.0=3)

The keywords HI and LO may be used when the highest and lowest scores form the endpoints of the range of scores that is to be recoded. We could designate the actual end value, as shown below:

RECODE   BSRI (−6.3 THRU −2.1=1)

Or, since −6.3 is the lowest value in the distribution of scores, we could simply state

RECODE   BSRI (LO THRU −2.1=1)

The LO and HI keywords are particularly helpful when the researcher is working with a large data file and is not sure what the lowest and highest values of the variable are.

7.3c The Newly Created Variable

Finally, the name of the new variable that is created as a result of the recoding is placed at the end of the RECODE statement and follows the keyword INTO. If we were to call this new variable SEXROLE, then

    RECODE BSRI (LO THRU −2.1=1) INTO SEXROLE

The effect of the complete RECODE statement (as it appears in Section 7.3) would be that a new variable (SEXROLE) would be created by SPSS^x based on employees' scores on the BSRI, such that each subject would also receive a score of either 1 ("masculine sex typed"), 2 ("feminine sex typed"), or 3 ("androgynous"), based on his/her BSRI score. These scores would then become a part of the SPSS^x data file, and could then be subsequently used to perform statistical analyses. For example, in a later chapter you will instruct the computer to "sort" the frequencies of PER-FORMANCE scores according to both GENDER and SEXROLE, the newly created variable. This will allow you to examine whether there is a higher percentage of effective employees who are androgynous instead of sex typed, and whether this relationship holds for both men and women. The above example illustrates how data transformation by the computer can help us "make sense" out of the data.

7.3d Placement of the RECODE Statement

The RECODE statement discussed above is to be entered in your data file between your DATA LIST statement and your first procedure statement. This permits the computer to create your new variable before conducting analyses that might include this variable. For example:

    DATA LIST RECORDS=1. . . . .etc.
    RECODE BSRI (LO THRU −2.1=1)(−2.0 THRU 2.0=3)(2.1 THRU
    HI=2) INTO SEXROLE
    procedure statement if analyses are requested
    (e.g., FREQUENCIES)
    BEGIN DATA

    data records

    END DATA

In the last section of this chapter, we will introduce you to a new procedure statement, called "LIST VARIABLES", which will replace the FRE-QUENCIES statement and which will allow us to view our newly expanded data file that includes SEXROLE. But first we will discuss another procedure for creating a new variable based on scores of two already existing variables: the IF command.

7.4   Using Two Variables to Create a New (Third) Variable: Transforming Task and Relations Scores into Leadership Style Categories

Let us consider another data transformation that might be helpful in making sense of the results of your study at E-Z Manufacturing: leadership STYLE. Recall that our discussion of leadership style in Chapter 5 explored whether or not people who are *both* highly relations and task oriented in their leadership style might be the most effective managers over the long run, since any manager over time is likely to encounter a variety of situations calling for both types of behavior. However, since the data that you have obtained from employees at E-Z Manufacturing include a range of scores on each of these styles, there is no way of easily comparing performance of individuals who score high on both variables to that of people who score high on one, but low on the other. That is, right now you have continuous scores on the RELATION and TASK variables, but you do not have any way of classifying people as primarily TASK ORIENTED (i.e., a person scoring high on the task scale and low on the relations scale), RELATIONS ORIENTED (a person scoring high on relations and low on task scales) or BOTH (an employee who scores high on both the task and relations scales). If we were interested in eventually testing the hypothesis that people who are both task and relations oriented in their leadership style are the most effective managers, then such classifications of only task oriented, only relations oriented, and both task oriented and relations oriented might be valuable. However, in order to create these classifications, it will be necessary to create another new variable, which we will call STYLE, that is formed on the basis of scores from both the TASK and RELATION variables. In other words, we are using two variables already in our data file to generate categories for a third variable that we plan to create.

7.5   Using the IF Command to Create a New Variable

There are two ways to go about creating a new variable from two existing variables. One is to use the COMPUTE procedure; the second is to use the IF command. Because the COMPUTE procedure for the transformation which we will desecribe is rather complex, we have opted to employ the IF command to transform employees' scores from the TASK and RELATION categories into a new categorical variable (STYLE). That is, you could create a new variable which would allow you to categorize employees at E-Z Manufacturing according to the extent to which each employee scores high or low on the TASK and RELATION scales. Let's assume that a score above the midpoint of each of these scales ("5") is indicative of a strong orientation to the leadership style being measured, and that a score below "5" is indicative of a weak orientation to that style. Thus, we will transform scores on both variables according to these criteria. Note that we are not concerned with employees who scored low on both TASK and RELATION, so we will not need a rule for classifying this group. Thus, as with your transformation of the BSRI scores into three categories of SEXROLE, this transformation would result in a new variable also having only the following three values:

"1" = TASK-ORIENTED STYLE   (TASK > 5; and RELATION < 5)
"2" = RELATIONS-ORIENTED   (TASK < 5; and RELATION > 5)
      STYLE
"3" = BOTH TASK- & RELATIONS-   (TASK > 5; and RELATION > 5)
      ORIENTED STYLE

You could create this new variable by including three IF statements in your file. These statements are listed below:

IF RELATION < 5 AND TASK > 5 STYLE = 1
IF RELATION > 5 AND TASK < 5 STYLE = 2
IF RELATION > 5 AND TASK > 5 STYLE = 3

Note that this command will have the result of creating a variable (STYLE) classifying your employees as TASK ORIENTED (people who score high on the TASK scale *and* low on the RELATION scales, transformed to a score = 1), RELATIONS ORIENTED (low task *and* high relations scores, transformed score = 2), and BOTH (people who score high on *both* task and relations orientation, transformed score = 3). As you will see later, this transformation will take you a long way toward making sense of your data because it will allow you to test whether people who are both task and relations oriented in their leadership style are more effective than are people who are either primarily task or relations oriented.

Further, this new variable will allow you to determine possible relationships between this new variable STYLE and our other new variable SEXROLE. For example, you could now instruct the computer to determine the relative percentage of androgynous employees who also exhibit a leadership style that is *both* task and relations oriented, compared to the number of sex-typed individuals who exhibit this leadership style. Again, these are issues that will be addressed in subsequent chapters, so for now we will turn our attention to obtaining a printout of your "new" data file which includes the scores on the two new variables, SEXROLE and STYLE.

7.5a Placement of the IF Command for Creating a New Variable

As with the RECODE statement, the IF commands should be placed after the DATA LIST statement but before any statements or procedures that will initiate data analysis. Although the order of the IF statements and the RECODE statement is interchangeable, we will place the IF statements immediately after RECODE.

```
DATA LIST   RECORDS=1/. . . . . etc.
RECODE   BSRI. . . . . . . . INTO SEXROLE
IF RELATION < 5 AND TASK > 5 STYLE = 1
IF RELATION > 5 AND TASK < 5 STYLE = 2
IF RELATION > 5 AND TASK > 5 STYLE = 3
BEGIN DATA
```

7.6 Obtaining a Printout of the Transformed Data File: The LIST VARIABLES Command

All the data transformation commands will be entered into your file between the DATA LIST statement and the BEGIN DATA statement. To be sure that you have done this correctly, it is a good idea to generate a printout of your modified data file after inserting these commands. To generate a printout of this modification of your data file, we will introduce a new SPSS[x] command: LIST VARIABLES. This command is useful for generating a listing of your data file after you have transformed scores on the variables of interest for your study. LIST VARIABLES will provide a listing of scores for all variables specified on the DATA LIST statement. In addition, it will provide a listing of scores for the newly created variables, SEXROLE and STYLE, defined by the RECODE and IF statements. In order to have all the variables in your file listed, you would state:

```
LIST VARIABLES = ALL
```

This command would be entered into your data file after the IF statements and before the BEGIN DATA statement. The values for all the variables

Table 7.1   Sample Printout of Transformed Data File

SUBJECT	BSRI	GENDER	RELATION	TASK	PERFORM	AGE	EDUC	SEXROLE	STYLE
1	-6.3	1	1	9	7	61	12	1.00	1.00
2	-5.4	1	2	8	6	64	11	1.00	1.00
3	-5.0	1	3	7	5	24	15	1.00	1.00
4	-4.8	1	8	4	6	31	13	1.00	2.00
5	-6.2	1	3	9	7	59	12	1.00	1.00
6	-5.8	1	2	8	1	42	12	1.00	1.00
7	-3.1	1	6	6	4	64	12	1.00	3.00
8	-5.2	1	7	3	5	64	12	1.00	2.00
9	-3.8	1	3	8	2	58	13	1.00	1.00
10	-4.9	1	6	2	1	60	12	1.00	2.00
11	-2.1	1	7	3	6	47	12	1.00	2.00
12	-2.2	1	6	7	4	28	12	1.00	3.00
13	-3.1	1	6	8	5	58	16	1.00	3.00
14	-2.5	1	4	9	4	28	12	1.00	1.00
15	-3.5	1	6	6	3	53	12	1.00	3.00
16	6.8	2	4	6	4	48	14	2.00	1.00
17	4.8	2	6	4	6	61	13	2.00	2.00
18	6.5	2	8	4	4	42	17	2.00	2.00
19	4.9	2	8	4	3	24	16	2.00	2.00
20	5.3	2	9	4	1	36	15	2.00	2.00
21	4.2	2	7	3	7	60	17	2.00	2.00
22	5.3	2	6	4	6	37	19	2.00	2.00
23	6.8	2	4	7	5	31	14	2.00	1.00
24	7.0	2	9	3	6	31	15	2.00	2.00
25	5.6	2	7	7	5	22	15	2.00	3.00
26	3.6	2	7	3	3	40	16	2.00	2.00
27	4.3	2	6	6	4	44	14	2.00	3.00
28	5.8	2	7	6	7	46	12	2.00	3.00
29	6.9	2	4	7	6	24	15	2.00	1.00
30	5.1	2	7	3	5	29	14	2.00	2.00

continued

in the study will now be listed in the output file and can be viewed on the screen or sent to the printer for hard copy. You can "eye-ball" the printout to make sure that the scores on BSRI, TASK, and RELATION do, in fact, yield the appropriate scores on the new categorical variables, SEXROLE and STYLE.

7.7   Sample SPSS^x Run Using RECODE, IF, and LIST VARIABLES

In order to recode BSRI into SEXROLE, to create a new variable STYLE from TASK and RELATION, and generate a printout of the transformed file, your SPSS^x file should have the following records appearing in the order given below:

Table 7.1   *Continued*

31	-1.3	1	6	9	8	21	16	3.00	3.00
32	1.8	1	9	6	5	20	13	3.00	3.00
33	-1.8	1	6	8	7	34	14	3.00	3.00
34	1.2	1	7	7	9	28	14	3.00	3.00
35	-2.0	1	4	8	4	29	16	3.00	1.00
36	1.8	1	9	8	8	39	14	3.00	3.00
37	-1.9	1	9	3	5	38	15	3.00	2.00
38	.8	1	4	6	7	46	17	3.00	1.00
39	-2.0	1	9	8	6	21	12	3.00	3.00
40	1.8	1	8	7	5	25	13	3.00	3.00
41	-.6	1	6	7	4	53	12	3.00	3.00
42	1.8	1	8	4	3	29	12	3.00	2.00
43	-1.9	1	4	8	9	25	12	3.00	1.00
44	-2.0	1	7	7	7	53	18	3.00	3.00
45	-1.3	1	8	9	8	54	12	3.00	3.00
46	-1.2	2	8	9	8	50	12	3.00	3.00
47	1.9	2	4	7	4	37	16	3.00	1.00
48	-.6	2	9	7	7	29	12	3.00	3.00
49	1.9	2	6	6	3	60	12	3.00	3.00
50	-.8	2	7	3	6	56	12	3.00	2.00
52	1.5	2	9	4	6	46	12	3.00	2.00
53	-2.0	2	6	7	7	57	12	3.00	3.00
54	1.9	2	4	8	6	34	16	3.00	1.00
55	-1.2	2	7	9	9	28	12	3.00	3.00
56	1.7	2	9	6	6	36	15	3.00	3.00
57	-1.9	2	6	8	8	23	13	3.00	3.00
58	1.5	2	9	8	8	27	14	3.00	3.00
59	-2.0	2	6	4	7	62	16	3.00	2.00
60	1.3	2	9	7	7	53	12	3.00	3.00

```
DATA LIST   RECORDS=1/ . . . . . . etc.
RECODE   BSRI (LO THRU −2.1=1)(−2.0 THRU 2.0=3)(2.1 THRU
  HI=2) INTO SEXROLE
IF RELATION < 5 AND TASK > 5 STYLE=1
IF RELATION > 5 AND TASK < 5 STYLE=2
IF RELATION > 5 AND TASK > 5 STYLE=3
LIST VARIABLES = ALL
BEGIN DATA

data records

END DATA
```

Note that in the above file the FREQUENCIES procedure has been removed as it is not needed for the present task. Also, SPSS[x] will not execute both the FREQUENCIES and the LIST VARIABLES procedures in the same run. So in the exercises below, be sure to remove the FREQUENCIES record that you entered in the last chapter from the data file.

Exercises

1. Transform BSRI scores to the categorical variable SEXROLE. In addition, create a new variable for leadership style (called STYLE) from the existing TASK and RELATION variables. To do this, enter the RECODE statement and three IF statements described in this chapter to your file. Remember to place them after the DATA LIST statement.

2. Enter the LIST VARIABLES statement described above in your data file immediately after your IF statements so that you can generate a printout of your transformed file. Remember that this statement should appear just before your BEGIN DATA statement. Don't forget to remove your FREQUENCIES command from the data file.

3. Generate a printout of your new output file, using the procedures described in the previous chapter. Your printout should like the one in Table 7.1.

4. (Optional) Create an SPSS[x] file of the following ages:
   64, 71, 63, 21, 42, 38, 59, 27, 51, 34
   Now use the RECODE command to transform the continuous variable, AGE, into a categorical variable, STATUS, having two levels according to the following criteria: 1 = all ages up to fifty, and 2 = all ages over fifty. Use the LIST VARIABLES command to generate a printout of the old variable, AGE, and the newly created variable, STATUS.

5. (Optional) Listed below are the scores of students on two ten point quizzes. Create an SPSS[x] file of the variables QUIZ1 and QUIZ2. Now use IF commands to create a new categorical variable, TREND, based on students' scores on *both* quizzes according to the following criteria: 1 = students scoring below 5 on QUIZ1 *and* above 5 on QUIZ2; 2 = students scoring above 5 on QUIZ1 *and* below 5 on QUIZ2; 3 = students scoring above 5 on *both* QUIZ1 and QUIZ2. Use the LIST VARIABLES command to generate a printout of scores on QUIZ1, QUIZ2 and TREND:

QUIZ1	QUIZ2
7	4
2	7
9	8
8	3
9	4
4	9
8	9
4	8
9	9

8 Summarizing Your Data with Descriptive Statistics

In this chapter we will discuss:

- using FREQUENCIES for obtaining descriptive statistics
- determining the descriptive statistics appropriate for different kinds of variables
- labeling variables and their values for readability
- dealing with missing data

8.1 Introduction

One of the primary reasons for doing social science research is to be able to make accurate statements regarding the behavior or attitudes of a large number of people. In most cases it is impossible to collect data from every member of this "target" group (statisticians refer to this group as the "population" of the research project), but even where this is possible it is very difficult for the human mind to comprehend large numbers of individual facts. For this reason researchers may want to summarize the general characteristics of the subjects from whom data have been obtained. The mean, median, mode, standard deviation, variance, and range are examples of summary statistics that enable a researcher to describe her/his findings in a brief, but precise, manner.

In Chapter 6, you were able to obtain a preliminary feel for the data from the employees at E-Z Manufacturing by inspecting the frequency distributions of each of the variables studied in the project. Yet if one of the corporate managers questioned you about various characteristics (e.g., age, education level, task orientation, etc.) of the employees in the study, you would no doubt have some difficulty communicating your impressions about these characteristics based solely upon what you know from the frequency distributions. In other words, you have no easy way to communicate your impression about how old or how educated the employees are, how they scored on various tests such as the BSRI or TASK orientation scale, etc., without showing the entire set of frequency analyses to the manager. However, by calculating descriptive statistics on each of the variables included in your project, not only would you acquire a better understanding of the data, but you would now have the means of communicating this information in a precise numerical form to others who are interested.

8.2   SPSS^x Programs for Obtaining Descriptive Statistics

SPSS^x contains two programs that compute summary statistics on single variables (technically known as *univariate* frequency distributions). These programs are CONDESCRIPTIVE and FREQUENCIES. In this chapter the FREQUENCIES program has been chosen over CONDESCRIPTIVE because it provides greater information without a substantial increase in preparation time. If, however, a data file contains a large number of interval or ratio variables, then CONDESCRIPTIVE is recommended because it is far more efficient in its use of computer time.

Both programs compute fourteen statistics, most of which are meaningful only if the data are interval or ratio level. In addition, as you saw in the previous chapter, the FREQUENCIES program prints out the number of responses for each unique value, information that is often useful in understanding data of any level of measurement. FREQUENCIES can optionally provide percentile scores and construct bar charts or histograms. CONDESCRIPTIVE, on the other hand, will optionally generate z-scores for each value, a capability that is lacking in the FREQUENCIES subprogram. Thus, if z-scores are desired, it is suggested that the student refer to the SPSS^x manual for more detailed information. If one understands the use of the FREQUENCIES procedure, s/he should have no trouble preparing a CONDESCRIPTIVE run.

In this chapter you will learn how to obtain descriptive statistics (using FREQUENCIES) for the variables in your study on leadership style and management at E-Z Manufacturing. In addition, the formats for Variable Labels, Value Labels, and Missing Values will be discussed in a supplementary optional section.

8.3   Using FREQUENCIES to Obtain Descriptive Statistics

As you already know, the FREQUENCIES statement directs the computer to run the FREQUENCIES program. Remember from the previous chapter that when you use the FREQUENCIES procedure, you must specify which variables are to undergo a frequency analysis. You may either list all the variables individually that you wish to have analyzed (as you did in Chapter 6), or you may simply list the first and last variables for analysis, joined by the keyword TO. Furthermore, in order to conserve both time and paper, it is advisable to include the statement "FORMAT= ONEPAGE" (preceded by a "/") after the list of variables in the statement.

One of the most desirable features of SPSS^x is that it generally provides the user with a wide variety of choices for processing data. On the negative size this feature often requires somewhat more preparation time and demands that the researcher be quite familiar with the statistical procedures being used. We hope to demonstrate in this and subsequent chapters that the user need not be intimidated.

The FREQUENCIES statement not only allows you to have any or all variables in a data file processed (counted and sorted according to individual values of each variable), but also permits a large number of descriptive statistics to be calculated. Since statistics can be calculated only after the data have been "sorted," these calculations are said to constitute a "subroutine." Do not worry about this terminology; the only consequence of using this, and the subroutines in later chapters, is that you must decide exactly what is to be done and include that in the complete procedure specification (e.g., FREQUENCIES, in this chapter).

To obtain *statistical* output on each of the variables listed in the FREQUENCIES statement, it is also necessary to use the STATISTICS subroutine statement, which includes a list of the statistics that are to be calculated. You may either use "ALL" to produce all fourteen descriptive statistics, or you may specify the particular statistics that are desired (see Table 8.1). If you choose to specify the particular statistics that you want calculated, in place of "ALL" you need only list the keywords corresponding to each statistic that you want included in the output. These keywords must be separated by spaces. To analyze BSRI to PERFORM for frequencies, and to have all available statistics calculated, the format would appear as follows:

```
FREQUENCIES   VARIABLES=BSRI TO PERFORM
    /FORMAT=ONEPAGE
    /STATISTICS=ALL
```

As with all statements of this type, subroutines are separated from one another with a slash. The above statement would result in the analysis of all (and only) the variables in your data file from BSRI to PERFORM. Thus, BSRI, GENDER, RELATION, TASK, and PERFORM would be included in the analysis; but variables before or after BSRI and PERFORM (e.g., SUBJ or SEXROLE) would not be analyzed. Obviously, summary

Table 8.1   Statistics Options for FREQUENCIES

Keyword	Statistics
MEAN	Mean
SEMEAN	Standard Error of the Mean
MEDIAN	Median (not interpolated)
MODE	Mode
STDDEV	Standard Deviation
VARIANCE	Variance
SKEWNESS	Skewness
SESKEW	Standard Error of Skewness
KURTOSIS	Kurtosis
SEKURT	Standard Error of Kurtosis
RANGE	Range
MINIMUM	Minimum Value
MAXIMUM	Maximum Value
SUM	Sum of the Scores
DEFAULT	Mean, Standard Deviation, Minimum and Maximum
ALL	All of the above statistics
NONE	No statistics

statistics will be computed only for those variables listed or included on the FREQUENCIES record. When all statistics are requested, the researcher will receive (among others) the Mean, Median, Mode, Standard Deviation, Variance, Range, Minimum, and Maximum.

If, on the other hand, you want only the mean, median, and standard deviation included in the output, the STATISTICS subroutine would be modified to incorporate the keywords referring to those statistics. Using Table 8.1 as a guide, the FREQUENCIES statement would now appear:

FREQUENCIES VARIABLES=BSRI TO PERFORM /FORMAT=ONEPAGE
/STATISTICS=MEAN MEDIAN STDDEV

To reiterate, then, once the researcher is satisfied that the collected data have been entered into the computer correctly (see Chapter 5), s/he will normally want to examine, in some detail, how the subjects responded to each item on the research instrument. In order to accomplish this efficiently, the researcher runs a FREQUENCIES procedure on selected variables from the data collected. To describe how a "typical" subject responded to each item, one would use appropriate "measures of central tendency" such as the arithmetic mean, median, and mode. Another important characteristic of any frequency distribution is how widely the subjects' responses varied—did most of them feel or act the same way or were there great differences in their responses? The most precise way to communicate this characteristic is to report appropriate "measures of dispersion" such as the range, variance, and standard deviation. This will enable the researcher to generalize about how this group of people feel or behave. Let us now examine how our SPSS[x] file might appear if we were requesting univariate statistical output for several of the variables in our data file on leadership style and management.

8.4   Sample SPSS[x] Program for Descriptive Statistics (FREQUENCIES)

```
DATA LIST   RECORDS=1/ 1 SUBJ . . .
FREQUENCIES VARIABLES=GENDER,PERFORM,BSRI
  /FORMAT=ONEPAGE
  /STATISTICS=ALL
BEGIN DATA

    data records

END DATA
```

8.5   Explanation of FREQUENCIES Output from the LEADERSHIP Data File

Let's assume that you are now ready to describe the employees at E-Z Manufacturing in greater detail and with more precision than could be gleaned from simply looking at the frequency distributions of the variables. Specifically, you're interested in knowing more about the gender of your subjects, you're interested in the subjects' responses to the Bem Sex Role Inventory, and you wish to look at their actual performance evaluations. That is, you are ready to obtain some basic descriptive statistics on the variables associated with these data. The FREQUENCIES statement that would enable you to produce descriptive statistics on these variables would appear:

```
FREQUENCIES VARIABLES=GENDER,PERFORM,BSRI
  /FORMAT=ONEPAGE
  /STATISTICS=ALL
```

The first step was to specify in the FREQUENCIES record the variable names assigned to each of these items of data. Those variable names are, of course, GENDER, PERFORM, and BSRI. Knowing that the GENDER variable had 2 values (male and female), the performance rating (PER-FORM) had 9 values (as it was measured on a 9 point scale), but that the Bem Sex Role Inventory (BSRI) scores could take on numerous different values ($-7.0, -6.9, -6.8, . . . +6.8, +6.9, +7.0$), the "FORMAT= ONEPAGE" was included to reduce the bulk of the output. This specification causes SPSS[x] to condense all frequency tables to no more than one

Table 8.2   Output from a FREQUENCIES Program

GENDER

VALUE LABEL		VALUE	FREQUENCY	PERCENT	VALID PERCENT	CUM PERCENT
		1	30	50.0	50.0	50.0
		2	30	50.0	50.0	100.0
		TOTAL	60	100.0	100.0	

MEAN	1.500	STD ERR	.065	MEDIAN	1.500
MODE	1.000	STD DEV	.504	VARIANCE	.254
KURTOSIS	-2.070	S E KURT	1.971	SKEWNESS	0.0
S E SKEW	.309	RANGE	1.000	MINIMUM	1.000
MAXIMUM	2.000	SUM	90.000		

VALID CASES   60   MISSING CASES   0

- -

PERFORM

VALUE LABEL		VALUE	FREQUENCY	PERCENT	VALID PERCENT	CUM PERCENT
		1	3	5.0	5.0	5.0
		2	1	1.7	1.7	6.7
		3	5	8.3	8.3	15.0
		4	9	15.0	15.0	30.0
		5	9	15.0	15.0	45.0
		6	12	20.0	20.0	65.0
		7	12	20.0	20.0	85.0
		8	6	10.0	10.0	95.0
		9	3	5.0	5.0	100.0
		TOTAL	60	100.0	100.0	

MEAN	5.533	STD ERR	.255	MEDIAN	6.000
MODE	6.000	STD DEV	1.978	VARIANCE	3.914
KURTOSIS	-.231	S E KURT	1.971	SKEWNESS	-.418
S E SKEW	.309	RANGE	8.000	MINIMUM	1.000
MAXIMUM	9.000	SUM	332.000		

BSRI

VALUE	FREQ	PCT	CUM PCT	VALUE	FREQ	PCT	CUM PCT	VALUE	FREQ	PCT	CUM PCT
-6.3	1	2	2	-2.0	5	8	33	1.9	3	5	75
-6.2	1	2	3	-1.9	3	5	38	3.6	1	2	77
-5.8	1	2	5	-1.8	1	2	40	4.2	1	2	78
-5.4	1	2	7	-1.3	2	3	43	4.3	1	2	80
-5.2	1	2	8	-1.2	2	3	47	4.8	1	2	82
-5.0	1	2	10	-.9	1	2	48	4.9	1	2	83
-4.9	1	2	12	-.6	2	3	52	5.1	1	2	85
-4.8	1	2	13	.6	1	2	53	5.3	2	3	88
-3.8	1	2	15	.8	1	2	55	5.6	1	2	90
-3.5	1	2	17	1.2	1	2	57	5.8	1	2	92
-3.1	2	3	20	1.3	1	2	58	6.5	1	2	93
-2.5	1	2	22	1.5	2	3	62	6.8	2	3	97
-2.2	1	2	23	1.7	1	2	63	6.9	1	2	98
-2.1	1	2	25	1.8	4	7	70	7.0	1	2	100

MEAN	.267	STD ERR	.490	MEDIAN	-.600
MODE	-2.000	STD DEV	3.793	VARIANCE	14.387
KURTOSIS	-.946	S E KURT	1.971	SKEWNESS	.187
S E SKEW	.309	RANGE	13.300	MINIMUM	-6.300
MAXIMUM	7.000	SUM	16.000		

page in length (this can be seen in Table 8.2). In this case we have also requested that all statistics be computed for each variable, even though not all of them can be appropriately used for each variable.

Let's now examine the output provided by the computer when we run the FREQUENCIES program listed above. Table 8.2 presents the output from the analysis of three variables from our data file: GENDER, PERFORM, and BSRI.

8.5a   *Output for GENDER*

The first variable printed in the output is GENDER. This represents a "nominal variable" because its values denote only that one is different from the other—that subjects who responded as male ("1") are not the same as subjects who responded as female ("2"). SPSS^x, however, has no way of knowing what level of data is being analyzed. It is for this reason that the researcher must be able to choose the appropriate statistics to use in interpreting the output. For example, SPSS^x calculates a mean of 1.5000 for the variable GENDER. Does this mean that the average respondent is midway between being male and female? We should hope not. The mean is not an appropriate statistic to use in describing a nominal variable.

Regarding GENDER, one may describe the subjects in the following way: "There were equal numbers of males and females in the sample for E-Z Manufacturing." This information is obtained from the column headed "FREQUENCY" which gives the actual count of subjects who were scored as "1's" and those scored as "2's". The equal number of males and females is not surprising to us, since we selected our sample of employees at E-Z Manufacturing on a number of different criteria, one of them being the gender of the individual. This means, of course, that 50.0 percent of the subjects were female, and 50.0 percent were male, information obtained from either the column headed "PERCENT" or "VALID PERCENT." One normally uses the VALID PERCENT column because this column takes into account situations where data are declared as MISSING. The only difference between the PERCENT and VALID PERCENT columns is the denominator upon which the percentages are calculated. The PER-CENT column uses all cases including those declared on a MISSING VALUES statement so that one can estimate for what percent of the subjects no valid answer was recorded. The VALID PERCENT column subtracts any cases declared missing before calculating the percentages. A more detailed example and discussion of how missing values influence the way in which you read the output are provided in Section 8.8.

The only measure of central tendency which is truly appropriate for nominal variables such as GENDER is the "MODE"—which is defined as the most frequently occurring value. In this example, the equal number of male and female subjects renders the mode somewhat meaningless. With nominal data there can be no meaningful use of the concept of "dispersion," so, of all the statistics calculated by SPSS^x only the MODE can really be used with nominal data. Perhaps what is becoming obvious to you is that descriptive statistics provide only minimal additional information over frequency distributions when the variable of interest is nominally scaled. This, of course, is nothing to be concerned about—there is really little to know about the gender of subjects other than how many (and what percent) were females and how many were males.

8.5b   Output for PERFORM

The second variable printed out in Table 8.2 is the subject's performance evaluation (PERFORM). This might be considered an example of an ordinal variable. The values are arrayed in a logical order with "1" being a rating of "not at all effective" through a rating of "9" meaning "extremely effective." One cannot be absolutely sure that all the intervals between the values are equal. That is, one can't know if the interval between a "2" and a "3" is the same as the interval between a "4" and a "5." We do know, however, that a "3" is more effective than a "2", that a "4" is more effective than a "3" and a "2," and that a "5" is more effective than any of the other three. The most conservative course of action is to consider PERFORM an ordinal variable. As you will later see, however, there are situations where it might be beneficial to view PERFORM as an interval variable, but for right now let's think of it as being ordinal. An ordinal variable enables us to use a few more of the statistics provided by the FREQUENCIES procedure.

To describe subjects in terms of their performance ratings, we can say that 5.0 percent were rated as "extremely effective" (Value=9), or, if we are more pessimistic, we can say that 5.0 percent were rated as "not at all effective" (Value=1). Here, using the MODE makes good sense, as it tells us that more subjects received the rating of "6" than any other. However, here is an example that illustrates how important it is that the researcher be familiar with his/her data in every way possible. There are actually two modal values in this distribution for PERFORM, looking at the frequency analysis. Both "6" and "7" occurred twelve times in the distribution; yet SPSS^x reports only the first mode (namely 6). Limitations in SPSS^x such as these could result in a misinterpretation of the data if the researcher used only descriptive statistics to understand the results of the study; the importance of looking at the data from every angle possible (e.g., both frequency analyses and descriptive statistics) is clearly born out by a situation like this. The fact that the modal values for PERFORM are 6 and 7, and the median, a statistic sometimes used to indicate centrality of the data, is also 6 indicates that there was a slight "positivity bias" in the supervisor's ratings of the employees' performance in leadership situations, that is, "6" and "7" are above the midpoint of the performance rating scale.

With ordinal data, the "RANGE" also may be used. In this example, the scores extend from 9 to 1, so the range is 8. This tells us that at least one subject was given the highest rating and at least one other was given the lowest rating. Had the range been 3, we would have wanted to look at the maximum and minimum to get some understanding of how the ratings were distributed. Had the maximum been 9 and the minimum 6, that would have suggested the subjects were all very closely rated at the effective end of the index. On the other hand, had the maximum been 4 and the minimum 1, that would have suggested a similar closeness of rating, but at the low end of the index.

8.5c Output for BSRI

The third variable, BSRI, represents the researcher's Golden Grail—interval or ratio data. Interval or ratio data represent the most precise measurement data and are the most useful types of data for statistical analysis. Every statistic provided by SPSS^x is appropriate, but only a few of them are commonly used in social science research. To describe the sample of employees at E-Z Manufacturing, we might choose to use such common descriptors as the Mean, Mode, Median, Range, Standard Deviation, and Variance.

The mean score on the Bem Sex Role Inventory was 0.267, half the subjects scored higher than −.600 (median), and −2.0 was the most frequently appearing score (mode). Thus, while the average score was within the range of androgyny (+2.0 to −2.0), there was a slight tendency for employees to be more feminine sex typed than masculine sex typed, as indicated by the fact that the mean lay above the midpoint of the BSRI scale (0.0). In addition, since the mean and median are some distance apart, one could reasonably assume that the distribution of BSRI scores was slightly skewed. Scores ranged from a −6.3 to a maximum of +7.0. A standard deviation of 3.793 was determined indicating a fairly wide spread of scores and, more specifically, that a "typical" distance from the mean for employees was about 3.793. Based upon this standard deviation value, one could state that about 68 percent of the respondents scored between a −3.52 (the mean minus one standard deviation) and a +4.06 (the mean plus one standard deviation). Notice that in the case of BSRI a good deal more information has been conveyed, in a more concise fashion, than was possible with either the nominal or the ordinal variable.

To summarize briefly:

- If the variable is **nominal**—then use only the frequency counts, valid percent values, and mode to describe the variable's "central tendency." No estimate of "dispersion" is appropriate.
- If the variable is **ordinal**—then still use the frequency counts, valid percent values, and mode to describe the variable's "central tendency." In some instances, the median may also be a valid index of central tendency. You may also estimate its "dispersion" by using the range (maximum value minus minimum value).
- If the variable is **interval** or **ratio**—then any of the statistics calculated by the FREQUENCIES procedure may be used. One usually reports at least the mean and the standard deviation to describe the frequency distribution of any interval or ratio variable.

8.6   What About All Those Other Statistics?

You have no doubt noticed that many more statistics have been provided in the output than what you were interested in using. You could have limited the output to include only those statistics of interest by specifying them in the "/STATISTICS=" subroutine (the specific terms required for doing this are found in Table 8.1). However, you will find that much of learning to use SPSS^x involves learning how to use and interpret the output which is generated by the program. With most runs, SPSS^x provides a great deal more output than you will ever use, so it is beneficial to become proficient at selecting only the output that is meaningful to your data or to the question you are attempting to address.

8.7   Labeling Variables and Values (Optional)

We have already pointed out that it is sometimes useful to provide extended labels for variables so it's possible to recognize and understand them more easily on the printout. Similarly, values within variables, particularly if they are categorical, often make for easier reading and understanding of the data if they are given a label. For example, it is much easier to understand the data in a column labeled "male" than one labeled "1." SPSS^x enables the user to label variables and values by including VARIABLE LABELS and VALUE LABELS statements in the file.

8.7a   The VARIABLE LABELS Record

This record allows the researcher to attach an extended label to any variable named in the data file. For example, we may want to have the label "PERFORMANCE EVALUATION ON LEADERSHIP TASK" printed each time the variable name PERFORM is used in an SPSS^x run.

The general format for the VARIABLE LABELS command is to give the actual variable name (eight characters or less), then a space, and finally the extended label that is to appear (up to 120 characters) enclosed in quotation marks. Several variable labels may be assigned on one VARIABLE LABELS command. Simply place a "/" after the extended label and enter the next variable name followed by its label. Should the list extend beyond the number of spaces allowed on a single record, a continuation may be made by advancing to the next record and indenting one space.

8.7b   The VALUE LABELS Record

This line is similar to the VARIABLE LABELS command except that it permits the attaching of an extended label (up to twenty characters) to *each of the values* of the variable named. The general format for VALUE LABELS is to give the variable name, a space, the numerical value, and then the label for each numerical value. Again, these labels must be enclosed within quotation marks. Value labels for several variables may be included on each VALUE LABELS command. As above, simply separate sets of variable names, values, and value labels by slashes. Be sure to indent any continuation lines at least one space.

Examples of the VARIABLE LABELS and VALUE LABELS commands are shown below. Perhaps it is intuitively obvious that these commands must follow the DATA LIST command, that is, you can't label a variable or value until it's been defined within the file. These statements also precede any commands that request a particular procedure involving data manipulation. In the example below, the FREQUENCIES statement is one such command. Also, you might note that *information contained in quotation marks in the VARIABLE LABELS and VALUE LABELS commands should not be split among lines.*

```
DATA LIST   RECORDS=1/ 1 SUBJ 1. . .
VARIABLE LABELS   PERFORM
   "PERFORMANCE ON LEADERSHIP TASKS"
VALUE LABELS   GENDER 1 "MALE" 2 "FEMALE"/
   STYLE 1 "TASK-ORIENTED" 2 "RELATIONS-ORIENTED"
   3 "BOTH TASK & RELAT"
FREQUENCIES VARIABLES=BSRI TO SEXROLE/. . .
BEGIN DATA

   data records

END DATA
```

The above VARIABLE LABELS statement requests that the extended label "Performance on Leadership Tasks" identify the variable PERFORM whenever it appears in the output. The VALUE LABELS statement requests that "male" and "female" appear on the output in conjunction with the numbers "1" and "2." It also requests labels for the values of STYLE so that it is possible to identify the various categories of only task oriented, only relations oriented, and both task and relations oriented.

8.8   How to Deal with Missing Data (Optional)

At times researchers are unable to obtain data sets that are 100 percent complete. Some subjects may refuse to answer particular questions, some data may not have been obtained for certain subjects, or some variables may not be applicable to some subsets within your sample.

When there are missing values for some of the variables in your data file, you have two basic courses of action from which to choose. The first is simply to leave blank spaces in the data file where missing values are located. This choice will result in SPSS^x automatically assigning what is called the "$SYSMIS" (system-missing value). On all subsequent SPSS^x runs these missing data will be printed with the value "." (i.e., a decimal point). While there are no problems created by choosing this first alternative, we believe there are a number of reasons to consider the second as the better choice. This second alternative involves constructing a "MISSING VALUES" statement.

The MISSING VALUES statement allows the researcher to assign up to three unique numbers which will identify that no data were collected on that variable for a particular case. The number(s) that we use to indicate a missing value must be unique; that is, it must not be one of the actual data values possible for that particular variable. By convention we usually assign the number "9" for each column of the variable. Therefore, for a variable such as GENDER which occupies only one column and has only two possible values ("1" for male and "2" for female), we would assign "9" as the missing value if one of our subjects failed to respond to that question. However, if the variable were IQ scores with over 100 values (three columns), then we would by convention assign 999 for its missing value. The format is to give the variable name and then the number that has been used to indicate missing data within parentheses. Missing values for several variables may be assigned on one MISSING VALUE command (and its continuations). Simply place a slash after each set of missing values declared.

An example of assigning "9" for missing values on the variable GENDER, "0" for missing values on PERFORM, and "99" for missing values on BSRI is shown below. We used "0" to indicate missing values on the variable PERFORM because this variable may have actual values of 9 (to indicate "extremely effective") within the data set, and therefore 9 would not be considered a unique number. We used "99" for BSRI because no values of BSRI exceeded 70 (assuming we remove the decimal place as we would do with data entry when the decimal is specified in the DATA LIST statement).

    MISSING VALUES   GENDER (9)/ PERFORM (0)/BSRI (99)

The MISSING VALUES statement is placed between the DATA LIST statement and the procedure (e.g., FREQUENCIES) statement. An appropriate position for the above MISSING VALUES record is after the VALUE LABELS statement.

    DATA LIST . . .
    VARIABLE LABELS . . .
    VALUE LABELS . . .
    MISSING VALUES . . .
    FREQUENCIES . . .
    BEGIN DATA

    data records

    END DATA

8.9   Output from FREQUENCIES When There Are Missing Values (Optional)

When there are missing values in the data file, it is critical that the researcher understand the difference between the "PERCENT" and "VALID PERCENT" columns that accompany the frequency tables. As was explained in Section 8.5a, when there are missing values, the VALID PERCENT column is used rather than the PERCENT column. The VALID PERCENT column subtracts any cases that are declared missing before calculating the percentages, whereas the PERCENT column calculates percentages based upon all cases (including those for which values are missing) in the data file. For example, in the case of questions asked only of a subgroup of the study (e.g., a question asked only of male employees), the presence of a large percentage of missing values (all of the female subjects) would mean that even if all thirty males gave the same response to an item, the PERCENT value could be no higher than 50.0 percent. In the above case, the VALID PERCENT column would register 100 percent which is far more useful in trying to make sense of the data. The value of 100 percent clearly indicates that all the subjects who were expected to answer the question (i.e., males) did in fact respond on that item.

8.10 Beyond Univariate Distributions

Social scientists are seldom satisfied with interpreting only univariate frequency distributions. Being of a curious nature, the scientist (social or otherwise) wants to know not just how many, how widely dispersed, but *why*. In our example above, any social scientist worth his/her weight in salt would want to know why the subjects responded as they did to the Bem Sex Role Inventory; why did some subjects receive high performance ratings while others received low ratings. These questions cannot be answered by looking at only one variable at a time. Generally, science is dedicated to locating significant relationships between variables. This dictates that the social scientist be familiar with techniques for looking at the distributions of two (or more) variables simultaneously. Most of the remainder of this book will be devoted to such techniques—techniques for locating and analyzing bivariate and even multivariate distributions.

Exercises

1a. Using the data file introduced in Chapter 5, calculate the appropriate statistics to describe the employees at E-Z Manufacturing on the following variables: TASK, RELATION, EDUC, AGE, SEXROLE, and leadership STYLE. Note that we are requesting analysis on the two variables that we created using RECODE and IF statements. This, of course, is possible only if you retain the RECODE and IF statements in your file.

Use the FREQUENCIES statement to obtain the descriptive statistics. This statement, remember, must appear *after* the RECODE and IF statements. You may choose to request all statistics, then select the relevant ones to describe each variable. Or, referring to Table 8.1, you may use keywords to request a set of particular statistics that would include those relevant to at least interval/ratio data (e.g., mean, median, mode, variance, standard deviation, minimum, maximum, and range). Also, make certain that you remove the LIST VARIABLES statement before submitting the program for analysis.

1b. Once you've obtained the printout, write a brief sentence or two describing the major characteristics of each variable. As part of your description, be sure to address the following points. How would you describe the education level and ages of the employees? What statistics would be appropriate to describe TASK and RELATION scores if you considered these ordinal variables? If you took the less conservative approach and considered them interval? What type of variables are SEXROLE and STYLE? Regarding these last two variables, what additional information do the descriptive statistics provide beyond what is already known from the frequency analyses? Briefly summarize the results of your analyses as you might report them to upper management.

2. (Optional) Below are the exam scores for a university class of twenty students. Construct an SPSS^x file and then use it to find the mean, variance, standard deviation, and other appropriate descriptive measures that best describe these data:

87, 89, 73, 67, 89, 90, 89, 93, 77, 79,
83, 79, 77, 83, 81, 86, 91, 98, 80, 75

3a. (Optional) Use the VARIABLE LABELS and VALUE LABELS statements to improve the readability of your printout. Specifically, use the VARIABLE LABELS statement to extend the name of PERFORM to the label "PERFORMANCE RATING"; use the VALUE LABELS statement to label "male" and "female" on the variable GENDER. Include other labels where you or your instructor deem appropriate.

3b. (Optional) Assume that one of your subjects (subject 11) in the LEADERSHIP DATA FILE created in Chapter 5 failed to provide information on the variable GENDER. Another (subject 25) was not rated on his leadership performance (PERFORM). Replace the values that are currently in your data file with a "9" for the subject whose gender was missing, and a "0" where the PERFORM value was missing. Be sure to insert a MISSING VALUES statement in your SPSS^x file. Now generate new frequency tables on GENDER and PERFORM, noting how the output for these data differs from those shown in Table 8.2. Also, calculate descriptive statistics on these two variables and comment on how they might have changed due to the missing values.

9 Crosstabulation: Understanding Bivariate Relationships

In this chapter we will discuss:

- running the CROSSTABS procedure
- determining appropriate statistics
- interpreting measures of association
- controlling for third variables in crosstabluation

9.1 Introduction

We now turn our attention to the topic of bivariate distributions—ones which characterize two variables simultaneously. Much of the research done in the social sciences involves data that are "categorical" or "discrete" rather than "continuous." In our data file on leadership effectiveness, we have three such categorical variables: GENDER, SEXROLE, and STYLE. As an example, leadership STYLE, a variable that we generated in Chapter 7, has three "discrete" categories: relations orientation, task orientation, and combined task and relations orientation. Responses to the Bem Sex Role Inventory (BSRI), on the other hand, can take on any two-digit values between -7.0 and $+7.0$. As such, BSRI is a "continuous" variable. The analysis of relationships involving discrete or categorical variables generally involves the construction of tables that present both variables simultaneously (i.e., bivariate distributions). Such tables are often referred to as "crosstabulations" because they tabulate or count the frequencies of values *across* two variables simultaneously.

Why might we want to carry out a crosstabulation? Let's return to our project on leadership effectiveness that we're conducting at E-Z Manufacturing. Consider the hypothesis, for example, that male employees are more likely to be task oriented than relations oriented, while the reverse pattern would occur for women employees. We could test this hypothesis by examining the frequencies obtained in a crosstabulation of the variables GENDER and STYLE. Our printout would contain a table that indicates (1) the number of men and women (separately) who are task oriented; (2) the number of men and women (separately) who are relations oriented; and (3) the number of men and women who are both task and relations oriented. There are numerous other questions relevant to our project that could be addressed by looking at bivariate distributions—for example, whether a particular SEXROLE (masculine, feminine, or androgynous) is most frequently associated with a particular leadership STYLE; or whether one's SEXROLE orientation is at all related to one's performance rating (PERFORM) on leadership tasks.

The CROSSTABS procedure in SPSS^x provides an easy method for constructing bivariate tables that will allow us to answer these types of questions. In addition, CROSSTABS calculates a number of statistics that allow us to estimate the strength of relationship between the two variables displayed in each of the tables. However, it is necessary to know something about the interpretation of these tables prior to submitting a CROSSTABS program because there is great flexibility in the way in which the tables can be printed.

9.2   What You Need to Know Before Running CROSSTABS

While learning to use the CROSSTABS procedure is quite simple, learning to interpret the output correctly requires some additional preparation. Recall from the previous chapter that there are restrictions on the types of mathematical/statistical techniques that can be appropriately applied to data below interval level. For that reason, one is always well advised to collect data of the highest possible level (this may sometimes be accomplished simply by the way the research instrument is designed). However, despite the researcher's best efforts, some variables defy measurement at anything but the nominal or ordinal level. In the analysis of crosstabulation tables, the interpretation procedure to be followed is determined by the variable which is measured at the *lowest* level. So as you will see, if your lowest variable is nominal, you will use a different procedure for interpretation than if your lowest variable is ordinal. If you should be dealing with variables measured at the interval or ratio level, other techniques should be used to analyze the data (see Chapter 10 on correlation).

Crosstabulation tables (and CROSSTABS) are appropriate *only when analyzing pairs of variables in which at least one of them is either nominal or ordinal.* While there are a large number of measures of association (statistics that estimate the strength of relationship between two or more variables) that are used to analyze specific pairings (such as a nominal dependent variable and an interval independent variable), one really needs only to be prepared to confront two general possibilities:

1. Tables in which at least one of the variables is nominal.
2. Tables in which both variables are at least ordinal.

9.3 Knowing Which Statistics to Use When

SPSS[x] has no way of knowing what level of data exists for each of your variables. Therefore, when a number of tables are generated for bivariate pairs, a variety of statistical tests may be produced on the printout. It is up to the researcher to know which of these statistics may be applied to the specific relationships being interpreted. Let's consider the two situations listed in the preceding section: (1) when one variable is nominal; and (2) when both variables are at least ordinal. We shall take these two situations in order.

9.3a   When At Least One of the Variables Is Nominal

When one variable is nominal, we must use the Chi Square test to interpret our output. This test allows a researcher to determine whether the obtained bivariate distribution of a pair of variables is different from that which would be expected if both variables were assumed to vary independently of one another. We might expect, for example, that Protestants and Catholics are equally likely to be Republican. Empirical observation, however, may suggest that this is not so and that Protestants are far more likely to be Republicans than are Catholics (this finding is hypothetical). Consider our own data on leadership effectiveness. We might expect that men and women (GENDER) are equally likely to be either task oriented or relations oriented in their leadership STYLE, i.e., we begin with the assumption that GENDER and STYLE are *statistically independent* of one another. We will be able to determine whether this idea is supported by looking at the results of the Chi Square test. The Chi Square test enables you to assess whether the obtained frequencies are sufficiently different from the expected frequencies so as to conclude that these two variables are not independent but that one variable is influencing the other.

CROSSTABS will calculate the Chi Square statistic and its related probability. This probability can then be used to determine whether the variables are independent of each other, or influenced by each other.

When the Chi Square value is computed, the data are first transformed into a crosstabulation or contingency table. From this table, the Chi Square value and a number of other statistics are generated.

9.3b   When Both Variables Are Ordinal or Better (i.e., Ordinal, Interval, or Ratio)

Under these conditions, one can choose from a variety of *measures of association* that estimate the strength of relationship between two or more variables. For simplification, we will choose a statistic named Kendall's tau to analyze these tables. Kendall's tau is widely used by social scientists and is the ordinal equivalent of the Pearson correlation coefficient. Once again, the data are first transformed into a contingency table before the Kendall tau is computed.

9.4   You Need to Know the Difference Between Independent and Dependent Variables

One final point to discuss before examining how to set up a CROSSTABS program is the matter of determining which of the variables in each pair is to be considered the dependent variable and which the independent variable. In experimental research designs, the independent variable is the stimulus which is manipulated by the researcher. The observed effects on behavior, attitudes, etc. represent the dependent variable. In other types of research, it is often more difficult to make this determination. For convenience, it is usually sufficient to consider independent variables to be the "causes" of behavior. Dependent variables, then, are the "effects" or changes in behavior. In the relationship between a subject's gender and sex role orientation (masculine, feminine, or androgynous), it is logical to assume that gender is the independent variable that may have some influence on sex role orientation, the assumed dependent variable. Does it make as much sense to assume that one's sex role orientation will change a person's gender?

It is important to determine the dependent variable correctly. If this is not done the tables may be constructed in such a way as to make the results extremely difficult to interpret. Traditionally, crosstabulation tables are constructed with the values of the independent variable listed horizontally across the top of the table. The dependent variable values are listed vertically on the left hand side of the table (See Table 9.2 for an example of how this table would appear). This configuration is easily accomplished with the CROSSTABS procedure by listing the dependent variable first and then the independent variable. With this in mind, we are now ready to begin discussion of the format for the CROSSTABS procedure.

9.5   Explanation of the CROSSTABS Procedure and Related Statistics

To obtain crosstabulation tables and the related statistics that will enable interpretation of these tables, three statements need to be discussed. The first is the CROSSTABS statement, the second is an OPTIONS statement which enables us to modify the format of the output, and the third is a STATISTICS statement which permits us to choose various statistical analyses.

9.5a   CROSSTABS

This record calls up the program which displays a "frequency matrix" or "contingency table" for two or more variables, i.e., a table indicating the frequency of subjects falling into each unique combination of categories. This program also enables us to obtain a number of statistics related to the frequency matrix by inclusion of a STATISTICS record. The specific table that is requested is designated in the specification field in the following way: the dependent variable is listed, the keyword BY follows, then the independent variable is listed. For example:

CROSSTABS   SEXROLE BY GENDER

It is possible to request more than one table with a single CROSSTABS statement by separating the table requests with a "/". For example:

CROSSTABS   SEXROLE BY GENDER/STYLE BY SEXROLE

The above statement requests two tables. The first looks at how gender influences sex role orientation, the second looks at how sex role influences leadership style. Interestingly, in the above statement, SEXROLE is considered a dependent variable in one table (i.e., it is influenced by GENDER) and an independent variable in the second (i.e., it is influencing leadership style). Thus, as mentioned earlier the distinction between an independent and dependent variable is not always readily apparent, since the same variable (e.g., SEXROLE) can be considered *either*, depending on the context and specific research question.

   One can also introduce "control" variables very easily. Suppose that you wish to know if education has the same effect on the income of women as men. Here education would be considered the independent variable, income the dependent variable, and gender (men vs. women) the control variable. In this case, the addition of this control variable results in the production of two separate tables, one showing the effect of education on income for men, and other showing the effect of education on income for women. Relating this concept to our project on leadership effectiveness, you might be interested in determining if one's SEXROLE orientation (masculine, feminine, or androgynous) has the same influence on leadership STYLE for males as females (GENDER). Again, GENDER would become a control variable, and would result in two separate tables. One table would contain only male subjects and the other only female subjects. Each table will, of course, crosstabulate the respondent's leadership STYLE with his/her SEXROLE orientation.

The format for requesting a control variable is simple. List the control variable after the independent variable in the CROSSTABS statement. Control variables are preceded by the keyword BY. For example, GENDER is listed as a control variable in the following statement:

CROSSTABS   STYLE BY SEXROLE BY GENDER

In general, there will be as many tables generated as there are values of the control variable. Because GENDER has only two values ("1" for male; "2" for female), two tables will be generated. If your control variable had three possible values, then three tables would be generated. Obviously, control variables will generally be discrete variables; and you should take care not to use a continuous variable as a control variable. If, for example, you used AGE as a control variable, SPSS^x would generate a different table for each different age in the sample. You would end up with pages upon pages of meaningless tables, and no doubt you would lose your favorable standing with your local computer center!

9.5b   The OPTIONS Statement

This statement allows you to select several optional ways of presenting the crosstabulation tables. While eighteen different options are available with the CROSSTABS procedure, we are interested in only one of them. When we specify "OPTIONS 4" we will cause column percentages to be printed. In other words, the number of cases in each cell of the table will be expressed as the percentage of the total cases in that column. For all our work with CROSSTABS, this OPTIONS record will remain the same, and will appear in the record after the CROSSTABS statement as:

OPTIONS   4

9.5c   The STATISTICS Statement

This record follows the OPTIONS record and allows you to select a number of statistics (Chi Square and measures of association) to be computed. You may select the statistics in one of two ways. By using the

Table 9.1   Statistics Options for CROSSTABS

Statistic	Number
Chi Square	1
Phi for 2 x 2 tables, Cramer's V	
for larger tables	2
Contingency Coefficient	3
Lambda	4
Uncertainty coefficient	5
Kendall tau-b	6
Kendall tau-c	7
Gamma	8
Somers' d	9
Eta	10
Pearson r	11

keyword "ALL", all available statistics will be computed (there are about ten in all). The alternative method is to list the numbers (separated by commas if you like) that correspond to the specific statistics that are available. These statistics and their corresponding numbers are listed in Table 9.1. For example, to request the Chi Square (which corresponds to "1" in Table 9.1) and Kendall's tau B (which corresponds to "6" in the table, the STATISTICS statement would appear:

STATISTICS   1, 6

9.6   Sample SPSS^x Program Using CROSSTABS

The sequence of an SPSS^x CROSSTABS file would appear as shown below. While it isn't necessary to include the OPTIONS and STATISTICS records in order for the crosstabulation tables to be generated, these records are required to obtain column percentages in the tables and various statistics. Also note that because the variables STYLE and SEXROLE are included in the analysis below, the RECODE and IF statements that were used to create these variables must be included in the SPSS^x run.

```
DATA LIST   RECORDS=1/1 SUBJ . . . .
RECODE BSRI (LO THRU −2.1=1) (−2.0 THRU +2.0=3) (2.1 THRU
   HI=2) INTO SEXROLE
IF RELATION < 5 AND TASK > 5 STYLE=1
IF RELATION > 5 AND TASK < 5 STYLE=2
IF RELATION > 5 AND TASK > 5 STYLE=3
CROSSTABS   STYLE BY SEXROLE/STYLE BY SEXROLE BY GENDER
OPTIONS   4
STATISTICS   1,6,7
```

BEGIN DATA

data records

END DATA

9.7   Understanding Bivariate Relationships in the Leadership Data File by Using CROSSTABS

One of the questions you are interested in addressing as part of your project at E-Z Manufacturing is to what extent the sex role orientation of managers (masculine, feminine, or androgynous) affects the ways in which they manage (STYLE). Based upon the research literature in this field, you hypothesize that sex role orientation (SEXROLE) may affect the way people manage (STYLE). In order to answer this question, it would be necessary to crosstabulate SEXROLE with STYLE. However, you also suspect that the effect of sex role orientation on style may be different for men than for women. What we are doing now is considering a third variable—a control variable. Accordingly, a second crosstabulation request of SEXROLE and STYLE using GENDER as a control variable would also be appropriate. These two crosstab requests are reflected the SPSS^x CROSSTABS file that is given as an example in the previous section (9.6).

The first table requested—STYLE BY SEXROLE—is called a zero-order table. It will sort the subjects into a number of cells based upon all possible combinations of paired values (see Table 9.2). The second request, STYLE BY SEXROLE BY GENDER, will produce two tables depicting the relationship between SEXROLE and STYLE, one for male employees and one for female employees. These two tables represent the "first-order partial crosstabulation tables," a lengthy phrase which merely indicates that a third variable—in this case GENDER—has been controlled.

In addition, three statistics have been requested. With the exception of the Chi Square, these so-called measures of association indicate how strongly two variables are related. In the above SPSS^x file, we have requested three statistics: 1,6, and 7. The "1" causes SPSS^x to calculate the Chi Square, the statistic that must be used if one or both variables in the table are nominal. The "6" and "7" cause Kendall's tau's to be computed, measures which can be used when both variables in the table are ordinal and which can provide estimates of explained or "common" variance. The Tau B ("6") is used if the table is square (the number or rows equals the number of columns); the Tau C ("7") is used if the table is rectangular (number of rows and columns not equal).

9.8   Explanation of CROSSTABS Output

There are two components to the CROSSTABS output. The first is interpreting the crosstabulation tables, the second is knowing how to apply and interpret the statistics. You should first look at all the cells in the table to determine whether or not the independent variable appears to have an effect on the dependent variable. The statistics then help convey information about the extent of the relationship that might exist between these two variables.

9.8a   Does SEXROLE Affect Leadership STYLE?

Let's begin by inspecting the output from the STYLE by SEXROLE crosstabulation (see Table 9.2a). This table is output with the title: "CROSSTABULATION OF STYLE BY SEXROLE". If you have specified variable and value labels in the SPSS^x file (which will greatly assist you in reading the output), they will appear on the printout as well (see Section 8.7 in Chapter 8). The upper number in each cell represents the number of subjects who have the unique combination of values on each variable. For example, in Table 9.2a, the upper left cell indicates that there were seven subjects whose leadership style was task oriented *and* whose sex role was "masculine." In that same cell, the bottom number, 46.7, tells us that 46.7 percent of all the people having a masculine sex role used a task-oriented leadership style. The use of OPTION 4 in our SPSS^x run ensures that each row is percentaged vertically. In other words, we can see that of those subjects with a masculine sex role orientation, (i.e., SEXROLE = 1), the greatest proportion—46.7 percent—exhibited a task-oriented leadership style.

One way to approach the table is to look at the first row total at the extreme right of the table. The number 25.0 percent indicates that of the entire sample, 25.0 percent exhibited task leadership style. However, the number in the upper left cell—again 46.7—indicates that a high percentage of employees with a masculine sex role orientation exhibited this leadership style. The percentage in the upper-middle cell—20.0—indicates that a fairly low percentage of employees who had a feminine sex role orientation exhibited task leadership style, and that most feminine sex-typed individuals (60.0 percent; middle cell) were relations oriented in their leadership style. One can also readily see that only a small percentage (16.7 percent) of androgynous individuals showed task-oriented leadership, while 66.7 percent showed a combined relations and

Table 9.2a-c Sample Output from CROSSTABS

9.2a
```
            STYLE                      BY  SEXROLE
- - - - - - - - - - - - - - - - - - - - - - - - - - - - -     PAGE  1 OF  1

                        SEXROLE
                COUNT  I
                COL PCT I                      ROW
                        I                      TOTAL
                        I  1.00I    2.00I    3.00I
        STYLE   --------+--------+--------+--------+
                1.00  I    7  I    3  I    5  I    15
                      I  46.7 I  20.0 I  16.7 I  25.0
                      +--------+--------+--------+
                2.00  I    4  I    9  I    5  I    18
                      I  26.7 I  60.0 I  16.7 I  30.0
                      +--------+--------+--------+
                3.00  I    4  I    3  I   20  I    27
                      I  26.7 I  20.0 I  66.7 I  45.0
                      +--------+--------+--------+
                COLUMN     15        15        30        60
                TOTAL    25.0      25.0      50.0     100.0


        CHI-SQUARE   D.F.    SIGNIFICANCE     MIN E.F.    CELLS WITH E.F.< 5
        ----------   ----    ------------     --------    ------------------

         16.46667     4         .0025           3.750      4 OF    9 ( 44.4%)


                    STATISTIC             VALUE       SIGNIFICANCE
                    ---------             -----       ------------

        KENDALL'S TAU B                  .35962          .0010
        KENDALL'S TAU C                  .34250          .0010
```

```
- - - - - - - -  C R O S S T A B U L A T I O N   O F  - - - - - - - - -
            STYLE                      BY  SEXROLE
    CONTROLLING FOR..
```
9.2b
```
            GENDER                     VALUE =       1.
- - - - - - - - - - - - - - - - - - - - - - - - - - - - -     PAGE  1 OF  1

                        SEXROLE
                COUNT  I
                COL PCT I                ROW
                        I                TOTAL
                        I  1.00I    3.00I
        STYLE   --------+--------+--------+
                1.00  I    7  I    3  I    10
                      I  46.7 I  20.0 I  33.3
                      +--------+--------+
                2.00  I    4  I    2  I     6
                      I  26.7 I  13.3 I  20.0
                      +--------+--------+
                3.00  I    4  I   10  I    14
                      I  26.7 I  66.7 I  46.7
                      +--------+--------+
                COLUMN     15        15        30
                TOTAL    50.0      50.0     100.0
```

continued

Table 9.2   *Continued*

CHI-SQUARE	D.F.	SIGNIFICANCE	MIN E.F.	CELLS WITH E.F.< 5
4.83809	2	.0890	3.000	2 OF 6 (33.3%)

STATISTIC	VALUE	SIGNIFICANCE
KENDALL'S TAU B	.36395	.0195
KENDALL'S TAU C	.40889	.0195

9.2c

```
- - - - - - - -  C R O S S T A B U L A T I O N  O F  - - - - - - - - -
       STYLE                      BY  SEXROLE
CONTROLLING FOR..
       GENDER                     VALUE =     2.
- - - - - - - - - - - - - - - - - - - - - - - - - - - -  PAGE  1 OF  1
```

		SEXROLE		
	COUNT			ROW
	COL PCT	2.00	3.00	TOTAL
STYLE				
	1.00	3	2	5
		20.0	13.3	16.7
	2.00	9	3	12
		60.0	20.0	40.0
	3.00	3	10	13
		20.0	66.7	43.3
	COLUMN	15	15	30
	TOTAL	50.0	50.0	100.0

CHI-SQUARE	D.F.	SIGNIFICANCE	MIN E.F.	CELLS WITH E.F.< 5
6.96923	2	.0307	2.500	2 OF 6 (33.3%)

STATISTIC	VALUE	SIGNIFICANCE
KENDALL'S TAU B	.38179	.0155
KENDALL'S TAU C	.42667	.0155

task style. Thus at first glance, it appears that sex role orientation does have some effect on leadership style. Further inspection of the table would suggest the following conclusions: (1) most masculine sex-typed individuals use a task-oriented leadership style; (2) most feminine sex-typed individuals use a relations-oriented leadership; and (3) androgynous individuals are most likely to use a combination of both task and relations-oriented styles.

Since both variables in Table 9.2a are nominal, the appropriate statistic to use is the Chi Square. Although the Chi Square statistic can be used with virtually any kind of data, it is very sensitive to small sample sizes. With small sample sizes, one or more cells may have an "expected frequency" of less than 5. Since the expected frequencies appear in the denominator of the calculating formula for the statistic, these small numbers can make a large difference in the interpretation—one such cell may actually make the difference between a statistically significant value and one that is not statistically significant.

SPSS^x provides enough information to warn you of the potential problem of small sample sizes. You can see in Table 9.2 the heading "CELLS WITH E.F.< 5." This message alerts you to the great care that needs to be used whenever one or more of the expected cell frequencies are less than 5. We urge the reader to be very cautious when reporting tables in which even one cell has an expected frequency of less than 5. When it makes sense, variables may be recoded into fewer values or categories using a RECODE statement as was discussed in Chapter 7. However, such recoding would not make sense for the variables in Table 9.2, so we simply need to proceed very cautiously with our interpretation of this Chi Square.

Looking at the values printed below the crosstab table, we find that Chi Square equals 16.467 and has a significance of 0.0025. Using the customary 0.05 significance level, we can say that there is a statistically significant relationship between sex role orientation and leadership style since 0.0025 is less than 0.05. Stated slightly differently, this means that SEXROLE and STYLE do not vary independently of each other, but rather that certain sex role orientations are more likely to be associated with certain leadership styles. Quite clearly, this statistically supported assertion is consistent with the numbers of masculine, feminine, and androgynous individuals exhibiting various leadership styles that we observed in the tables. Chi Square does not indicate the strength or direction of the relationship, it merely informs us whether the patterns within the bivariate distribution are likely to have been due to chance or to the independent variable.

9.8b Is GENDER an Important Variable to Consider?

As you recall, you suspect that the apparent relationship between SEX-ROLE and leadership STYLE might be different for male subjects than for female subjects. The second crosstabulation request (STYLE BY SEXROLE BY GENDER) controls for the effects of GENDER on this relationship. Two tables (Table 9.2b and Table 9.2c) are generated by this request—one for females and one for males—and they must be considered together. Using the same interpretation strategy as before, we can examine the relationship between leadership style and sex role orientation for male and female employees separately. What we find is really quite consistent with what we've already learned from the simple STYLE BY SEXROLE table. Consider male employees only (Table 9.2b). Most who are masculine sex typed (46.7 percent) exhibit a task-oriented leadership style; most who are androgynous show a combination of task and relations style. Now consider the female employees only (Table 9.2c). Here again the largest percentage of the androgynous females show a combination of leadership styles while those who are primarily feminine sex typed tend to show a relations-oriented leadership style.

The variables, of course, are still nominal, and therefore the Chi Square is the appropriate statistic. We must interpret each table separately, but eventually must combine the findings on our own. For male employees (Table 9.2b), we see the relationship, although close, is no longer significant ($X^2=4.8381$; p=0.0890 which is greater than 0.05). Yet for women, the relationship between sex role and leadership style continues to be significant ($X^2 = 6.96923$; p=.0307). Therefore gender can be considered a significant factor when considering leadership style and sex roles. While our goal is not to show you every possible trick for interpreting your data, we are attempting to show you how the CROSSTABS procedure may be used as a powerful tool for understanding some rather complex relationships that exist among several different variables.

9.9   Rethinking the Nature of the Variables SEXROLE and STYLE (Optional)

While we have done a rather thorough job of examining the relationship between sex role orientation and leadership style, we have not really addressed the question of *how strong* this relationship is. It may not seem important given that some aspects of the relationship disappeared when we controlled for gender, but what if we had made use of some rather obscure laws of logic? Remember that tables containing two ordinal variables may be interpreted with the more powerful Kendall's tau (more powerful because they are what statisticians refer to as proportional reduction of error measures). Remember also that the definition of an ordinal variable is that its values must be arranged in a logical order such that they range from "high" to "low" or from "being present" to "being absent." Might there be some way to consider leadership style and sex role orientation as ordinal variables?

9.9a   Changing a Categorical (Nominal) Variable to an Ordinal Variable

As we have already defined it, leadership STYLE involves the predominance of a task orientation, a relations orientation, or a combination of both. This is the same as saying that leaders who are identified as task oriented exhibit far *more* evidence of task orientation than those who are identified as relations oriented. Also then, leaders who have a combination of both orientations would have more task orientation than those identified as relations oriented, but less than those identified as "purely" task oriented. Therefore, if the value "BOTH" appeared between the values of TASK and RELATION, then leadership style could qualify, statistically speaking, as an ordinal variable.

It is left to the reader to construct the actual argument, but with respect to sex role orientation the same change would also allow us to treat this as an ordinal variable. The remaining task is to find a way to transform the categorical variables of STYLE and SEXROLE into ordinal variables. If you recall in Chapter 7, we rearranged the continuous variable BSRI into the categorical variable SEXROLE by using the RECODE procedure. There is no reason why we couldn't use this same strategy to reorder a categorical variable such as SEXROLE into an ordinal variable. RECODE will permit the rearrangement of the three values for each of our variables so that each has an underlying order. For example, as SEXROLE now stands, "1" = masculine sex typed, "2" = feminine sex typed, and "3" = androgynous. However, we have suggested that there exists an underlying continuum or order for this variable such that "masculine" lies at one extreme and "feminine" lies at the other, with "androgynous" somewhere between the two (i.e., masculine←androgynous→feminine). To represent this continuum or order within our variable, we would need to renumber our categories such that "1" = masculine, "2" = androgynous, and "3" = feminine.

9.9b   SPSS^x Records Needed to Rearrange and Relabel STYLE and SEXROLE

To transform both STYLE and SEXROLE into ordinal variables and to add identifying variable labels, you would need to add several records to your SPSS^x file. These additional records are provided in boldface print in the following sample file:

```
DATA LIST   RECORDS=1 / 1 SUBJ. . .
RECODE   BSRI. . . . .INTO SEXROLE
IF RELATION < 5. . .
IF RELATION > 5. . .
IF RELATION > 5. . .
RECODE STYLE (2=3), (3=2)/ SEXROLE (2=3), (3=2)
```

```
VALUE LABELS STYLE 1 'TASK' 2 'BOTH' 3 'RELATIONS' /
SEXROLE 1 'MASCULINE' 2 'ANDROGYNOUS' 3 'FEMININE' /
CROSSTABS   STYLE BY SEXROLE
OPTIONS   4
STATISTICS   1,2,6,7
BEGIN DATA
```

data records

END DATA

9.9c   The Consequence of Treating STYLE and SEXROLE as Ordinal Variables

You should see from Table 9.3 that the recoding procedure has accomplished our goal. Both variables can be considered, statistically and mathematically, to be ordinal variables, so it is now appropriate to apply

Table 9.3   Output from CROSSTABS: STYLE and SEXROLE as Ordinal Variables

```
- - - - - - - - - - -  C R O S S T A B U L A T I O N  O F  - - - - - - - - -
      STYLE                        BY  SEXROLE
- - - - - - - - - - - - - - - - - - - - - - - - - - -  - PAGE  1 OF  1

                      SEXROLE
              COUNT  I
              COL PCT IMASCULIN ANDROGYN FEMININE   ROW
                     IE         OUS               TOTAL
                     I   1.00I    2.00I    3.00I
      STYLE   --------+--------+--------+--------+
               1.00  I    7  I     5  I     3  I    15
      TASK           I 46.7  I 16.7  I 20.0  I  25.0
                     +--------+--------+--------+
               2.00  I    4  I    20  I     3  I    27
      BOTH           I 26.7  I 66.7  I 20.0  I  45.0
                     +--------+--------+--------+
               3.00  I    4  I     5  I     9  I    18
      RELATIONS      I 26.7  I 16.7  I 60.0  I  30.0
                     +--------+--------+--------+
              COLUMN      15       30       15       60
              TOTAL     25.0     50.0     25.0    100.0


   CHI-SQUARE   D.F.   SIGNIFICANCE    MIN E.F.    CELLS WITH E.F.< 5
   ----------   ----   ------------    --------    ------------------

    16.46667      4       .0025          3.750     4 OF    9 ( 44.4%)

          STATISTIC          VALUE        SIGNIFICANCE
          ---------          -----        ------------

   CRAMER'S V                .37044
   KENDALL'S TAU B           .27037          .0104
   KENDALL'S TAU C           .25750          .0104
```

Kendall's tau. Our new contingency table is square (3 rows and 3 columns) so we must use the Kendall's tau B. This statistic can be viewed as a correlation coefficient in that the values may range from -1.00 to $+1.00$. From the statistics provided below the table, we see that Kendall's tau B has a value of 0.27037 with a probability (under "Significance" column) of 0.0104, indicating a statistically significant relationship since 0.0104 is less than 0.05. The fact that no sign precedes the tau value indicates a "positive" relationship between the two variables (a negative relationship is designated by a negative sign). A positive relationship means that as one variable increases in value, the other also increases. "Increase" refers to the magnitude of the values read by the SPSS[x] program. Therefore, for our two variables, a positive tau B indicates that as SEXROLE orientation "increases" from "masculine" to "androgynous" to "feminine", the leadership STYLE "increases" from "task" to "both" to "relations" orientation. In other words, employees with feminine sex role orientation are more likely to exhibit relations-oriented leadership styles than are masculine or androgynous employees. While we arrived at this same interpretation before going through all these variable manipulations, we can now communicate this relationship in the universal language of statistics through the Kendall's tau B.

9.9d   Estimating the Common Variance Between STYLE and SEXROLE

The value of applying Kendall's tau does not stop with the conclusion that we were able to make in the previous section. Realize that one of the goals of science is to discover how changes in one variable bring about or are related to changes in another. Statisticians refer to these changes as "variance." While the concept of variance is not usually applied to ordinal data, there is statistical evidence that establishes the legitimacy of "variance" as a measure of ordinal variability. The point is not to discuss what variance really means, but to consider what additional information the variance might tell us about the relationship between STYLE and SEXROLE.

If one variable (e.g., STYLE) were perfectly related to another (e.g., SEXROLE), then *all* the variance in the dependent variable would be accounted for by changes in the independent variable. Explaining all of the variance between two variables would be equivalent to explaining 100 percent of the variance—the closer to 100 percent, the stronger the relationship between the variables. By mathematically squaring Kendall's tau, we can obtain an estimate of the proportion of the variance in the dependent variable accounted for by changes in the independent variable. Multiplying this square by 100 will yield the percent of explained or "common" variance. Referring back to our tau value of 0.27037, squaring and multiplying this number gives us an estimate of 7.3 percent explained variance between STYLE and SEXROLE. In other words, slightly over 10 percent of the differences in leadership style can be explained by different sex role orientations. While this may not appear to be a very large explained variance, one has to bear in mind the fact that for social science research, the average explained variance is in the order of 15–20 percent.

At this point, of course, one could continue the investigation on our ordinal variables by controlling for GENDER, interpreting Kendall's tau and explained variance for men and women separately. Our point is to suggest that the really good researcher attempts to do as much as possible to interpret tables as precisely as possible. This, in the long run, is most easily accomplished by using the language of statistics. Nominal data simply do not lend themselves to such statistical analyses, but ordinal data provide a number of opportunities for the use of well-defined, widely accepted rules of statistical analysis.

9.10   If You're Feeling a Bit Of Anxiety about Bivariate Analyses . . .

If the analysis of crosstabulation tables seems rather complicated to you, then you've experienced things as they should be. SPSS^x, as you have just seen, makes the calulation of many statistics very easy, but the valid interpretation of these statistics takes real expertise and practice. The value of SPSS^x and computer-based data analysis is that it enables you to explore all possible opportunities for analyzing and interpreting data. Nominal and ordinal variables are really more difficult to interpret than interval and ratio variables, the staple of the natural sciences and some areas of the social and behavioral science. It is to the bivariate analysis of interval and ratio variables that we shall turn in the next chapter.

Exercise

1. Using the CROSSTABS procedure, run the program given in Section 9.6 in which you crosstabulate SEXROLE (androgenous, feminine, masculine) by leadership STYLE (task, relations, or both).
2. Check to see that your output is similar to the one given in Table 9.2.
3. Note the value of Chi Square and interpret this statistic. State carefully what we can conclude about the relationship between SEXROLE and STYLE.
4. (Optional). Below are the data collected from a sample of fifty-five licensed automobile drivers. The variables measured are: Gender (1

= male, 2 = female), number of Accidents in the last five years (0 = none or 1,1 = 2 or more), and number of Miles Driven in each of the last five years (0 = less than 12,000, 1 = more than 12,000). Enter these data, construct an SPSS^x file, then run the zero order crosstabulation table and interpret it. How does your interpretation change when you control for the number of miles driven in each of the last five years?

Gender	Accidents	Miles Driven	Gender	Accidents	Miles Driven
1	1	1	2	0	0
1	1	1	2	0	0
1	1	1	2	0	0
1	1	1	2	0	0
1	1	1	2	0	0
1	1	1	2	0	0
1	1	1	2	0	0
1	1	1	2	0	0
1	1	1	2	0	0
1	1	1	2	0	0
1	1	1	2	0	0
1	1	1	2	0	0
1	1	1	2	0	0
1	1	1	2	1	0
1	0	1	2	1	0
1	0	1	2	1	1
1	0	1	2	1	1
1	1	0	2	1	1
1	0	0	2	1	1
1	0	0	2	1	1
1	0	0	2	1	1
2	0	0	2	0	1
2	0	0	2	0	1
2	0	0			

10 Correlation

In this chapter we will discuss:

- SPSS[x] programs for determining correlations
- interpreting the output from the PEARSON CORR procedure
- calculating nonparametric correlation coefficients
- creating scatter diagrams with SPSS[x]

10.1 Introduction

In the previous chapter we demonstrated how to use the CROSSTABS procedure to examine the relationship between two or more variables. The CROSSTABS procedure is most appropriately used with data that are nominal or ordinal. While it is possible, and often necessary, to recode interval variables (age, for example) into a small number of categories for the construction of contingency tables, some detail and precision are lost. SPSS[x] provides other procedures that are more effective and efficient for evaluating the relationship between two or more interval (or ratio) variables. These procedures involve the calculation of correlation statistics.

Correlation statistics are used to determine the degree and direction of relatedness between any two interval or ratio variables. The range of the correlation statistic is from −1.00 to +1.00. The closer the value is to an absolute value of 1.00 (either positive or negative), the greater the degree of relatedness. The direction of the relationship can be either positive or negative. Shoe size and height, for example, are positively correlated; as the one variable (height) increases, so also does the other (shoe size). When two variables are negatively correlated, an increase in the first is related to a decrease in the second. Thus, the larger the automobile, the lower the miles per gallon it can achieve. Sometimes changes in one variable are unrelated to changes in the second variable. For example, height and intelligence are unrelated; tall people can be either smart or dull, and the same holds for short people. In such cases the correlation between the variables centers around zero; hence, there is no correlation.

10.2   Examining Correlations in Our Leadership Project

In our project on sex roles and leadership at E-Z Manufacturing, we would have reason to explore a number of possible relationships between variables using correlational procedures. In one sense, correlations between almost any two interval/ratio variables in a study like this one might yield valuable information. For example, by using correlational procedures, we could identify possible relationships between one's score on the BSRI and one's age or education level, variables which are all at least intervally scaled.

Perhaps an even more fruitful approach, however, could be taken by correlating BSRI scores with such variables as TASK (which indicates how task oriented a person tends to be in leadership situations) and RELATION (which indicates how relations oriented a person tends to be). As we just mentioned, from the previous chapter we already know that SEXROLE orientation and leadership STYLE are related; we might also expect that low BSRI scores (those indicating a more masculine sex type) would be associated with higher TASK orientation (i.e., a negative correlation), and that high BSRI scores (indicating a feminine sex type) would be associated with high RELATION orientation (i.e., a positive correlation).

You may recall from Chapter 8 on Summarizing Your Data with Descriptive Statistics that we had previously taken the conservative approach and treated variables such as TASK, RELATION, and PER-FORM, which were scored on 1-to-7 or 1-to-9 Likert scales, as ordinal variables. Arguments for treating variables like these as interval variables are frequently advanced by social scientists, since such treatment allows considerably more powerful statistical analyses, including the use of procedures like the Pearson r. For this reason, it could be advantageous to consider the variables TASK, RELATION, and PERFORM as interval rather than ordinal variables. If one is willing to accept this modification, we could now perform a number of Pearson correlations that might help us answer questions regarding the relationships among BSRI scores, TASK scores, RELATION scores, and PERFORMANCE scores. Specifically, we might run correlations on all possible pairs of these variables to determine how they are interrelated.

10.3   SPSS[x] Programs For Determining Correlations

PEARSON CORR and NONPAR CORR are two SPSS[x] programs that can be used to determine the correlation coefficient. As the name implies, PEARSON CORR yields the Pearson product-moment correlation coefficient ("r"). The hypothesis tests of significance given in the SPSS[x] PEARSON CORR procedure can only be used when the data are normally distributed and are at least interval. The NONPAR CORR program computes Spearman's "rho" and Kendall's "tau," nonparametric tests that are appropriate for use when the data are ordinal and/or not normally distributed. A related program called PLOT is sometimes used in conjunction with the correlation programs. This program prints out a scatter diagram of the data points for each pair of variables being considered. As such it will enable you to visualize the way in which two variables are related, showing "clusters" of points in similar directions, curvilinear relations, and so on.

In the following pages, we will focus on the PEARSON CORR procedure as the technique to analyze the relationship between two variables that are at least interval. Once the format for this procedure is understood, it is quite easy to go back and substitute with the NONPAR CORR if so desired. Brief explanation of the NONPAR CORR and PLOT programs have been included as optional sections.

10.4   Explanation of PEARSON CORR, and Related OPTIONS, and STATISTICS Records

In order to obtain the correlation coefficient and various other related statistics, the PEARSON CORR record is generally used in conjunction with a STATISTICS record and OPTIONS record. Each of these records is described below.

10.4a   The PEARSON CORR Record

The words PEARSON CORR in the control field call up the program that is necessary for the Pearson "r" to be calculated. This record results in correlation coefficients being calculated for pairs of variables listed in the specification field. Variables to be correlated may simply be listed in succession on the record:

PEARSON CORR   BSRI, PERFORM, TASK, AGE

The format above requests that each variable in the statement be correlated with every other listed variable. Variables to be correlated may also be joined with the keyword WITH. If the WITH format is used, generally it is not important which variable of the pair is placed first and which is placed second in the request. Correlations between several pairs of variables have been requested in the following statement:

PEARSON CORR   BSRI WITH PERFORM/BSRI WITH TASK/BSRI WITH AGE

This statement produces three correlation coefficients, one for each pair of variables. When a number of correlations involving some of the same variables are requested (as in the statement above where BSRI is correlated with PERFORM, TASK, and AGE), a simpler form may be used:

PEARSON CORR   BSRI WITH PERFORM, TASK, AGE

The above format follows the general form of: "VARIABLE 1, VARIABLE 2 WITH VARIABLE 3, VARIABLE 4, VARIABLE 5." Thus, the computer is instructed to perform the operations on the following pairs—variable 1 and variables 3, 4, and 5, then variable 2 and variables 3, 4, and 5. Any number of variables may be inserted before or after the keyword WITH. The variables listed before the keyword WITH create the rows of a correlation matrix in the output and the variables listed after the keyword WITH create the columns of the matrix. Note that the "WITH" keyword produces correlations of only the specified pairs of variables, i.e., the above format would not yield correlations between variable 3 and variable 4, nor 3 and 5 or 4 and 5.

Another way of requesting a number of different correlations is to use the general format "VARIABLE 1 TO VARIABLE 5." This statement instructs the computer to perform the operations on all possible two-variable combinations from variable 1 all the way to variable 5. For example, the statement

PEARSON CORR   BSRI TO PERFORM

would yield correlations on all possible pairs of variables in the data file between BSRI and PERFORM.

10.4b   The STATISTICS Record

This record follows the PEARSON CORR statement and is required only if you want to select particular statistics in addition to the Pearson "r," which is automatically calculated. The number "1" in the specification field causes the printing of the number of valid cases in the data, the mean, and standard deviations of the distributions for each of the variables included in the previous line. The number "2" causes the cross-product deviations and covariance for each pair of variables to be calculated, information that is sometimes helpful to have.

10.4c   The OPTIONS Record

This record follows the STATISTICS statement and is used to produce a specific format or configuration for the output. There are a number of OP-TIONS that one might request: a "3" in the specification field would cause significance values to be based on a two-tailed test rather than a one-tailed test, the default option. When there is no way to determine the direction of the relationship in advance—as in most exploratory research—this option is appropriate. A "6" would cause only the non-redundant correlation coefficients to be printed. When some formats are used in the PEARSON CORR statement, the correlations for each pair of variables are printed twice. For example, when you simply list the variables BSRI and AGE in the PEARSON CORR statement, BSRI is correlated with AGE, and AGE is then correlated with BSRI. Obviously, such correlations are redundant, and OPTION 6 eliminates this redundant output.

10.5   Sample SPSS^x Program for Correlation (PEARSON CORR)

The following SPSS^x file requests three correlations, one for each possible pair of variables in the statement. In addition, the number of cases, the mean and standard deviation for each variable are requested by the STATISTICS record. By including a "6" on the OPTIONS record, redundant output is eliminated.

```
DATA LIST   RECORDS=1/SUBJ. . .
PEARSON CORR   BSRI, AGE, EDUC
STATISTICS   1
OPTIONS   6
BEGIN DATA

data records

END DATA
```

10.6   Explanation of PEARSON CORR Output from BSRI, AGE, and EDUC Correlations

The complete output from a PEARSON CORR procedure for correlations on BSRI, AGE, and EDUC is presented in Table 10.1. The first informa-

Table 10.1   Sample Output from PEARSON CORR

```
-- P E A R S O N   C O R R E L A T I O N   C O E F F I C I E N T S --

VARIABLE              VARIABLE              VARIABLE
PAIR                  PAIR                  PAIR
--------              --------              --------
BSRI      -.3013      BSRI       .4303      AGE       -.2157
WITH     N( 60)       WITH     N( 60)       WITH     N( 60)
AGE      SIG .010     EDUC     SIG .000     EDUC     SIG .049
```

tion provided in the output is a list of the variables requested on the PEARSON CORR line.

Note that you could have included any of the variables defined on the DATA LIST record and SPSS^x would have obligingly calculated correlation coefficients. However, it is up to the user to recognize which pairs to request. In this case, for example, you must first determine which of the variables are interval, then from this list you choose pairs of variables that are logically or theoretically likely to be related. For this example a variable list—BSRI, AGE, and EDUC—was specified.

For each variable in the PEARSON CORR statement, the number of valid cases, the arithmetic mean, and the standard deviation are provided. If statistic "2" was requested in the STATISTICS record, the cross-product deviation and covariation terms for each of the three nonredundant pairs is included in the request. Immediately below these values are printed the correlation coefficients for pairs of variables. For each pair you are again given the number of valid cases used in calculating the correlation coefficient, Pearson's "r", and the significance level of that value. As is the custom, a significance level (value) of .05 or less is taken to mean that there is a "statistically significant" relationship between a pair of variables.

All three relationships that were analyzed in the sample SPSS^x file are "statistically significant." A significant correlation does not necessarily imply a strong correlation, but it does indicate that the correlation is a reliable one and therefore is probably not due solely to chance. Education (EDUC) is positively correlated with responses on the Bem Sex Role Inventory (BSRI), and age (AGE) is negatively correlated with both BSRI responses and educational level (EDUC). While the correlations between BSRI and AGE (−.3013) and EDUC and AGE (−.2157) are undeniably small, they do indicate that at least some of the variation in one variable is related to variation in another. Specifically, older employees tend to have lower BSRI score, that is, they tend to be more masculine sex typed. This finding might logically be explained by the fact that older employees at E-Z Manufacturing are typically male. Furthermore, the fact that younger employees are typically more educated is certainly in line with the recent emphasis on hiring college graduates for many of the positions within corporations. The much higher positive correlation (+.4303) that exists between BSRI scores and educational levels (EDUC) may initially be construed as indicating that more education results in a more feminine sex type. To understand this somewhat peculiar relationship, however, requires that we go beyond the two variables being correlated. It happens that most of our younger employees are female; most of our younger employees also are more educated. Therefore, since our more educated employees are more likely to be female, it should not come as a surprise to us that the more educated employees score higher on the BSRI (i.e., they are more feminine sex typed).

Correlations such as the one between BSRI and EDUC illustrate the great care that sometimes must be taken in interpreting correlation statistics. The statement that more education results in a more feminine sex type is clearly misleading without making reference to the fact that other variables— gender and age— are involved here as well. Thus, the importance of knowing your data as intimately as possible as you interpret statistical output cannot be overemphasized. And while some of the correlational statistics you obtain may not provide a great deal of insight into the questions being addressed, they may suggest directions for further statistical analysis using more sophisticated procedures that can investigate the relationships among a number of variables simultaneously.

As an aid in interpreting correlation coefficients, you can calculate what is termed the "coefficient of determination." The coefficient of determination is a measure of the proportion of variance in one variable that can be explained by the other. In other words, it tells you how much of the change in the first variable is accounted for by a change in the second variable, and vice versa. This statistic can be obtained by squaring the value of the correlation coefficient (r^2). For example, the correlation between BSRI and AGE is -0.3013. Squaring this value gives us a coefficient of determination of 0.091. It is often more convenient to transform this value into a percentage (simply multiply by 100) and for this pair of variables we can say that about 9.1 percent of changes in the responses on the Bem Sex Role Inventory can be explained by changes in the educational levels of the subjects.

Although we have correlated only three variables in the above example, many research questions could be posed that would necessitate further use of the PEARSON CORR procedure. For example, we might expect TASK and RELATION scores to be negatively correlated, i.e., those who show a strong task-oriented leadership style may tend to be weak in relations-oriented leadership style. We might also expect correlations between BSRI scores and TASK scores and between BSRI scores and RELATION scores. We might want to explore possible correlations between TASK and PERFORM scores, and RELATION and PERFORM scores. As you can see, a wealth of potential information lies in the appropriate use of the correlation statistic.

10.7   Nonparametric Correlation Using NONPAR CORR (Optional)

The Pearson "r" discussed above is a parametric test and can be used only when the data are at least interval and are normally distributed. In a great deal of social science research, one or both of these requirements will not be met. Where the data are not normally distributed but at least ordinal, nonparametric tests such as Spearman's rho and Kendall's tau may be used.

In order to obtain Spearman's rho or Kendall's tau, it is necessary to replace the PEARSON CORR record (see Section 10.5) with a record reading NONPAR CORR in the control field. Variable names are entered in exactly the same manner as described for the PEARSON CORR procedure above. However, the STATISTICS record does not apply to this program, and therefore this record must be removed from the file. Furthermore, only Spearman's rho will be calculated unless an OPTION is specified. To obtain the Kendall's tau and Spearman rho statistics, you must follow the NONPAR CORR line with OPTIONS 6. If, for example, you were interested in taking the more conservative approach and treating TASK, RELATION, and PERFORM as ordinal variables, you could request nonparametric correlational analyses in the following manner:

```
DATA LIST   RECORDS=1/1 SUBJ. . .
NONPAR CORR   TASK, RELATION, PERFORM
OPTIONS   6
BEGIN DATA

data records

END DATA
```

The output from the above program (see Table 10.2) prints only the nonredundant correlation coefficients. The first matrix presents the Kendall's tau correlation coefficients and the second presents Spearman's rho correlation coefficients. Interpretation of these statistics is identical to that of the Pearson r.

10.8   Obtaining Scatter Diagrams Using PLOT (Optional)

When analyzing data, it is often useful to have a visual picture of the association between two variables. This is especially important if one has reason to suspect that a nonlinear relationship will best describe the association. These nonlinear relationships may take many forms and are not to be considered any less meaningful than linear relationships. There

Table 10.2   Sample Output from NONPAR CORR

-- KENDALL CORRELATION COEFFICIENTS --

RELATION   -.2624
              N(60)
              SIG .005

PERFORM   .3184   .1297
              N(60)   N(60)
              SIG .001   SIG .098

              TASK   RELATION

" . " IS PRINTED IF A COEFFICIENT CANNOT BE COMPUTED.

-- SPEARMAN CORRELATION COEFFICIENTS --

RELATION   -.3268
              N(60)
              SIG .005

PERFORM   .4033   .1719
              N(60)   N(60)
              SIG .001   SIG .094

              TASK   RELATION

are techniques for dealing with curvilinear relationships, but these are beyond the scope of this manual. Nevertheless, you might want to know how to construct two-dimensional graphs of associations to be able to understand better the empirical relationships. To construct such graphs you can use the PLOT program. PLOT provides a great variety of techniques to tailor the formatting of these graphs. It is not our intention to cover these variations, but rather to demonstrate how quickly you can construct scatter diagrams from your data. Figure 10.1 illustrates the output from the PLOT request below:

PLOT   PLOT=PERFORM WITH AGE

The above statement requests a scatter diagram of the variables PERFORM and AGE. The repetition of the term "PLOT" is required in the PLOT statement because of the many formatting options that the researcher might utilize. For most purposes, it is only necessary to remember to substitute "PLOT PLOT=" for PEARSON CORR as the conventions for listing variables are identical to those for the other correlation procedures. Since it is customary to place the dependent variable on the vertical axis and the independent variable on the horizontal axis, as with the CROSSTABS procedure discussed earlier, it is a good habit to always place the dependent variable first in the PLOT request.

Figure 10.1: Results of PLOT Program

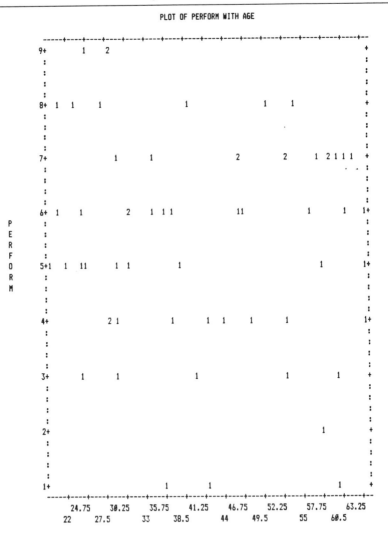

Note on the scatter diagram in Figure 10.1 that when data points lie on identical coordinates, they are indicated by a number greater than one—there are five instances in which there are identical pairs of scores (indicated by the number "2" on the scatter diagram) in this illustration of PERFORM and AGE. Examination of this output would suggest that there is virtually no relationship between these two variables of PER-FORM and AGE. Thus, in this scattergram there is no pattern of scores moving up and to the right (positive correlation) or down and to the right (negative correlation). If one runs a PEARSON CORR on these two variables, an "r" of -0.0520 would be obtained. This represents a relationship that is very weak and not statistically significant, thus confirming our preliminary interpretation based on the scatter diagram.

10.9   After Correlation . . .

The correlation statistic, as we have used it, is useful for identifying the strength and direction of relationships between pairs of variables. As such it gives us a handle on how some variables in our study might be related to others. For example, we have already seen that BSRI scores are related to AGE and EDUC, and in the exercises that follow we will investigate relationships between BSRI, RELATION, TASK, and PERFORM. Yet, interpretation of correlation statistics precludes causal inference, and therefore it is sometimes only a first step in the analysis of studies which attempt to investigate the complex relationships among many variables or to test various hypotheses that might strengthen arguments of causality.

Depending on the nature of one's study, the type of data collected, and the orientation of the researcher (psychology, sociology, human re-sources, etc.), the next steps for data analysis may be somewhat different. For example, regression analysis is heavily utilized by sociologists while analysis of variance is often a favorite tool of experimental psychologists. Because our project at E-Z Manufacturing crosses the boundaries of several disciplines, we will in fact be able to look at the data from several perspectives. Chapter 11, for example, introduces the student to multiple regression and path analysis, while Chapters 12–14 examine hypothesis testing with such procedures as the t-test and analysis of variance. Each approach enables us to understand the results of our project in a better, albeit, different way.

Exercises

1a.   As part of your project on leadership analysis at E-Z Manufacturing, you suspect that BSRI scores may be related to TASK scores, RELA-TION scores, and overall performance (PERFORM). Furthermore,

you anticipate a negative correlation between TASK and RELA-
TION. Using a correlation program, determine the strength and direc-
tion of these relationships. In addition, use a two-tailed test (OP-
TIONS 3) to determine whether these are signficant correlations.
You are also interested in finding out whether there are correlations
between (a) TASK and PERFORM and (b) RELATION and PER-
FORM.

1b. Interpret each of the six correlations requested above. How strong
and in what direction is each correlation? Which correlations are
significant? How might you account for the positive correlation between BSRI and RELATION? the negative correlation between BSRI
and TASK? Are you surprised by the fairly low correlation between
BSRI and PERFORM? Is PERFORM related to any of the variables
that you examined in this exercise?

2. (optional) Using the PLOT program, illustrate the relationships between TASK and RELATION, and BSRI and TASK in scatter diagrams. Study the scattergrams noting how they can be used to represent correlations in a pictorial manner.

3. (optional) For this exercise assume that you have collected the following data from ten college students:
   1. the number of hours studied for a class exam
   2. the student's score on the 100 point exam

Hours Studied	Quiz Score
2	38
3	39
2	52
5	60
5	72
4	79
5	82
6	88
7	81
7	94

Construct an SPSS^x file and produce a scatter diagram. What kind
of relationship do you think the points on the diagram show? Run
the PEARSON CORR procedure to see if your above answer was
correct.

11 Multiple Regression Analysis

In this chapter we will discuss:

- the nature of multiple correlation and regression analysis
- using the SPSS^x REGRESSION procedure
- interpreting the output of the REGRESSION procedure
- uses of the unstandardized and standardized regression equations
- constructing and evaluating path diagrams

11.1 Introduction

It was once believed in the social sciences that for every effect there existed one and only one cause. This belief resulted in a variety of social theories called "determinisms" that included racial, physical, economic, political, religious, and technological determinism. While relatively simple and easy to understand, these single-factor theories oversimplified and distorted reality.

Largely because of the rapidly increasing availability of computers, the emphasis in the social sciences has shifted from the study of simple two-variable (bivariate) relationships of cause and effect to multivariate relationships—ones that analyze the effect of several variables simultaneously on a single dependent variable. Let's consider a very simple example from our data file on leadership. We have already shown in a previous chapter that there are correlations between such two-variable pairs as AGE and BSRI, and EDUC and BSRI (see Chapter 10). Yet these somewhat simple relationships between BSRI and each of these two variables may be substantially more complex when we begin to consider how all three variables relate *simultaneously*. By analyzing all three variables simultaneously, we can obtain a more complete picture of how each of these variables is related to the other. Before the advent of computers, multivariate techniques involving three or more variables such as the rather simple one described above were extremely laborious to calculate and understandably were seldom used. The unfortunate result was that while pieces of the puzzle were seen, often the bigger picture was missed entirely!

11.2 Multiple Correlation and Regression

Multivariate techniques involving measures of association produce a multiple correlation coefficient and multiple regression analysis. The multiple correlation coefficient—usually written as "R"—is simply the correlation between the actual scores on a single dependent variable and the scores predicted by the linear combination of any number of independent variables. Like the Pearson r for bivariate correlation, Multiple R varies on a scale of -1.00 to $+1.00$ and can be squared to express the proportion of the total variation in the dependent variable that is explained by the linear combination of the independent variables. It provides a convenient summary measure of the adequacy of a given set of independent variables in accounting for changes in a dependent variable.

While correlations tell us how two or more variables are related, regression analysis enables us to make predictions about the values of dependent variables when the value of a specific independent variable is known. For example, your college G.P.A or grade point average (a dependent variable of sorts) was predicted by the scores you received on the college entrance examination (an independent variable). Multiple regression, like simple regression, is used to make predictions about the value of the dependent variable; however, the prediction is now based upon the relationship of the dependent variable with two or more independent variables.

Use of the multiple correlation coefficient and regression analysis for statistical inferences is warranted only when the following four conditions are met: (1) the respondents are chosen randomly, (2) the dependent and independent variables are interval level and normally distributed, (3) the effects of the independent variables on the dependent variables are linear, and (4) the independent variables are not correlated with one another.

However, regression is considered a "robust" technique, i.e., one that is very forgiving of moderate violations of the above four conditions. Thus, the researcher can still be confident in conclusions despite such violations. Probability sampling will, in general, provide a close enough approximation to random selection and makes it relatively simple to satisfy the first condition. Regarding the second condition, ordinal variables are commonly used without serious problems and moderate deviations from normal distributions do not seem to bias the results greatly. The third condition can often be met by employing mathematical transformations to closely approximate linear relationships. In practice, the final condition can be met if the intercorrelations between the independent variables are no greater than 0.60. Even though social research seldom meets all four of these conditions completely, the multiple correlation coefficient and regression analysis are powerful tools that may be used to understand complex human behavior, so long as the researcher is aware of the limitations imposed by the data.

11.3   Multiple Regression and the Leadership Data File

Although not the major concern of our project at E-Z Manufacturing, one of the topics most amenable to regression analysis in our study is that of the subjects' scores on the Bem Sex Role Inventory (BSRI). Based upon past research, one would expect to find that BSRI scores most likely would be related to the subject's gender, age, and educational level. We could analyze the combined effect of these three variables on BSRI by performing a multiple regression analysis.

11.4   SPSS^x Program for Multivariate Correlation

REGRESSION is the SPSS^x program that is used to perform multiple correlation and regression. REGRESSION is used to calculate (among other statistics) the multiple correlation coefficient (R); in addition, this program may be used to generate the line of regression required for predicting values of a dependent variable, given a set of values for the independent variables. In this chapter we will focus on the program REGRESSION as a means of determining how well a set of two or more independent variables together explain variation in a single dependent variable. We will also consider the matter of predicted relations. Finally, we will briefly comment on the use of REGRESSION in performing a form of causal analysis known as "path analysis."

11.5   Format for REGRESSION Program

The REGRESSION statement calls up the program that is required to compute the multiple correlation coefficient (R) as well as perform the multivariate regression analysis. For our purposes, the specification field will consist of three parts: a request for descriptive statistics (this is optional); a list of all the variables in the regression/correlation analysis; and specification of the dependent and independent variables. Each of these parts is outlined in more detail in the next section.

1. In the specification field the word "DESCRIPTIVES" means that you wish the routine to compute the means, standard deviations, and

correlation matrix for all variables specified in the analysis. As was mentioned previously, this part of the REGRESSION statement is optional and need not be included for the program to run successfully.

2. All the variables that the researcher intends to use in the correlation and regression analysis are then listed in the VARIABLES= subcommand. For example, the following record

```
REGRESSION   DESCRIPTIVES/VARIABLES=BSRI,
AGE, GENDER, EDUC/
```

indicates that four variables—BSRI, GENDER, AGE, and EDUC—will be included in the regression analysis. In addition, descriptive statistics on these four variables have been requested with DESCRIPTIVES. Note that the separate stages of the REGRESSION command are separated with the "/".

3. The last part of the REGRESSION statement makes the actual request for a regression analysis. This is accomplished by using the "DEPENDENT=" subcommand. First, one must list the variable chosen to be the dependent variable. This must be followed by a "/". Next, one provides all the independent variables, preceded by the keyword ENTER, to be analyzed together. The word "ENTER" is essentially another subcommand that represents the researcher's choice of method by which the independent variables will be analyzed. An example might appear as follows:

```
REGRESSION   DESCRIPTIVES/VARIABLES=BSRI,
AGE, GENDER, EDUC/
DEPENDENT=BSRI/ ENTER AGE, GENDER, EDUC
```

The above format for the "DEPENDENT=" subroutine indicates that for this analysis BSRI will be treated as the dependent variable, and AGE, GENDER, and EDUC will be used as independent variables. When all the remaining variables from the "VARIABLES=" list are to become independent variables, as an alternate method we could simply use the word ENTER and omit the variable names.

It is possible to initiate several regression analyses by using a separate DEPENDENT= subcommand for each one. A sample request for two different regression problems is presented below:

```
REGRESSION   DESCRIPTIVES/
VARIABLES=BSRI,AGE,GENDER,EDUC/
DEPENDENT=BSRI/ENTER AGE,GENDER,EDUC/
DEPENDENT=EDUC/ENTER AGE,GENDER
```

In each case above, a different variable is being used as the dependent variable, and different sets of independent variables are being correlated with the dependent variable. Again, observe the need to separate each part of the REGRESSION statement with a "/". There are many other ways of setting up the REGRESSION statement, but the forms illustrated here will work for all of our uses.

11.6   Sample SPSS[x] REGRESSION Program for Multiple Correlation

A sample SPSS[x] program for carrying out multiple regression and correlation analysis is given below. In this example, we have chosen BSRI as the dependent variable and AGE, GENDER, and EDUC (education) as the independent variables.

```
DATA LIST   RECORDS=1/1 SUBJ. . .
REGRESSION   DESCRIPTIVES/
   VARIABLES=BSRI,AGE,GENDER,EDUC/
   DEPENDENT=BSRI/ENTER AGE,GENDER,EDUC
BEGIN DATA
```

data records

```
END DATA
```

11.7   Explanation of the REGRESSION Output

As with any statistical program, there are two aspects of understanding the output of the REGRESSION program. First, one must understand the statistical information that has been provided; and second, the information must be used and interpreted to aid in understanding the results of the study. Because the output from REGRESSION is quite complex, we have divided the discussion of REGRESSION output into several components: (a) a listing of the output, (b) using the information in the output to generate a regression equation, and (c) interpreting the output from an actual run using the sample program listed in Section 11.6.

11.7a   The Statistical Output from REGRESSION

The following statistical information (see Table 11.1) is automatically printed with each REGRESSION run as constructed in Section 11.6:

1. The mean and standard deviation for each variable in the list
2. A Correlation Matrix—the correlation coefficients (Pearson r's) between each of the variables in the list

Table 11.1　　Sample Output From REGRESSION

```
* * * *   M U L T I P L E   R E G R E S S I O N   * * * *


Listwise Deletion of Missing Data

          Mean  Std Dev  Label

BSRI       .267   3.793
AGE      41.467  14.171
GENDER    1.500    .504
EDUC     13.700   1.916

N of Cases =    60

Correlation:

           BSRI      AGE      GENDER     EDUC

BSRI      1.000    -.301      .687      .430
AGE       -.301    1.000     -.028     -.216
GENDER     .687    -.028     1.000      .228
EDUC       .430    -.216      .228     1.000


* * * *   M U L T I P L E   R E G R E S S I O N   * * * *

Equation Number 1    Dependent Variable..   BSRI

  Descriptive Statistics are printed on Page    3

Beginning Block Number  1.  Method: Enter     AGE     GENDER    EDUC


Variable(s) Entered on Step Number  1..   EDUC
                                    2..   AGE
                                    3..   GENDER


Multiple R          .77597     Analysis of Variance
R Square            .60213                    DF     Sum of Squares     Mean Square
Adjusted R Square   .58082     Regression      3         511.10861       170.36954
Standard Error     2.45577     Residual       56         337.72472         6.03080

                              F =     28.24991     Signif F =  .0000


----------------- Variables in the Equation -----------------

Variable          B        SE B      Beta       T  Sig T

EDUC          .469939    .175482   .237389    2.678  .0097
AGE          -.062169    .023110  -.232276   -2.690  .0094
GENDER       4.709651    .651395   .626070    7.230  .0000
(Constant) -10.658023   2.763116            -3.857  .0003
```

3. Multiple Correlation Coefficient (R)
4. R Square: this is usually referred to as the "coefficient of multiple determination" and is a measure of the proportion of variance in the dependent variable that can be explained by the two or more independent variables acting together. In other words, it tells one how much of the change in the dependent variable is accounted for by changes in the independent variables.
5. Adjusted R Square: this statistic is a more conservative estimate of the percent of variance explained and should be used when the sample size is small. It is simply the previously defined "R Square" adjusted for the number of independent variables in the equation and the number of cases in the sample.
6. Variables in the equation: this is a summary table of the information to be used in the regression analysis. It lists the values needed to actually write a prediction equation for this particular regression analysis and this particular sample of respondents. We shall discuss this further in the next section.

11.7b   How to Make Predictions about the Dependent Variable by Using REGRESSION Output

REGRESSION enables the researcher to generate the line of regression necessary for making predictions about values of the dependent variable. Such a technique is of substantial value in the social and behavioral sciences since much of the work of applied social scientists deals with the attempt to predict human behavior. For example, college admissions officers attempt to predict the future G.P.A of applicants based upon such independent variables as high school rank, ACT scores, achievement motivation, etc. Market researchers wish to predict the effect on toilet paper sales of such independent variables as the softness, scent, color, packaging, etc., of the product. Such attempts at prediction make use of regression equations, and most employ two or more independent variables.

Let's consider a typical example. A market researcher surveys a large number of households and finds that the sales of toilet paper (the dependent variable which we shall call "Y" and which is measured in thousands of rolls) were related to the product's scent (an independent variable which we call X_1, measured on a scale of 1–10) and its strength (a second independent variable which we call X_2, measured on a scale of 1–100). The number of rolls of toilet paper sold could be predicted by using the general *unstandardized regression equation*:

$$Y = a + b_1(X_1) + b_2(X_2) + b_n(X_n)$$

where "a" refers to the y-intercept and "b_1, b_2," etc. refer to the slope values of the line of regression (or line of best fit).

In order to obtain the predicted sales for a particular type of toilet paper (i.e., "Y"), one would have to know the values for each of the terms on the right hand side of the equation. These include the values for "a" (y-intercept) and "b's" (slopes), as well as for X_1, X_2, and so on. The numerical values for the y-intercept and slopes are calculated as part of the REGRESSION program, and these values are obtained from the "VARIABLES IN THE EQUATION" table in the REGRESSION output (take a look at Table 11.1 for an example). The value for "a" is listed in the output as the "CONSTANT", the value for b_1 is listed as the "B" for the product's scent (X_1); and the value for b_2 is listed as the "B" for the product's strength (X_2). Let's assume that after running the REGRESSION program, the values for the equation are determined such that

$$Y = 1.99 + .274 (X_1) + .090 (X_2).$$

The values for X_1 and X_2 in the above equation are, of course, determined by the actual ratings of the scent and strength of the particular toilet paper about which we are making predictions. If a new type of tissue is produced with a scent rating (X_1) of "5" and a strength rating (X_2) of "75", the market person would predict a yearly sales figure of 10.11 thousand (or 10,110) rolls [1.99 + .274(5) + .090(75)].

The market researcher is now able to report to management how well a particular toilet paper having certain scent and strength characteristics would sell. While this may be enough information for management, some might also wish to know which of the two characteristics had the more important independent impact on sales. The above equation makes it difficult to compare the relative effects of strength and scent as each is measured in different units. Our market researcher could construct the *standardized regression equation.* To do this s/he would need only look again at the "VARIABLES IN THE EQUATION" table and use the values under the heading "BETA" (as an example, see Table 11.1). In our hypothetical situation, this would result in the following equation:

$$Y' = .21(X_1) + .34(X_2)$$

There is no value for the "CONSTANT" because equations with standard-ized regression coefficients (BETA's) *always have the value of zero for the constant.*

Now it can be determined that "strength" has the greater independent effect on sales (.34 standard units of change in sales for each standard unit increase in strength compared to .21 standard units in sales for the same standard unit increase in scent), and future product development might well include efforts to increase the strength rather than change the scent of the tissue. For comparing the relative effects of independent variables, the researcher must use the standardized regression coefficients (BETA's) that are computed by subprogram REGRESSION. For predicting values of the dependent variable (in original units) the unstandardized regression coefficients (B's) and the constant must be used.

11.7c   Interpreting the Output from a Typical SPSS[x] REGRESSION Run

Although the previous example was somewhat lengthy and involved, it illustrates how one can go about using the information from REGRESSION to interpret and predict relationships among variables. This same process of interpretation can be applied to the SPSS[x] run in which REGRESSION output was requested from the multivariate analysis of the AGE, GENDER, and EDUC on BSRI scores, the sample program appearing in Section 11.6. The output from this program is listed in Table 11.1.

At first glance, the output of the REGRESSION run seems overwhelming. However, if taken one step at a time, you can easily determine the simultaneous impact of two or more independent variables on one dependent variable. Referring to Table 11.1, the first information provided is the "descriptive statistics"—mean, standard deviation, and, if specified, extended label for each of the variables present on the "VARIABLES=" list. These statistics are optional and have been generated in response to the keyword "DESCRIPTIVES" that appears on the first line of the regression line. This keyword also caused the correlation matrix of all the variables to be printed, which appears next in Table 11.1. Many researchers feel most comfortable when they can quickly review these descriptive statistics and it is usually desirable to request them.

The remaining information provides us with the calculated values for the multiple correlation coefficient (R) (which tells us how strongly AGE, GENDER, and EDUC together are related to BSRI), all regression coefficients (both unstandardized and standardized), and the constants that would be required to construct the regression equations. In Table 11.1, the value for Multiple R is .77597, indicating a strong correlation between the combined independent variables (AGE, GENDER, EDUC) and the dependent variable (BSRI). The "Adjusted R Square" value informs us that our equation accounts for 58 percent of the variance in BSRI scores. This is a very large value for most social science research where the average may be as low as 15 percent explained variance.

It is also possible to ascertain from the output whether the slope of the regression line is significantly different from zero (basically this tells us whether our correlation is a signficant one that can therefore be generalized to the population). A significant *t* value (i.e, <.05) indicates that the slope of the regression line is indeed different from zero. The *t* values for EDUC, AGE, and GENDER have probabilities of .0097, .0094, and .0000 respectively. Since these probabilities are all less than .05, then each of these factors can be considered significant.

Finally, one finds the information needed to replace the "B's", "Beta's", and "a's" in the following regression equations:

1. The unstandardized regression equation tested in the above regression request can be written as follows:

$$BSRI = a + B_{GENDER} + B_{AGE} + B_{EDUC}$$

or

$$BSRI = (-10.7) + (4.7)(GENDER) + (-.06)(AGE) + (.47)(EDUC)$$

2. The standardized regression equation tested in the above regression request can be written as follows:

$$BSRI' = (BETA_{GENDER}) + (BETA_{AGE}) + (BETA_{EDUC})$$

or

$$BSRI' = (.63)(GENDER) + (-.23)(AGE) + (.24)(EDUC)$$

One could now enter the values for any individual's age (in years), gender ("1" if male and "2" if female), and education (also in years) into the first equation and calculate the predicted score that the individual would achieve on the Bem Sex Role Inventory. The second equation indicates the relative importance of the three independent variables on the BSRI score. Gender has the largest BETA coefficient and, therefore, exerts the greatest influence on the score. Education is the second most important, and age is the least important of these three.

11.8   Why Bother with All of This?

One of the stated advantages of regression analysis was that it permits the researcher to be more realistic about the causation of human behavior. Very little of human behavior can be attributed to only one cause, or even to a number of causes operating at precisely the same instant. Rather, it is often the case that some independent variables affect the dependent variable through one or more "intervening" variables. To be able to estimate these "indirect effects," one can employ one of the many techniques that constitute "path analysis." The actual construction of path diagrams is beyond the scope of this manual; however, we can briefly illustrate the interpretation of such procedures using the example on AGE, GENDER, EDUC, and BSRI given above.

11.9 Multiple Regression and Path Analysis

We have previously demonstrated how to determine the simultaneous effects of age, gender, and education on a respondent's score on the Bem Sex Role Inventory (BSRI). One might also hypothesize that age and gender are related to the respondent's educational attainment and therefore these variables actually have an *indirect* effect on the BSRI score. That is, younger people are likely to have higher educational levels and for this reason are likely to score more androgynous on the BSRI. Furthermore, males may be more likely than females to have higher educational levels and therefore have more androgynous scores than females. To test these hypotheses we would need only to do one additional regression run beyond the one that we carried out in the preceding example. While we will not go through the actual steps involved in setting up a path diagram in this manual, suffice it to say that this extra run would provide some additional standardized regression coefficients which could be used to construct the path diagram in Figure 11.1.

The values in Figure 11.1 represent the "path coefficients" (p), each

Figure 11.1: Example of a Path Diagram

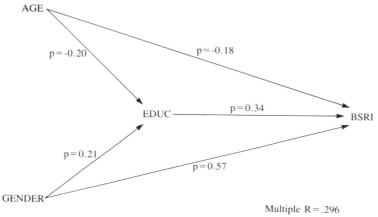

Multiple R = .296

of which estimates the strength of relationship between the two variables linked by an arrow. The relative importance of each independent variable is determined by the magnitude of its path coefficient. Thus, you can see that GENDER has the greatest effect on BSRI, and AGE has the least effect. Indirect effects are determined by multiplying together the path coefficients for all arrows in a given path. For example, to determine the indirect effects of GENDER on BSRI scores, one need only multiply the path coefficient between GENDER and EDUC (0.21) by the path coefficient between EDUC and BSRI (0.34). This procedure yields 0.07. Values under 0.10 are not usually considered meaningful, so in this example, all indirect effects are so small that they do not contribute to our understanding of the causes of BSRI scores.

When path analyses are encountered in published research, the most significant indirect effects will generally be discussed, but the reader needs to be able to determine the magnitude of all such effects in order to verify that any significant indirect relationships have not been overlooked. This is especially important as path analysis techniques permit the construction of very realistic causal arguments illustrated by very complex diagrams with arrows running every which way. In such complex cases it's not at all unusual for the author to overlook indirect relationships; and it behooves the reader to be able to double-check the adequacy of published interpretations.

11.10   Some Final Thoughts

Path diagrams tell the researcher some things that single multiple regression equations don't. First, multiple regression does determine the direct effects of each independent variable on the dependent variable as measured by the standardized regression coefficients, but path analysis also allows one to assess the indirect effects. In some cases it may very well be that one variable has no direct effect on another, and therefore, multiple regression analysis would show no relationship. Path analysis, in such a case, would provide a more accurate understanding of the complexity of the relationships through the computation of indirect effects. In more complex models, path analysis also permits the researcher to examine the relationships among independent variables, something that cannot be done with a single multiple regression equation.

Finally, path analysis is an important theoretical tool because it requires one to spell out *all* relationships in a causal model. The researcher is forced to consider both direct as well as indirect effects among independent variables. Through this careful analysis, explanations in the social sciences can be greatly improved.

Exercises

1. In this chapter, we demonstrated that gender, age, and education were significant determinants of a respondent's score on the BSRI. Use the REGRESSION procedure to examine how well scores on the BSRI as well as the respondent's age, gender, and education predict her/his performance (PERFORM) in leadership situations in the organization.
   a. identify the dependent variable and independent variables.
   b. set up the REGRESSION statement in the space below.

   Interpret the output from REGRESSION.
   a. What is the value of R, and what does it mean?
   b. How much of the variance in PERFORM can be explained by age, gender, education, and BSRI score?
   c. Using the values for the slopes (b) and y-intercept (a) in the unstandardized regression equation, what level of performance would you predict in a thirty-year-old woman with fifteen years of education and a BSRI score of +3.2?
   d. Using the BETA values from the output table, which variable has the greatest independent effect on PERFORM?

2. (Optional) Social scientists have long been concerned with the problem of unemployment. One cross-cultural research project collected the following data:

Country	Unemployment Rate	Political Stability	Level of Economic Development	Rate of Urbanization
England	7.2	2.6	1.46	1.1
Finland	2.6	8.1	.83	0.7
Ghana	7.1	5.0	.02	0.2
Greece	7.8	2.1	.09	0.9
Israel	3.8	8.1	.40	0.9
New Zealand	3.0	8.6	1.71	0.8
Norway	2.1	8.6	1.41	1.2
Taiwan	4.8	7.2	.80	0.6
USA	3.2	8.0	2.34	1.8
Uruguay	5.2	3.2	.46	0.9

a. Construct both the unstandardized regression equation and the standardized regression equation for the combined independent effects of political stability, economic development, and rate of urbanization on the unemployment rate.

b. What proportion of the variation in unemployment rates is left *unex-plained* by the above three independent variables?

c. If you were told that Canada had the following values: political stability = 8.2; level of economic development = 2.11; and rate of urbanization = 1.6, what would you predict as its unemployment rate?

d. Which of the three independent variables has the greatest effect on a country's unemployment rate?

e. Fill in the path coefficient (i.e., the standardized regression coefficients) values on the causal diagram below:

12 The *t*-Test: Testing Differences Between Two Groups or Conditions

In this chapter, we discuss:

* the appropriate application of the *t*-test
* the SPSS^x T-TEST command statement
* the interpretation of the T-TEST output table for independent means
* the format for running paired *t*-tests

12.1 Introduction

In the four preceding chapters, we have accomplished three goals with our statistical analyses. We have described our employees at E-Z Manufacturing by obtaining a number of different summary statistics on them; we have demonstrated that some variables are associated with other variables and therefore can be predicted by those variables; and we have tested several specific hypotheses regarding the influence of an independent variable on a nominally-scaled dependent variable. In the next three chapters we will explore further how statistics can be used to test hypotheses. In our project at E-Z Manufacturing, this means examining the effect of such factors as sex roles and leadership style on performance in leadership situations. Specifically, we will focus on three statistical procedures designed to test hypotheses about means: the *t*-test, one-way analysis of variance, and factorial analysis of variance. In this chapter, we deal exclusively with the *t*-test.

The *t*-test is used to determine whether the difference between the means of two groups or conditions is due to experimental manipulation or selection, or simply to chance. Thus, this procedure establishes the probability of the outcome of an experiment, and in doing so enables the researcher to reject or accept the null hypothesis (the null hypothesis states that the experimental manipulation had no effect, therefore the means of the groups will be equal). In this respect, the *t*-test is an inferential statistic used to test hypotheses and, therefore is similar to the chi square analysis (Chapter 9). Whereas the chi square is applied to situations involving nominal data, the *t*-test is used when the data are at least interval level. Under ideal conditions, these types of inferential statistics allow the researcher to infer a causal relationship between the independent and dependent variable.

Because the *t*-test is a parametric test, certain conditions about the data must be met in order to use the test most effectively. These include: interval or ratio level data, groups that have similar variances (known as homogeneity of variance), and a normal distribution of the variable. Although the *t*-test is sometimes used when some of these conditions are not satisfied, the researcher must realize that in such situations the conclusions drawn from the *t*-value regarding the effect of the independent variable are less reliable.

There are two distinct applications of the *t*-test. When a randomized and/or between-subjects design is used, the *t*-test for independent samples is the appropriate test. Use of either a within-subjects design (also called a "repeated measures" design) or a subject-by-subject matched design requires analysis with the *t*-test for paired samples (also known as the direct difference *t* or the *t*-test for dependent or correlated samples).

12.2   Applying the *t*-Test to the Leadership Data File

We would be interested in testing a number of hypotheses for our project on sex roles, leadership style, and performance at E-Z Manufacturing. Yet, while we might generate quite a few different research hypotheses, only a handful of these hypotheses could actually be evaluated with the *t*-test. Remember that in order to use the *t*-test appropriately (1) only two-group (or condition) comparisons may be made, and (2) the data must meet the conditions listed above. Since many of the hypotheses to be addressed in this project involve situations that do not meet these conditions, they would have to be evaluated using other inferential statistical procedures.

One question that we might be interested in addressing as part of this project (and that could be evaluated with the *t*-test) is whether GENDER (an independent variable) affects scores on (a) the TASK scale and (b) the RELATIONS scale (both dependent variables). In other words, you might have strong *a priori* reason to believe that men would exhibit a higher TASK orientation than women, since research indicates that task orientation is a stereotyped masculine characteristic. Comparing the scores of women on TASK orientation against those of men on TASK orientation with the independent *t*-test would enable you to confirm whether this was indeed the case. On the other hand, you might expect women to exhibit a higher RELATIONS orientation (a stereotyped feminine characteristic) than men, an hypothesis that could also be tested with the independent *t*-test. But let's not stop there. Ultimately we're interested in what factors affect the performance (PERFORM) of your employees in leadership situations, so why not determine whether GENDER affects overall performance (PERFORM) as well? Although in this instance there may be no clear *a priori* reason to suspect that it should, it is certainly a question worth investigating.

Our interest goes beyond simply testing for the effect of gender on performance; of greater interest is whether SEXROLE (i.e., whether one is androgynous, masculine sex type, or feminine sex type) affects performance. However, here it might be beneficial to frame our question in a slightly different way. We might be interested not so much in whether there are differences in performance (PERFORM) depending on one's SEXROLE (masculine, feminine, or androgynous), but rather whether there are differences in performance depending on whether an individual is androgynous or sex typed (*either* masculine or feminine). As you will see later, to answer this question, we would need to form a single group of sex-typed individuals consisting of both masculine and feminine sex typed men and women. The performance of this group could then be compared against the performance of the androgynous group of men and women.

12.3   SPSS[x] Program for *t*-Tests

Now that we have seen how the *t*-test might be applied to the Leadership Data File, let's turn our attention once again to SPSS[x]. Both the independent and the paired *t*-tests are available on SPSS[x] under the T-TEST program. The hypotheses described above all require use of the *t*-test for independent samples, and for this reason we will focus our discussion on the format for the *t*-test for independent samples. The format for the *t*-test for correlated samples is quite similar and will be discussed only briefly in a later, optional section.

12.4   Understanding the Format of the T-TEST Statement

The words T-TEST in the control field are used to call up the *t*-test routine. The format of the specification field changes depending on whether independent or paired samples are being compared.

12.4a   The t-Test for Independent Samples

When comparing independent samples, the specification field for the T-TEST statement must contain information about both the independent variable and the dependent variable. Only one independent variable may be listed in any T-TEST statement, but the analysis of up to fifty dependent variables (far more than we'll need in our project!) may be requested within a single T-TEST statement.

The specification field of the T-TEST statement for independent samples always begins with the GROUPS= subcommand. Following this subcommand, the name of the independent variable (or any other variable which is used to define the groups being compared) is listed. If, for example, we wanted to compare the performance of men and women on a particular dimension (i.e., broken down according to the GENDER of the subject), then the initial part of the T-TEST statement would appear:

   T-TEST   GROUPS=GENDER(1,2) /

In the above statement, the levels or categories of the variable to be compared are designated in parentheses following the name of the independent variable. Thus, where "1" = males and "2" = females, the above statement indicates that for the variable GENDER, males (1) and females (2) are to be compared. In situations where there are more than two categories of the variable, the actual categories to be compared are designated in parentheses. If, for example, we have three categories of SEXROLE (1 = masculine; 2 = feminine; 3 = androgynous), but we wanted to compare only the performance of masculine and androgynous types, our T-TEST statement would read:

T-TEST   GROUPS=SEXROLE(1,3) /

The dependent variables to be included in the analysis follow the VARIABLES= subcommand. If you wanted to analyze gender differences in scores on two dependent variables, say TASK and RELATION, the statement would appear as:

T-TEST   GROUPS=GENDER(1,2) / VARIABLES=TASK RELATION

Note that the GROUPS= and VARIABLES= subcommands in the specification field must be separated by a slash. When a number of dependent variables are to be analyzed, the list may be abbreviated by listing the first and last variables in the list joined by the keyword TO. An example is shown below:

T-TEST   GROUPS=GENDER(1,2) / VARIABLES=TASK TO PERFORM

This statement would result in three *t*-tests comparing males to females on all variables in the data file from TASK to PERFORM. In this case, TASK, RELATION, and PERFORM would be included in the analysis. You might want to note that the keyword TO can be used in the manner shown above only when the variables being analyzed lie adjacent to one another in the data file.

12.4b   The OPTIONS Statement

The T-TEST program will run without the OPTIONS record, and most options are not important for our needs. OPTIONS 6 results in a printout having an 80-character width, a format that is more readable for printers that use narrow 80-column paper.

12.5   Sample SPSS^x Program for the Independent T-TEST

The appropriate records and sequence for an SPSS^x job using the T-TEST routine would appear as indicated below. As it is set up in the example, three *t*-tests will be performed. These *t*-tests compare the scores of females against males on each of the dependent variables listed (TASK, RELATION, PERFORM). No OPTIONS statement has been included in the sample program, but as mentioned before, an OPTIONS statement may be used in conjunction with the T-TEST program. If so, this record is placed immediately after the T-TEST statement.

```
DATA LIST    RECORDS=1/1 SUBJ. . .
T-TEST    GROUPS=GENDER(1,2) / VARIABLES=TASK TO PERFORM
BEGIN DATA
```

data records

```
END DATA
```

12.6   Interpreting the Output from an Independent T-TEST Run

In order to intepret the output from T-TEST, you must understand both the output table and the meaning of the numbers within the table.

12.6a   Understanding the T-TEST Table

A typical printout from a T-TEST for independent samples appears in Table 12.1. The specific printout presented here illustrates the output from

Table 12.1   Sample Output from T-TEST

GROUP 1 - GENDER EQ   1.
GROUP 2 - GENDER EQ   2.

- - - - - - - - - - - - - - - - T - T E S T - - - - - - - - - - - - - - - - - -

| VARIABLE | | NUMBER OF CASES | MEAN | STANDARD DEVIATION | STANDARD ERROR | * F VALUE | 2-TAIL PROB. | * POOLED VARIANCE ESTIMATE | | * SEPARATE VARIANCE ESTIMATE | |
| | | | | | | | | T VALUE | DEGREES OF FREEDOM | 2-TAIL PROB. | T VALUE | DEGREES OF FREEDOM | 2-TAIL PROB. |

RELATION
GROUP 1	30	5.8000	2.310	.422							
					1.85	.102	-2.04	58	.046	-2.04	53.23	.047
GROUP 2	30	6.8667	1.697	.310							

TASK
GROUP 1	30	6.7333	2.050	.374							
					1.09	.819	1.93	58	.059	1.93	57.89	.059
GROUP 2	30	5.7333	1.964	.359							

PERFORM,
GROUP 1	30	5.3667	2.141	.391							
					1.38	.390	-.65	58	.519	-.65	56.55	.519
GROUP 2	30	5.7000	1.822	.333							

the sample program listed in Section 12.5 in which gender effects on TASK, RELATION, and PERFORM were requested. For each dependent variable (there are three in Table 12.1), the number of cases, mean, standard deviation, and standard error are provided. Another set of values indicating the F value and two-tailed probability of F is also provided. These columns are used to determine whether homogeneity of variance, one of the conditions for appropriate use of the t-test, has been satisfied. If the probability of the F value is less than .05, then the variances in the groups being compared are different, and the condition of homogeneity of variance has not been satisfied.

The results of the F test determine whether to use the "pooled variance estimate" columns or the "separate variance estimate" columns in evaluating the t statistic. Note that the t values are the same in each of the columns, but that the degrees of freedom are different, and as a result, the two-tailed probability of t may be different as well.

The rules for using pooled versus separate variance estimates are easy.

1. IF THE VARIANCES FOR THE TWO GROUPS ARE SIMILAR (i.e, the 2-TAIL PROB. > .05), then use the output under the "pooled variance estimate" column. These columns represent the more conventional method of evaluating t based upon degrees of freedom equal to N-2 (this is the method that is described in most introductory statistics or research methods textbooks).
2. IF THE VARIANCES FOR THE TWO GROUPS ARE SIGNIFICANTLY DIFFERENT (i.e., the 2-TAIL PROB. of F < .05), use the output under the "separate variance estimate" column. Evaluation of the t statistic in this column is based upon an adjusted degrees of freedom which takes into account the nonsimilar variances in the two groups.

As you can see in Table 12.1, the probability for each of the F values is greater than .05. Thus, in all three t-tests that have been performed, the variances of the two groups are similar, and therefore the output under the "pooled variance estimate" should be used.

12.6b   Interpreting the t-values

Does gender influence relation and task scores? or overall performance? For our analyses of GENDER effects on RELATION, TASK, and PERFORM, the 2-TAIL PROB. under the "pooled variance estimate" column indicates whether there is a significant difference between the two groups being compared. As is customary, if the two-tailed probability is less than .05, then the null hypothesis can be rejected and we can conclude that there is a significant difference between the groups that can be attributed to GENDER. Our analyses in fact show that there is a signficant difference in the way men and women (GENDER) score on the RELATION test. Specifically, women show a significantly higher mean score of 6.87 compared with the lower mean of 5.80 for men. However, the results of the second and third *t*-tests indicate that, if one uses a two-tailed probability, there are no gender differences on either TASK or PERFORM scores, since $p > .05$. Therefore, gender does not appear to be an important variable in determining scores on the TASK scale or overall performance in leadership situations.

12.7   Format for a Paired T-TEST Run (Optional)

The paired *t*-test is used when a repeated measures or subject-by-subject matched design has been used. For example, if we wanted to determine whether TASK scores, in general, are higher (or lower) than RELATION scores, the paired *t*-test would be used. As you recall from Chapter 5, a TASK score and RELATION score was obtained for each subject, and therefore this aspect of the study incorporated a repeated measures design.

The SPSS^x format for implementing the paired *t*-test is as follows: in the specification field, the subroutine PAIRS= is designated, followed by the variables (joined by the keyword WITH) that are to be compared. For example:

    T-TEST   PAIRS = TASK WITH RELATION

An alternative method is simply to list all the variables that you want compared. For example, the statement

    T-TEST   PAIRS = TASK RELATION PERFORM

would result in the comparison of all possible combinations of variables. The above statement would generate three paired *t*-tests: TASK versus RELATION; TASK versus PERFORM; and RELATION versus PER-FORM. (You might have realized that the two latter comparisons listed above do not make a whole lot of sense with respect to our project at E-Z Manufacturing; they were included primarily to demonstrate the format for using paired T-TEST).

The output for the paired T-TEST is similar to that of the independent T-TEST with several minor differences. With the paired *t*-test, no F value is calculated to determine whether the variances for the variables (or levels of the independent variable) are similar. Accordingly, there is only one t value and associated probability. In addition, there are several statistics included in the paired T-TEST output which do not appear in the output for the independent T-TEST. These consist of the differences between the means of the two conditions, the standard deviation and standard error of the difference, and the correlation between the two variables (or conditions) that are being compared.

12.8   Using the T-TEST Procedure to Answer Questions about the Employees at E-Z Manufacturing: Preparing for the Exercise

A question relevant to our project at E-Z Manufacturing is whether sex typed individuals are different in their performance (PERFORM) from androgynous individuals. Specifically, we would like to combine both masculine and feminine sex typed employees into one group, and compare the performance (PERFORM) of this new group with that of androgynous employees.

In order to combine masculine and feminine sex types into a single group, we would want to use the RECODE statement. Recall from previous chapters that the variable BSRI was recoded into three categories (1 = masculine, 2 = feminine, and 3 = androgynous) to form the new variable SEXROLE. We now want to form a single group within SEXROLE for masculine and feminine types, so all we need do is recode feminine types (designated as "2") into the same category as masculine types (designated as "1"). The RECODE statement that would accomplish this combination is:

RECODE   SEXROLE (2=1)

Using your powers of logic, you could probably surmise that this RECODE statement should appear after the RECODE statement for BSRI but before the T-TEST record in the SPSS^x run.

To summarize briefly, we could now investigate the effect of being androgynous versus being sex typed (the independent variable) on performance (PERFORM) in leadership situations (the dependent variable). Again, recall that there may be both male and female employees within each of the two categories of the recoded SEXROLE variable.

Exercises

1a. Compare the leadership performance (PERFORM) of androgynous and sex-typed employees at E-Z Manufacturing as outlined in Section 12.8. As part of this exercise, you must (1) include the original

RECODE BSRI INTO SEXROLE statement, and (2) recode SEX-ROLE into two categories as described above. Before running the SPSS[x] program, take several minutes to make sure you know what records must be included in your run. To prepare for your run, answer the following questions:

a. Should you run a paired *t*-test or independent *t*-test?
b. What are the independent and dependent variables?
c. Where will you place the RECODE SEXROLE record?
d. How will the T-TEST statement appear? Write it out in the space below.

1b. Interpret the results of the *t*-test by answering the following questions.

a. Which group showed the higher performance?
b. Should you use the pooled or separate variance estimate to interpret the *t*-value? Explain your answer.
c. What *t*-value did you obtain?
d. Does this *t*-value indicate a significant difference between the groups? Explain your answer.
e. What conclusion can you draw regarding the effect of sex-typing on leadership performance?
f. If the *t*-value is significant, can you provide a possible explanation as to why the one group of employees performed better than the other?

2. (Optional) Exercise in T-TEST for paired comparisons. Compare RELATION scores with TASK scores using the paired *t*-test. Is there a significant difference in the scores on the two measures?

3. (Optional) As the vice-president of sales for a large computer firm, you are interested in what type of training you should emphasize for your sales force. One group of trainees goes through a program that emphasizes the longstanding record of the company in terms of both sales and service (e.g., share of the market, availability of immediate service, etc.). A second group of trainees attends a program that focuses on understanding the technology of the computer and its applications to various fields in which your company typically does business. Each group is then instructed to use the information they have just learned as the primary sales pitch for their products.

After taking elaborate steps to control for the many extraneous variables that might affect computer sales in general, you collect data on sales (dollar amounts) for various regions of the country for a three month period and break them down according to which emphasis was used in selling the product. The results are as follows (in thousands of dollars):

	Sales/Service Emphasis	Technology/Application Emphasis
Northeast	588	410
Mid-Atlantic	340	305
Southeast	295	312
Midwest	520	365
Deep South	243	125
Plains	85	102
Southwest	62	21
West	630	605
Northwest	272	136

a. What type of *t*-test should you run?
b. Set up the T-TEST statement as it should appear in your file.
c. Interpret the output of the T-TEST run:
  • Do you use pooled or separate variance?
  • What *t*-value did you obtain?
  • Is there a significant difference between types of sales strategies?
  • What conclusion can you draw from this analysis?

13 One-Way Analysis of Variance (ANOVA)

In this chapter we discuss:

- analysis of variance and individual comparisons
- the SPSS^x ONEWAY command statement
- the interpretation of the oneway analysis of variance and the individual comparison tests

13.1 Introduction to Analysis of Variance (ANOVA)

In Chapter 12, we were able to test several hypotheses about the data obtained from the employees at E-Z Manufacturing by using the t-test. As you recall, however, we were limited to testing only those hypotheses which involved the comparison of two groups. Several hypotheses worth investigating in our project involve the comparison of more than two groups simultaneously; for example, the influence of sex role (masculine, feminine, or androgynous) or leadership style on overall performance might be worth examining. In this as well as other cases, however, there are three levels of the independent variable (and so three groups), and in order to analyze data from these types of designs, it is necessary to use analysis of variance (ANOVA) procedures.

As with the t-test, ANOVA is used to determine whether there is significant variation among groups within an experiment. The ANOVA procedure produces an F value, the probability of which enables the researcher to accept or reject the null hypothesis, that is, to conclude whether or not an independent variable is influencing the dependent variable. As with other parametric tests, ANOVA is most appropriately used when the data are interval or ratio level, when the groups show similar variances, and when the data are normally distributed.

ANOVA may be used when two or more groups are being compared, and in this respect, ANOVA has wider application than the *t*-test. Thus, a one-way ANOVA may always be used in place of the *t*-test since ANOVA may be used to make two-group comparisons. However, whereas the *t*-test may not be applied when three or more conditions are being analyzed, use of the ANOVA is totally appropriate under these conditions.

While all ANOVA's are conceptually based upon a comparison of variance resulting from the independent variable, to the estimated variance resulting from random fluctuation (e.g., F = Between-Group Variance / Within-Group Variance), variations in the procedure for carrying out the ANOVA occur when different types of experimental designs are employed. For example, the procedure for performing a "randomized, between-group ANOVA" is computationally different than that for a "repeated measures ANOVA". Each ANOVA, however, yields an F statistic which is evaluated in essentially the same way, and when the probability of occurrence of the F value is less than .05, we conclude that there is significant variation among groups, i.e., variation which can be attributed to the independent variable.

13.2 The Need for Individual Comparisons

When three or more groups are being analyzed in the ANOVA, there frequently arises the need to carry out more specific two-group comparisons in order to determine where the major treatment effect is occurring. These two-group comparisons are commonly referred to as "individual" comparisons or "follow-up" tests. Let's assume, for example, that you are a clinical psychologist who has designed an experiment to assess the effectiveness of different types of therapy on the treatment of phobias in a sample of eighty men and women. You assign each subject to one of four groups (either a control group or one of three therapy groups), and after an adequate treatment period, you rate the amount of improvement each subject has shown (higher score = more improvement). The mean improvement scores (hypothetical, of course!) for the four groups are as follows:

Group 1	Control	12
Group 2	Psychoanalytic	18
Group 3	Client-centered	23
Group 4	Cognitive behavioral	41

You perform an ANOVA on the four groups, and find that there is significant overall variation (or differences) among the groups. From this analysis, you can conclude that the independent variable (therapy) is having an effect, but you are unable to state with any confidence where the effect is occurring. Is psychoanalytic therapy more effective than receiving no treatment at all? Is cognitive-behavioral therapy more effective than either psychoanalytic or client-centered therapies? Might there also be a signficant difference between psychoanalytic and client-entered approaches? These questions require that we carry out more specific individual comparisons between the pairs of groups in which we're interested.

There are a number of guidelines that one needs to know in order to properly carry out these two-group comparisons. For example, most researchers agree that it is appropriate to perform individual comparisons only if the result of the overall ANOVA is significant. Furthermore, one must decide at some point in the experimental process whether these comparisons are to be *a priori*—planned before the data are collected— or *a posteriori*—decided upon after collecting and studying the data. Even then, one must decide which specific *a priori* or *a posteriori* technique (since there are many) best suits the situation (or researcher). While we are not able to review all the relevant guidelines for performing individual comparisons within this text, suffice it to say that these comparisons are generally considered an important and necessary part of the analysis of an experimental design in which there are three groups or more.

13.3   Using a One-Way ANOVA to Test Hypotheses from Our Leadership Project at E-Z Manufacturing

There are several hypotheses of major interest in our project on sex roles and leadership that would mandate the use of ANOVA for hypothesis testing. And, of course, there are other instances in which ANOVA might be done for the purpose of exploratory analysis or might be used in place of the *t*-test (e.g., the analyses that were carried out in the previous chapter).

Let's consider one of the major questions that our project at E-Z Manufacturing was designed to answer: is leadership style an important factor in determining good performance in situations requiring leadership? Recall for a moment that each employee in our data file from E-Z Manufacturing has been categorized according to his/her leadership style (STYLE). Those employees who scored high on the TASK scale and low on the RELATIONS scale were placed in the task-oriented category (and were assigned a value of "1"); those scoring high on RELATIONS but low on TASK were placed in the relations-oriented category ("2"); and those scoring high on both scales were placed in the "both" category ("3"). Clearly we would be interested in finding out whether one's leadership style (STYLE) influences performance (PERFORM) in various leadership situations. In this case we would be analyzing the effect of an independent variable (STYLE) with three levels (or groups: Relations, Task, or Both) on a single dependent variable, performance (PERFORM). An analysis of this type would require use of the one-way ANOVA for a between-group design.

In addition to the hypothesis addressed above, there might also be an interest in determining whether SEXROLE (masculine, feminine, or androgynous) influences leadership performance (PERFORM). You may recall that this question was partly addressed in the previous chapter on *t*-tests by the exercise in which we examined how sex-typed employees performed in comparison to androgynous employees. We may find, for example, that masculine sex-typed employees are perceived as more effective leaders than feminine sex-typed employees, since masculinity has been traditionally associated with leadership in our society. We have chosen to use the question of how sex role (SEXROLE) affects TASK scores and overall leadership performance (PERFORM) to illustrate how to set up and interpret an SPSS^x run on analysis of variance.

13.4   SPSS^x Programs for a One-Way Analysis of Variance

Several SPSS^x programs may be used to calculate the F statistic, including BREAKDOWN, ONEWAY, and MANOVA. Both ONEWAY and BREAKDOWN are used when single factor, between-group designs are analyzed, MANOVA may be used when a repeated measures design is analyzed.

Our discussion will focus on the use and understanding of ONEWAY. This program has been chosen for two reasons: (1) the analysis of data from our Leadership Data File involves a between-group design, for which ONEWAY is appropriate; and (2) ONEWAY allows us to carry out several types of individual follow-up comparisons whereas BREAKDOWN does not.

13.5   Understanding the Format for the ONEWAY Statement

Several records are included for a typical SPSS^x run for performing an analysis of variance. In addition to the mandatory ONEWAY record, both OPTIONS and STATISTICS records may be included depending on the type of output and statistics desired.

13.5a   Format for the ONEWAY Record

The control field for this statement contains the word ONEWAY. For our purposes, there are two main categories of information that are to be stipulated in the ONEWAY specification field. First, the dependent and independent variables must be listed (in that order) and separated by the keyword BY. The inclusive levels of the independent variable follow in parentheses. Second, the desired group comparisons must be indicated.

The dependent variables (there may be anywhere from 1 to 100) are listed first, followed by the keyword BY and then the single independent variable with its minimum and maximum values (or levels) enclosed in parentheses. For example,

ONEWAY   PERFORM TASK BY SEXROLE (1,3)

requests an analysis of variance on the dependent variables PERFORM and TASK across all three levels of the independent variable SEXROLE. Note that the numbers in parentheses indicate the minimum and maximum values of SEXROLE, and thus all levels between the designated numbers (in this case, "2") will be included in the analysis as well. Had there been a fourth level of SEXROLE (designated "4"), this level would not have been included in the analysis because it lies outside the maximum value ("3") specified in the ONEWAY statement.

13.5b *Specifying Individual Comparisons in ONEWAY*

It is possible to request either *a priori* or *a posteriori* comparisons from SPSS^x within the ONEWAY statement. If you have planned the individual comparisons before executing the experiment, it is appropriate to request *a priori* comparisons (they are sometimes referred to as "contrasts"). In essence, when *a priori* contrasts are specified, SPSS^x merely calculates *t*-values for each two-group comparison requested. Although the procedure for specifying *a priori* contrasts is simple and straightforward, we will not discuss it here—you need only refer to the SPSS^x manual if you're interested in learning about the procedure.

If your comparisons are unplanned, *a posteriori* techniques are preferred. SPSS^x provides a choice of seven different *a posteriori* tests (referred to as "range" tests). The list includes:

Code Name	Description
LSD	Least significant difference
DUNCAN	Duncan's multiple range test
SNK	Student Newman Keuls
TUKEYB	Tukey's alternate procedure
TUKEY	Tukey's honestly significant difference
LSDMOD	Modified LSD
SCHEFFE	Scheffé test

Requesting any of the above "range" tests results in every possible two-group comparison within the experiment. To request a range test, the RANGES= subcommand is used in the ONEWAY statement, followed by the code name (given above) of the particular range test desired. For example:

ONEWAY   PERFORM TASK BY SEXROLE (1,3)/ RANGES=LSD

specifies that the Least Significant Difference test be implemented after the overall ANOVA is carried out. Note that as with other instances where subcommands were used, each subcommand within a statement must be separated from other subcommands with a slash (/). If you want to request more than one range test, a separate RANGES= subcommand must be used for each type of comparison requested. The following statement

ONEWAY   PERFORM TASK BY SEXROLE (1,3)/
     RANGES=LSD/
     RANGES=SCHEFFE

will produce two overall F values (one for each dependent variable) as well as the results of both the Least Significant Difference and the Scheffé *a posteriori* comparisons (these will be carried out on both dependent variables). As was mentioned previously, the choice of one particular range test over another depends in part upon the demands of the experimental situations. Your instructor can provide you with information that helps you understand the advantages and disadvantages of each test; in addition, s/he can help you decide which range test seems most appropriate for a particular situation.

13.5c   The STATISTICS Record

You may choose several optional statistics beyond the F value and individual comparisons by including the STATISTICS command. STATISTICS "1" and "3" in particular may aid in the understanding of the results of the analysis. STATISTICS 1 provides a plethora of descriptive statistics for each group (e.g., mean, standard deviation, standard error, 95 percent confidence intervals, etc.). If you are concerned about satisfying the requirement of homogeneity of variance, STATISTICS 3 provides several numbers that enable you to determine whether you have met this condition.

13.5d   The OPTIONS Record

Missing values, formatting options, and determining a harmonic mean when groups sizes are unequal can be dealt with by selecting various

OPTIONS. If you are working with an "unbalanced" design, it is often advantageous to select OPTIONS 10. This option not only determines a harmonic mean of groups sizes (a kind of weighted average "n" when groups sizes are unequal), but it also determines "homogeneous subsets" for all range tests. The concept of homogeneous subsets is explained in Section 13.7c.

13.6   Sample SPSS^x Exercise for ONEWAY Analysis of Variance

An example of a ONEWAY program which analyzes the influence of SEXROLE (masculine, feminine, or androgynous) on leadership performance (PERFORM) and task orientation (TASK) is given below. This program also specifies that the LSD range test be performed. Note that because SEXROLE (one of the variables that we created early on by using the RECODE procedure) is included as one of the variables in the ONEWAY statement, this variable must be defined for SPSS^x by including the original RECODE BSRI statement.

```
DATA LIST   RECORDS=1/ 1 SUBJ. . .
RECODE   BSRI (LO THRU −2.1=1) (−2.0 THRU +2.0=3)
(2.1 THRU HI=2) INTO SEXROLE
ONEWAY   PERFORM TASK BY SEXROLE (1,3)/
RANGES=LSD
STATISTICS 1 3
OPTIONS 10
BEGIN DATA

data records

END DATA
```

13.7   Interpreting ONEWAY Output

For the most part, the output from ONEWAY is straightforward. For each dependent variable, an analysis of variance table with the F ratio and probability is produced. In addition, this table includes the other information typically found in the ANOVA summary table: sources of variance, sums of squares, degrees of freedom (D.F.), and mean squares. Finally, a number of descriptive statistics are also produced if you requested STATISTICS 1.

As Table 13.1 indicates, an F ratio of 8.59 was obtained for the SEXROLE on PERFORM analysis. The associated probability for this F

value (F-PROB) is .0006. Since .0006 < .05, this indicates that SEX-ROLE has a significant influence on leadership performance. Results of SEXROLE on TASK (Table 13.2) yield an F ratio of 6.57 with an associated probability of .0027, again indicating a significant effect, that is, F-PROB < .05.

13.7a   (Optional) Have you satisfied the condition of homogeneity of variance?

Homogeneity of variance statistics (if you specified STATISTICS 3) enable you to determine whether or not this condition has been fulfilled. A significant value (i.e., p < .05) for the Cochran C and/or the Bartlett-Box F indicates that the variances for the groups are significantly different. If this should be the case, then there is no homogeneity of variance, and under this condition, one must be very cautious in interpreting the F value. In addition, an F_{max} value is calculated by dividing the maximum group variance by the minimum group variance. This number may be interpreted by referring to the standard "Distribution of F_{max} Statistics" table found in many statistics textbooks.

The results of the homogeneity tests for both analyses illustrated in Table 13.1 indicate that there are similar variances in the groups. Therefore, we can be confident that the F-values are accurate indicators of our experimental manipulation, and so we can move on to the next step of interpreting the printed F-values.

13.7b   Probing the Data: Results of Individual Comparisons

The results of the particular individual comparison or follow-up test requested in the ONEWAY statement are included in the output below the summary table. As seen in Tables 13.1 and 13.2, for each dependent variable, SPSS[x] generates a matrix consisting of a row of the Groups and a column of the Groups. Wherever an asterisk occurs in the matrix, the pairs of groups are significantly different at the .05 level.

We find from our LSD analysis of SEXROLE on TASK (Table 13.2) that feminine sex typed employees (Group 2) are significantly lower in task orientation than either masculine (Group 1) or androgynous types (Group 3). This finding is not surprising since research has shown that men (who are more typically masculine sex typed) tend to be more task oriented, while women (more typically feminine sex typed) tend to be more relations oriented in leadership styles.

And now we come to the findings that will help convince management at E-Z Manufacturing that our consulting fee was worth the price! From our LSD analysis of SEXROLE on PERFORM (Table 13.1) we see that Group 3 (androgynous employees) shows significantly higher leadership performance (PERFORM) than either Group 1 (masculine sex type) or Group 2 (feminine sex type). Furthermore, there is no significant difference between the performance of masculine and feminine sex types. Thus, an androgynous sex role orientation does seem to make for better leadership, and your recommendation to upper management would be to promote androgynous individuals to positions of leadership within the corporation. What about the finding that masculine and feminine types showed no difference in their leadership performance? This might initially

Table 13.1   Sample Outlet from ONEWAY: Perform by Sexrole

```
- - - - - - - - - - - - - - - - - - - - - - - - - - - O N E W A Y - - - - - - - - - - - - - - - - - - - - - - - - - - -


      Variable  PERFORM
   By Variable  SEXROLE

                        ANALYSIS OF VARIANCE


                              SUM OF        MEAN         F      F
           SOURCE      D.F.   SQUARES       SQUARES      RATIO  PROB.

BETWEEN GROUPS          2     53.4667       26.7333      8.5864 .0006

WITHIN GROUPS          57     177.4667      3.1135

TOTAL                  59     230.9333

                              STANDARD     STANDARD
GROUP       COUNT     MEAN    DEVIATION    ERROR     MINIMUM    MAXIMUM    95 PCT CONF INT FOR MEAN

Grp 1        15      4.4000   1.9567       .5052     1.0000     7.0000     3.3164 TO    5.4836
Grp 2        15      4.8000   1.6562       .4276     1.0000     7.0000     3.8829 TO    5.7171
Grp 3        30      6.4667   1.7167       .3134     3.0000     9.0000     5.8256 TO    7.1077

TOTAL        60      5.5333   1.9784       .2554     1.0000     9.0000     5.0223 TO    6.0444


Tests for Homogeneity of Variances

    Cochrans C = Max. Variance/Sum(Variances) = .4022, P = .639 (Approx.)
    Bartlett-Box F =                            .230 , P = .795


      Variable  PERFORM
   By Variable  SEXROLE
MULTIPLE RANGE TEST
```

Continued

seem to contradict your expectations (or stereotypes) about "good managers" having masculine traits. However, recall that earlier we noted that some situations call for relations-oriented leadership (a feminine stereotype) while others call for task-oriented leadership (a masculine stereotype). Thus, depending on the particular situation, masculine traits are sometimes more effective than feminine traits, other times feminine traits are more effective than masculine traits. The end result, of course, is that neither set of traits is particularly more effective over a range of situations calling for different types of leadership skills.

Table 13.1   *Continued*

```
LSD PROCEDURE
RANGES FOR THE  .050 LEVEL -

       2.83   2.83

HARMONIC MEAN CELL SIZE =    18.0000
THE ACTUAL RANGE USED IS THE LISTED RANGE *      .4159

  (*) DENOTES PAIRS OF GROUPS SIGNIFICANTLY DIFFERENT AT THE  .05# LEVEL


                      G G G
                      r r r
                      p p p

      Mean     Group  1 2 3

      4.4000   Grp 1
      4.8000   Grp 2
      6.4667   Grp 3   * *
   HOMOGENEOUS SUBSETS   (SUBSETS OF GROUPS, WHOSE HIGHEST AND LOWEST MEANS
                          DO NOT DIFFER BY MORE THAN THE SHORTEST
                          SIGNIFICANT RANGE FOR A SUBSET OF THAT SIZE)


SUBSET  1

GROUP      Grp 1       Grp 2
MEAN       4.4000      4.8000
- - - - - - - - - - - - - - - -

SUBSET  2

GROUP      Grp 3
MEAN       6.4667
```

13.7c   What Are Homogeneous Subsets?

If you are analyzing a balanced design (one with equal numbers of subjects in each group), or if you choose OPTIONS 10 when you are analyzing an unbalanced design, SPSS^x prints out a list of "homogeneous subsets." As the name implies, each subset consists of all the group means that do *not* differ significantly from each other. The formation of these homogeneous subsets enables the user to determine specifically where the greatest effect from experimental manipulation lies. In our analysis of SEXROLE on PERFORM, Groups 1 and 2 form a homogeneous subset because they are not significantly different from one another, and both are significantly different from Group 3, as discussed above.

Table 13.2   Sample ONEWAY Output: Task by Sexrole

- O N E W A Y -

Variable   TASK
By Variable   SEXROLE

ANALYSIS OF VARIANCE

SOURCE	D.F.	SUM OF SQUARES	MEAN SQUARES	F RATIO	F PROB.
BETWEEN GROUPS	2	46.6000	23.3000	6.5704	.0027
WITHIN GROUPS	57	202.1333	3.5462		
TOTAL	59	248.7333			

GROUP	COUNT	MEAN	STANDARD DEVIATION	STANDARD ERROR	MINIMUM	MAXIMUM	95 PCT CONF INT FOR MEAN	
Grp 1	15	6.4667	2.3865	.6162	2.0000	9.0000	5.1451 TO	7.7882
Grp 2	15	4.7333	1.5796	.4079	3.0000	7.0000	3.8586 TO	5.6081
Grp 3	30	6.8667	1.7367	.3171	3.0000	9.0000	6.2182 TO	7.5152
TOTAL	60	6.2333	2.0532	.2651	2.0000	9.0000	5.7029 TO	6.7637

Tests for Homogeneity of Variances

   Cochrans C = Max. Variance/Sum(Variances) =   .5082, P =   .084 (Approx.)
   Bartlett-Box F =   1.453 , P = .234

Maximum Variance / Minimum Variance   2.282

Continued

Exercises

1a. In this exercise, we are interested in finding out whether the type of leadership style (TASK, RELATIONS, or BOTH) has any bearing on overall leadership performance. Using the ONEWAY program, determine whether leadership STYLE affects performance in leadership situations (PERFORM). Also, select at least one range test (e.g., Scheffe, LSD, Tukey) to determine where significant group differences lie. There are several points that you will want to review before compiling the ONEWAY run.

a. Because STYLE is a variable created with three "IF" statements

Table 13.2   *Continued*

```
- - - - - - - - - - - - - - - - - - - - - - - O N E W A Y - - - - - - - - - - - - - - - - - - - - - - - -
     Variable  TASK
   By Variable  SEXROLE
MULTIPLE RANGE TEST


LSD PROCEDURE
RANGES FOR THE  .050 LEVEL -

      2.83  2.83

HARMONIC MEAN CELL SIZE =    18.0000
THE ACTUAL RANGE USED IS THE LISTED RANGE t      .4439

   (t) DENOTES PAIRS OF GROUPS SIGNIFICANTLY DIFFERENT AT THE  .050 LEVEL
                        G G G
                        r r r
                        p p p

     Mean     Group    2 1 3

     4.7333   Grp 2
     6.4667   Grp 1    t
     6.8667   Grp 3    t
   HOMOGENEOUS SUBSETS    (SUBSETS OF GROUPS, WHOSE HIGHEST AND LOWEST MEANS
                           DO NOT DIFFER BY MORE THAN THE SHORTEST
                           SIGNIFICANT RANGE FOR A SUBSET OF THAT SIZE)
   SUBSET  1

   GROUP      Grp 2
   MEAN       4.7333
   - - - - - - - - - -

   SUBSET  2

   GROUP.     Grp 1      Grp 3
   MEAN       6.4667     6.8667
```

162 Computer-Based Data Analysis

(refer to Chapter 7), these IF statements must appear in your SPSS^x program.

b. The independent variable for this exercise is STYLE, the dependent variable is PERFORM.

c. Include STATISTICS 1 (to obtain descriptive statistics) and 3 (to determine homogeneity of variance).

d. Include OPTIONS 10

1b. Interpret the output from the above analysis by answering the following questions.

a. Is your F-value significant?

b. Do your groups have similar variances?

c. Based on the results of the *a posteriori* range tests, which groups differ from each other?

d. Suggest an explanation as to why employees having both high task and relations orientations do better in situations involving leadership?

2. (Optional) Determine whether SEXROLE (masculine, feminine, androgynous) influences RELATIONS scores. Include a range test to compare individual groups. Is the F-value signficant? What do the results of the range test tell you? Provide an explanation for your findings.

3. (Optional) You are interested in whether diet or exercise might lower serum cholesterol levels in a group of patients who have been diagnosed as having high cholesterol (250 mg or above). You divide your forty-five patients into three equal groups. The patients in the first group (the control) simply have their cholesterol levels checked and are told to have a second test taken in three months. The patients in the second group are given detailed instructions for modifying their diet to include fewer saturated fats and more fiber. This second group, the diet modification group, has its cholesterol rechecked after three months. The patients in the third group agree to a daily exercise program whereby they spend thirty minutes of their lunch hour participating in an aerobic workout. As with the other two groups, this third group, the exercise group, has their cholesterol rechecked after three months. The data given below represent the level of cholesterol for patients in each group after the three month interval.

Control (1)	Diet Modification (2)	Exercise (3)
340	272	233
278	219	276
290	228	293
224	227	298
300	261	220

Control (1)	Diet Modification (2)	Exercise (3)
204	203	202
244	185	237
292	206	218
281	230	262
251	200	245
230	219	291
318	310	240
250	182	299
281	250	270
310	206	305

Carry out an analysis of variance using the ONEWAY procedure to determine whether a modified diet or exercise affects cholesterol levels.

a. Make certain you know the independent and dependent variables.
b. Set up a data file so you have two variables: "CHOL" (for cholesterol) as one of your variables, and "TREAT" (for type of treatment) as the other variable. You would want to designate patients inthe control group as "1" on the variable TREAT, those in the diet modification group as "2", and those in the exercise group as "3".
c. Include STATISTICS 1 for descriptive statistics and 3 for homogeneity of variance.
d. Request that at least one range test be performed.

Interpret the output by answering the following questions:
a. Is the F-value significant?
b. Do the groups have similar variances?
c. Based on the results of the *a posteriori* range tests, do any groups differ from each other?
d. What conclusions can you draw from the ONEWAY analysis?

14 Two-Way Analysis of Variance: Factorial ANOVA

In this chapter, we discuss:

- the logic of factorial ANOVA
- main Effects and interactions in a 2 x 2 design
- the SPSS^x ANOVA command statement
- interpretation & discussion of the a 2 x 2 ANOVA Output

14.1   Introduction to Factorial ANOVA

In Chapter 13, we saw that a one-way analysis of variance permits the researcher to do more sophisticated analyses than does the t-test (i.e., ANOVA allows a comparison of the effects of more than two groups or levels of the independent variable). The same can be said of factorial ANOVA in comparison to one-way ANOVA. That is, factorial ANOVA also allows a comparison of more than two levels of the independent variable, but it improves on one-way ANOVA in that the researcher can *simultaneously* assess the effects of two (or more) independent variables on a single dependent variable within the same analysis. Thus, factorial ANOVA yields the same information that two one-way ANOVA's would, but it does so in one analysis.

But that's not all. Factorial ANOVA also allows the investigator to determine the possible *combined* effects of the independent variables. That is, it also assesses the ways in which these variables interact with one another to influence scores on the dependent variable. Although understanding such "interaction effects" can be a complex and difficult task, it is essential to the progress of science, since in the real world many variables interact with one another to determine behavior. In this chapter we plan to provide a basic introduction to factorial ANOVA and the SPSS^x program that performs this powerful statistical analysis. You will see that while the interpretation of the results of a factorial ANOVA may require both thought and skill, the procedure for conducting this analysis using SPSS^x is not much different from that of a one-way ANOVA. Further, the conceptual basis of factorial ANOVA is essentially the same as that of one-way ANOVA, and the interpretation of the resulting F-values is also based on the same logic as in the one-way ANOVA.

As with one-way ANOVA, computation of factorial ANOVA assumes interval or ratio measures, homogeneity of variance among groups, and normally distributed data. As also discussed in the previous chapter, different types of experimental designs (e.g., randomized, between-group versus a repeated measures design) will call for different procedures in the computation of the ANOVA. Since our leadership study is primarily a between-group design, this is the procedure we will employ here. Another consideration in the computation (and interpretation) of factorial ANOVA concerns the number of independent variables ("factors") to be included in the analysis. The nature of the analysis and the resulting output will differ for a "two-way" versus a "three-way" factorial ANOVA. Although it would be possible to conduct a three-way ANOVA on the data from our leadership study (e.g., the factors could be GENDER, SEXROLE, and STYLE), we will limit our presentation to the various possible two-way ANOVA's that could be performed.

14.2 The Need for a "Factorial Combination" of Independent Varariables

A basic requirement for factorial ANOVA is that the levels of the two independent variables have been "completely crossed" in a factorial combination. This simply means that each level of the first independent variable must be combined with each level of the other independent variable. In the simplest two-way ANOVA (2 x 2 design), for example, four different groups of subjects would be needed. If the first factor was GENDER (male versus female) and the second was SEXROLE (recoded into sex typed versus androgynous), four combinations would be required to permit a factorial ANOVA (each unique combination is referred to as a "cell"):

1. Sex-typed Males
2. Sex-typed Females
3. Androgynous Males
4. Androgynous Females

Assuming that leadership performance effectiveness (PERFORM) is the dependent variable, this factorial combination will allow us to compare the overall PERFORM scores of men versus women (GENDER) and the overall PERFORM scores of sex typed versus androgynous employees (SEXROLE).

What is crucial to the "factorial combination" of these two independent variables is that we are also able to assess the possible interaction effect of the two variables combined. Thus, we might find that androgynous men and women are equally effective leaders, but sex typed *men* are more effective than sex typed *women*. In other words, leadership performance is determined by the combined effects of SEXROLE and GENDER. Another way of stating an interaction effect such as this is to say that the effect of one factor (i.e., GENDER) depends on the level of the second factor (SEXROLE). In this example, the effects of GENDER— that is, male leaders performing better than female leaders—occurs *only* for sex-typed men and women. At the second level of SEXROLE (androgynous employees), there is no gender difference (i.e., male and female leaders are equally effective). Note that we would not have been able to discover an effect like this one without using a factorial design.

14.3   Applying Factorial ANOVA to the Leadership Data File

In previous chapters, the variables STYLE and SEXROLE have been related to a variety of other variables, including GENDER, TASK, RELATION, and PERFORM. However, we have thus far carried out only a limited investigation of the variables EDUCation and AGE. In this chapter, we will momentarily turn our attention away from leadership performance to explore relationships between SEXROLE, GENDER, EDUC, and AGE using factorial ANOVA designs. In particular, we might be interested in determining whether SEXROLE and GENDER (independent variables) are related to the age and education levels (dependent variables of a rather odd sort) of the employees at E-Z Manufacturing.

A factorial ANOVA would also indicate whether there is an interaction effect of SEXROLE and GENDER on age and education. For example, it might be found that there is a significant difference in education levels of sex-typed versus androgynous men, but no such difference between sex-typed and androgynous women. This type of "exploratory" analysis is often helpful in gaining insights regarding the relationships among variables within a study.

Consider the following. Our analyses have already shown that androgynous employees tend to perform better in leadership situations than sex-typed employees. Suppose that we now find that androgynous men have higher education levels than sex-typed men, but that this difference in education does not exist for androgynous and sex-typed women. A clear strategy for future hiring of potential management leaders at E-Z Manufacturing might include recruiting tactics aimed at male college graduates or even men holding master's degrees. However, the corporation's affirmative action program of hiring women managers might best be aimed at women of all education levels since (based on our hypothetical results) education levels aren't different between androgynous and sex-typed women.

In the following we will discuss the basics for understanding the nature of factorial analysis using EDUC as the dependent variable, and GENDER and SEXROLE as independent variables. We will then present the procedures for conducting this analysis using SPSS$^{X.}$ Although this analysis represents a diversion from the main thrust of the project at E-Z Manufacturing, it provides a good example of an interaction effect, thereby giving us the opportunity to discuss the interpretation of such effects. You will then be asked to conduct a similar analysis using AGE as the dependent variable in the exercise at the end of the chapter. Finally, as a second exercise we will return to one of the major concerns of our project, and determine how GENDER and STYLE together might affect leadership performance (PERFORM).

14.4   Understanding the Components of Factorial ANOVA

Recall from the previous chapter that all ANOVA's are conceptually based upon a comparison of variance resulting from the independent variable(s) to the variance resulting from random fluctuation. Factorial ANOVA is conceptually based on the same type of ratio computations; the difference is that a 2 x 2 factorial ANOVA yields three F-ratios, instead of only one as in the one-way ANOVA. In the next two sections we will briefly review the reasons for this and show how to interpret these three F-values.

14.4a   "Sources of Variance" in Factorial ANOVA

The reason that three F-ratios are computed is that conducting factorial ANOVA is like performing two one-way ANOVA's to assess the "main effects" of each of the two independent variables, and a third analysis to assess the "interaction effect." Specifically, in a between-group design, between group variance can be separated into three sources: the main effect from Factor A (SEXROLE); the main effect from Factor B (GENDER); and the interaction effect from A x B (SEXROLE by GENDER). A separate F-ratio is computed to determine how much of the variance in the dependent variable can be attributed to each of these three effects. Each F-value simply represents the ratio of the variance from that particular effect to random variance (sometimes called "residual" variance). Thus, three sources of between-group variance—Factor A, Factor B, and the interaction of A x B—result in three F-values. As in the one-way

ANOVA, the significance of each effect is decided by looking at the probability associated with each F-value (i.e., if p < .05, the effect is significant).

14.4b   Interpreting the Results of Factorial ANOVA

The interpretation of main effects from a 2 x 2 factorial ANOVA is straightforward. If p < .05 for a particular factor, then there is a significant effect for that factor, and subsequent statistical comparisons are not necessary, since there are only two group means associated with the main effect. All we have to do is examine the means for the levels of the factor to determine which group is significantly higher or lower than the other.

The interpretation of a significant interaction is more complicated. This would require a comparison of "cell means" relevant to the factorial combination of the two independent variables. In our example of SEX-ROLE and GENDER on education, this would involve a comparison of each of the four groups described earlier, i.e., the mean education levels for (1) sex-typed men, (2) sex-typed women, (3) androgynous men, and (4) androgynous women. Further, because there are more than two groups, it would be necessary to compute individual comparisons (see Chapter 13) such as the Scheffe or Newman-Keuls test. Unfortunately SPSS^x does not carry out individual comparisons for factorial ANOVA, so the researcher must do these analyses by hand. For now, suffice it to say that these comparisons permit us to draw conclusions regarding interaction effects, such as those described in Section 14.3 (i.e., where there was a significant difference between educational levels of sex-typed men versus androgynous men, but no difference between sex-typed women and androgynous women).

14.5   Using SPSS^x to Conduct a 2 x 2 Factorial ANOVA

It is possible to conduct factorial ANOVA's using either the MANOVA or ANOVA programs in SPSS^x. Although MANOVA has wider application than ANOVA since it permits analysis of repeated measures designs, it is a far more complicated procedure. ANOVA is adequate for analysis of between-group designs, and since our comparisons are of this type, our discussion will be limited to the ANOVA program.

14.6   Understanding the Format of the ANOVA Statement

The procedure for conducting factorial ANOVA with SPSS^x is similar to that for conducting a one-way ANOVA. There are two basic statements involved: the mandatory ANOVA record and the optional STATISTICS record. We will briefly discuss the OPTIONS record, but will not employ it in the present example.

14.6a   Format for the ANOVA Record

The control field for this record contains the word ANOVA. As we saw with the ONEWAY record in Chapter 13, the specification field of the ANOVA record must contain information regarding the dependent variable(s) and the independent variables. Here also the dependent variable(s) must be listed first, followed by the keyword BY and then the two independent variable(s), with their minimum and maximum values enclosed in parentheses. Thus, the record to conduct a factorial ANOVA using EDUC as the dependent variable with SEXROLE and GENDER as the two independent variables would be as follows:

ANOVA   EDUC BY SEXROLE (1,2) GENDER (1,2)

14.6b   The STATISTICS Record

You may choose several optional statistics beyond the F-values by including the STATISTICS command. For our purposes, the STATISTICS 3 statement is the only one necessary. This request has the effect of printing the means and "counts" (i.e., the number of subjects indicated in parentheses beneath the means) for each *level* of each independent variable (e.g., the levels of GENDER are "1" = male and "2" = female), and the means and counts for each of the four *cells* representing the factorial combination of independent variables. These means are essential for interpreting both main effects and the interaction effect.

14.6c   The OPTIONS Record

Missing values, formatting options, and variations in the type of ANOVA computations are specified on this record. None of these options are particularly relevant to our discussion, so this record has not been included in our sample run. If, however, you should want to include variables with missing values, specify OPTIONS 1.

14.7   Sample SPSS[x] Exercise for Factorial ANOVA

An example of the ANOVA procedure for computing a 2 x 2 ANOVA described in the preceding section is given below. Note that because SEXROLE (one of the variables we created using the RECODE procedure in previous chapters) is included in the ANOVA statement, this variable must be defined for SPSS^x by including the original RECODE BSRI statement. Also, since we are limiting our analysis to only two levels of SEXROLE (sex typed versus androgynous), the RECODE SEXROLE statement must also be included to reduce this variable from three levels to two. Thus, the records needed for this run are:

```
DATA LIST   RECORDS=1/ 1 SUBJ. . .
RECODE   BSRI (LO THRU −2.1=1)(−2.0 THRU +2.0=3)(2.1 THRU
   HI=2) INTO SEXROLE
RECODE   SEXROLE (2=1) (3=2)
ANOVA   EDUC BY SEXROLE (1,2) GENDER (1,2)
STATISTICS 3
BEGIN DATA

   data records

END DATA
```

14.8   Interpreting ANOVA Output

Interpreting the output from a 2 x 2 factorial ANOVA involves examining the three *F*-values associated with the two main effects and the interaction effect. An analysis of variance table with *F*-values and corresponding probabilities is produced for each dependent variable, along with the means and counts requested by the STATISTICS 3 statement (see Table 14.1). SPSS^x actually prints out more information than is useful in the ANOVA table. Specifically, the *F*-values printed in the rows labelled MAIN EFFECTS (2.038), 2-WAY INTERACTIONS (14.309) and EXPLAINED (6.128) are essentially meaningless for our interpretation, so they can be ignored. The remaining three *F*-values printed in the rows labelled SEXROLE, GENDER, and SEXROLE GENDER are the ones of interest for interpreting the results regarding the main effects and the interaction effect. These will be discussed below.

14.8a   *Interpreting the Main Effects*

Following the printing of the means and counts in Table 14.1 is the ANOVA summary table. For the main effect of SEXROLE on EDUC, an *F*-value of 0.206 was obtained, with a corresponding probability ("SIGNIF OF F") of .652. Since the *p* value is greater than .05, we accept the null hypothesis and conclude that there is no difference in the mean education level of sex-typed versus androgynous employees. Actually, there is no need to examine the means for these two categories since the

Table 14.1   Sample Output from Factorial ANOVA Program

'ANOVA' PROBLEM REQUIRES   374 BYTES OF MEMORY.

＊ ＊ ＊ C E L L   M E A N S ＊ ＊ ＊

            EDUC
         BY SEXROLE
            GENDER

TOTAL POPULATION

     13.70
   (60)

SEXROLE
        1   2

     13.80   13.60
   (30) (30)

GENDER
        1   2

     13.27   14.13
   (30) (30)

            GENDER
               1   2
SEXROLE
        1   12.53   15.07
           (15) (15)

        2   14.00   13.20
           (15) (15)

        ＊ ＊ ＊ A N A L Y S I S   O F   V A R I A N C E ＊ ＊ ＊

            EDUC
         BY SEXROLE
            GENDER

SOURCE OF VARIATION	SUM OF SQUARES	DF	MEAN SQUARE	F	SIGNIF OF F
MAIN EFFECTS	11.867	2	5.933	2.038	.140
SEXROLE	.600	1	.600	.206	.652
GENDER	11.267	1	11.267	3.869	.054
2-WAY INTERACTIONS	41.667	1	41.667	14.309	.000
SEXROLE GENDER	41.667	1	41.667	14.309	.000
EXPLAINED	53.533	3	17.844	6.128	.001
RESIDUAL	163.067	56	2.912		
TOTAL	216.600	59	3.671		

        60 CASES WERE PROCESSED.

171

F-value was not significant. However, looking at the means supports this statistical conclusion: 13.80 years of education for sex-typed employees and 13.60 years for androgynous employees. Turning to the F-value of 3.869 for the main effect of GENDER with its associated probability of .054, we see that this difference is marginally significant. Examining the means for these two groups indicates that women at E-Z Manufacturing have a higher average education level (14.13 years) than do men (13.27 years). However, one must always be cautious in drawing conclusions about main effects when there is a significant interaction effect, which is the case in this analysis. So let's now turn our attention to this effect.

14.8b   Interpreting the SEXROLE by GENDER Interaction.

Table 14.1 reveals an F-value of 14.309 for the two-way interaction, with a probability of .000. Since this p < .05, we would conclude that there is a significant interaction between SEXROLE and GENDER in the average level of education for employees at E-Z Manufacturing. In order to interpret this interaction, it is necessary to examine the four cell means printed out for the factorial combination of these two variables in Table 14.1. However, since there are more than two means, we should compute *a posteriori* comparisons to determine which ones are signficantly different. As pointed out in Section 14.4b, SPSS^x does not compute these comparisons, so your authors have done these comparisons by hand using the Newman-Keuls method. These analyses revealed that there is a significant difference in the mean education level of sex-typed men versus sex-typed women, but there is no significant difference in the average level of education of androgynous men and women. Examination of the relevant cell means in Table 14.1 shows that sex-typed women have a significantly higher average education level (15.07 years) than do sex-typed men (12.53 years), but that the average number of years for androgynous women (13.20) is not significantly different from that of androgynous men (14.00). Thus, as we saw in several of the examples of possible interactions described earlier in this chapter, the present interaction suggests that the gender difference indicated by the main effect of GENDER occurs only for sex-typed employees.

Perhaps it is not surprising that androgynous men and women do not differ in their average education level, but explaining the result indicating that sex-typed women at E-Z are better educated than sex-typed men requires some speculation. One possible explanation for this difference is that sex-typed men were more likely to have dropped out of high school to go to work at E-Z Manufacturing. As we have said, this explanation is purely speculative, and more research would be needed to investigate these questions further. But that is why we referred to this factorial

ANOVA as "exploratory" at the beginning of this chapter. It is often such analyses that provide direction for future research. In practical terms for E-Z Manufacturing, exploring relationships between education, age, sex roles and leadership could yield potentially valuable information for establishing guidelines for the recruitment, hiring, and promotion of individuals to management level positions at the corporation.

14.9 Exploring Other Relationships in Our Project by Using Factorial Analyses

We have provided a concrete example of a 2 x 2 factorial ANOVA to introduce you to this important tool and the SPSS^x program that enables you to perform it on the computer. At the end of this chapter, you are given two more exercises in factorial ANOVA. In the first exercise, you are asked to determine how SEXROLE and GENDER are related to AGE (used as a dependent variable). While this exercise has only tangential relevance to our project, it is very similar to the sample provided in this chapter, and therefore, you should not have any difficulty understanding the output from the analysis.

The second exercise returns our attention to one of the major reasons for carrying out our project at E-Z Manufacturing. We will address the question of whether the GENDER of the employee and STYLE of leadership (independent variables) affect PERFORMance in leadership situations (the dependent variable). Recall that we have already investigated the relationship between GENDER and PERFORM and found that gender did not have a significant influence on leadership performance (PERFORM). That is, the overall PERFORM scores of men and women were not significantly different. In addition, we determined that leadership STYLE (whether an individual was task oriented, relations oriented, or both task and relations oriented) *was* a signficant factor in leadership performance (PERFORM). That is, we found that employees who were both task and relations oriented in their leadership style were more effective than employees who were either task or relations oriented only. By using a factorial ANOVA, we can now see whether there might be an interaction between our two independent variables, STYLE and GENDER.

Exercises

1a. In this exercise, we are interested in conducting a 2 x 2 factorial ANOVA with AGE as the dependent variable and SEXROLE and

GENDER as independent variables. That is, we want to know whether there is an age difference in sex-typed versus androgynous employees and between male versus female employees at E-Z Manufacturing, as well as whether or not there is an interaction between SEXROLE and GENDER in the ages of the employees. Perform this analysis using the ANOVA program. As discussed in this chapter, be sure to keep the following points in mind in conducting your analysis:

   a. Because the variable SEXROLE was created using the "RECODE" statement to transform BSRI, this RECODE statement must be included.

   b. Because the original SEXROLE variable had three levels (1= masculine sex typed, 2 = feminine sex typed, 3 = androgynous), the RECODE SEXROLE statement must also be included in order to combine masculine and feminine employees into one category.

   c. The dependent variable must be listed first on the ANOVA record, followed by the keyword BY and the independent variables.

   d. Include the STATISTICS 3 record to obtain a printout of the means needed to interpret your results.

1b. Interpret the output from the above analysis by answering the following questions:

   a. Are your *F*-values for the two main effects significant? What do they tell you about age differences in sex-typed versus androgynous employees and men versus women at E-Z manufacturing?

   b. Is the *F*-value for the SEXROLE x GENDER interaction significant? What can you conclude from this?

   c. Assume that you conduct *a posteriori* comparisons on the four cell means and that you find that the largest mean is significantly different from the other three, but there was no significant difference among the other three. Interpret this result.

   d. Suggest an explanation for the results of the interaction in part C. Why might this one group be significantly older than the other three groups of employees?

2. Perform a 3 x 2 factorial ANOVA to determine the effects of leadership STYLE (relations, task, or both) and GENDER on PERFORM. In order to carry out this analysis, you need only modify the ANOVA record that you used in the above run—the other records may all remain the same. Answer the following questions about the results that you obtain:

   a. Are the main effects of GENDER and STYLE significant? Interpret the *F*-values associated with the effects.

   b. Are these findings consistent with what we obtained from previous analyses carried out in Chapters 12 and 13, in which GENDER showed no effect on PERFORM, but STYLE showed a significant effect?

c. Is the interaction effect significant? What does this tell you about the combined effects of GENDER and STYLE?

3a. (Optional) A researcher was interested in the effects of the number of roommates (Factor 1, called NUMB) and room size (Factor 2, called SIZE) on satisfaction with residential life at college (the dependent variable, called SATF). She factorially combined two levels of NUMB (1 = one roommate; 2 = two roommates) and two levels of SIZE (1 = small room; 2 = large room) in a dormitory and measured SATF on a ten-point scale (where 0 = dissatisfied and 9 = satisfied). Create an SPSS^x file of the following data and conduct a 2 x 2 ANOVA:

NUMB	SIZE	SATF
1	1	6
1	1	5
1	1	6
1	1	7
1	2	7
1	2	8
1	2	7
1	2	9
2	1	2
2	1	1
2	1	1
2	1	0
2	2	8
2	2	7
2	2	6
2	2	7

3b. (Optional) Interpret the output from the above analysis by answering the following questions:

a. Are the F-values for the two main effects significant? What do they tell you about the effects of one versus two roommates and small versus big rooms on satisfaction?

b. Is the F-value for the NUMB x SIZE interaction significant? What can you conclude from this?

c. Assume that you conduct a posteriori comparisons on the four cell means and that you find that smallest mean is significantly different from the other three, but there was no significant difference among the other three. Interpret this result.

d. Apparently the number of roommates makes no difference in large rooms, and the size of room makes no difference when one only has one roommate. Suggest an explanation for this result.

15 Computer-Based Data Analysis, SPSS^x, and the E-Z Project

In this chapter, we discuss:

- computer analysis as a research tool
- a review of SPSS^x statistical procedures
- a review of the results of the leadership study
- applying computer skills in future research

15.1 Computer Analyses of Research Data

It seems appropriate to conclude with a review of what we have learned in this book about the use of the computer—and the SPSS^x statistical package in particular—in the analysis of data obtained in a research project such as the hypothetical study at E-Z Manufacturing. This manual has introduced you to an extremely powerful tool and has helped you develop the skills needed to use it in analyzing data. In the first several chapters, you learned a number of general concepts about how computers work and how data analysis packages operate within computer systems. Beginning with Chapter 5, you learned how to create a computer data file consisting of scores and data obtained from many subjects on several distinct variables related to a research question. You learned how to edit that file to correct data entry errors and to obtain a printout of the file. You also learned how to generate simple frequency distributions of the scores on each variable in the file, as well as how to transform existing variables into newly-created variables. We saw that this procedure could be helpful in getting an overall "feel" for the data, but that drawing meaningful conclusions from this cursory description of the data was next to impossible. We then proceeded to the statistical analysis of the data so that we could obtain a deeper understanding of the results. It was at this point that we introduced you to the wide range of descriptive and inferential statistics that could be computed using SPSS^x on our data file.

In Chapter 8, you learned how to generate a variety of descriptive statistics, such as the mean, median, mode, range, and standard deviation. This "number crunching" SPSS^x routine saves the researcher from hours of tedious labor that would be required to compute these statistics by hand. It's also much more accurate. These statistics can be very useful in helping the researcher "get to know" the data by obtaining single numbers that summarize the entire set of scores for each variable. They are also essential in making comparisons between important groups in the study (e.g., comparing mean leadership performance scores of men versus women). Chapter 9 introduced you to a routine for creating frequency matrices and contingency tables for scores in various combinations of levels of two or more nominal variables (e.g., the number of task oriented male versus female employees). In Chapter 10 you learned various correlational subroutines that are useful in describing direction and degree of relationships between variables (e.g., the correlation between BSRI and TASK scores), and in predicting scores on one variable from another variable. Using the more sophisticated analysis of multiple regression, Chapter 11 was able to demonstrate the interrelationship of several variables simultaneously, and using path analysis, to suggest possible causal relationships between variables.

The above statistical analyses took us a long way toward understanding our data and the relationships between variables relevant to our basic research questions dealing with how sex roles, leadership style, and various demographic variables contribute to effective leadership performance. However, in order to determine whether there were real differences among the various groups being studied, we had to rely on several inferential statistics that permit such conclusions. Thus, in Chapter 12 we learned how to use the t-test procedure to analyze differences between mean scores of groups on the same dependent variable (e.g., RELATIONS) at two levels of a single independent variable (e.g., GENDER). In Chapter 13, a more sophisticated procedure was introduced (ONEWAY ANOVA) which allowed the researcher to test for significant differences between three or more groups (e.g., mean PERFORM scores of masculine sex typed, feminine sex typed, and androgynous employees). We concluded in Chapter 14 with an extremely powerful procedure (Factorial ANOVA) which permits simultaneous testing for differences between levels of two independent variables (e.g., GENDER and SEXROLE) in addition to assessing their interactive, or combined, effects on the dependent variable.

We assume this introduction has given you an appreciation for the value of the computer in helping the investigator answer both simple and complex research questions. The computer not only saves time and effort, but it can enable the researcher to pose and answer questions that would be difficult, if not impossible, to address by "eyeballing" the data or by hand computations. We believe that the basic skills you have learned in conducting the above analyses on our hypothetical research project will be easily transferable to future projects that you may undertake. Indeed, you should have acquired a better understanding of research methods from the exercises in this manual, and we hope that you will be motivated to apply this knowledge and skill to whatever career you pursue.

This, of course, brings us back to one of the motivating factors for this project in the first place—the large consulting fee that upper management at E-Z Manufacturing is paying you for conducting this study! What are you going to be able to report to them that might be helpful in the development of their affirmative action program? Let's consider some of the conclusions and recommendations that you might make to them on the basis of your research and data analysis.

15.2   Sex Roles, Leadership Style, and Leader Effectiveness: A Review

Recall from Chapter 5 that upper management is interested in identifying criteria that can be used for making sound decisions about which individuals (especially female employees) to promote to leadership positions at E-Z Manufacturing. They hired you to conduct a study investigating important variables related to both gender and leadership effectiveness. Your literature review revealed that both sex role stereotypes and leadership style have been related to performance effectiveness in the past, so you decide to measure all these variables in a selected group of men and women at E-Z Manufacturing. Further, you obtained measures on the demographic variables, age and education level, in order to explore potential relationships between these variables and those of sex roles, leadership style, and leadership performance. After collecting and analyzing the data in the manner described in the preceding chapters, you must now prepare a report to be presented at the next board meeting.

What do you tell the eager execs that will convince them that you are worth your huge fee? Before you panic, recognize that it will not be possible to report everything you have learned from your study to these busy people. Since you're recognized as a distinguished social scientist, it will not be necessary to present all the minute details of methodology and statistics discussed in this book—they are going to assume that your conclusions are warranted by sound methods and analyses. Indeed, this is another argument for the value of the computer: it has done all the work that permits you to present a meaningful summary and make recommendations that the executives can understand and implement. To be sure, some tables and figures will lend credibility to your conclusions and facilitate your presentation. However, we will not concern ourselves here with this issue, nor will we pretend that what follows is a "prototype" of such a report. Instead, we will simply review some of the important and interesting findings of this hypothetical study as a way of helping you to integrate the diverse analyses that you conducted in the previous chapters in the context of the original research issues described above. Before going on, it might be useful for you to glance over your printouts and jot down some of your own conclusions to compare with ours.

First, we learned that sex role stereotyping does seem to exist at E-Z Manufacturing. Many male employees view themselves as primarily "masculine," and many female employees view themselves as stereotypically "feminine." However, you were able to identify a group of male and female employees who are "androgynous," that is, they see themselves as possessing attributes that are *both* masculine and feminine. You also discovered that there are consistent differences in leadership style among employees: some are primarily task oriented, others are relations oriented, and still others combine task and relations orientations in their leadership style. Further, you uncovered the interesting fact that most of the masculine sex typed employees are task oriented, most of the feminine sex typed employees are relations oriented, and most of the androgynous employees combine task and relations orientations in their leadership style. Thus, traditional stereotypes of a task oriented leadership style in men and a relations oriented style in women appear to hold primarily for sex typed employees. Finally, you found that sex typing seems to be related to increased age and lower levels of education.

While the above results are interesting in themselves (as well as theoretically important from a scientific point of view), the E-Z executives are now anxiously awaiting your interpretations and conclusions regarding their planned affirmative action program. The key to this goal is in the results concerning your measure of leadership performance effectiveness. Indeed, you probably breathed a sigh of relief upon examining these results and discovering that there were many worthwhile relationships to report. (You should note that in the "real world," there is never a guarantee that this will be the case—many major projects dead end with inconclusive results, a possibility that you should be prepared for and certainly should warn your clients about before agreeing to conduct the study!) One important finding is that there were no significant overall differences between men and women in performance effectiveness. Thus, there is no basis for anxiety about promoting women to traditionally male leadership positions. Thus, stereotypes about men and leadership do not appear to hold at E-Z Manufacturing; women appear to be equally as capable as men, and you can recommend that the affirmative action program be implemented without hesitation.

But which women (and men, for that matter) should be promoted? Your results demonstrated that androgynous men and women are more effective than sex typed employees, so this is a good group to target for promotion. Further, you have evidence as to why this relationship holds. Recall that androgynous employees were more likely to exhibit a combination of task and relations strategies than were sex typed individuals. Other analyses revealed that individuals exhibiting the combined leadership style are more effective than are people who are exclusively task or relations oriented. Thus, the overall pattern of results suggests that the affirmative action program (and promotions for male employees as well) is most likely to be successful by promoting those individuals who are androgynous and/ or exhibit a combination leadership style. It is important to emphasize the value of this knowledge: the net effect of this strategy will be to increase the effectiveness, productivity, and profit potential of E-Z Manufacturing as a whole by having the best possible people in leadership positions (a conclusion that will be music to the ears of E-Z execs). Finally, you might conclude your report by noting some of the interesting relationships between age, education, and other relevant variables that might assist in developing recruitment, hiring, and promotion guidelines within the corporation.

15.3   Caveat and Conclusion

We believe that enough has been said to give you a feel for the kinds of conclusions and recommendations that could result from a study such as the hypothetical one presented in this manual. As we have emphasized repeatedly, these data are hypothetical, and your authors can now confess that we constructed them so that they would come out this way. While the results have not been concocted "out of the blue," the real world of research is not so likely to be as neat and clean. The data do correspond with some actual research in the literature, but there are conflicting data as well. Our goal was to construct a data set that would be manageable for leading you through the various procedures introduced in this text and would yield meaningful results that would be fairly easy for you to understand. We hope that we have accomplished this goal. We also hope that in the process you have acquired the skills needed to address research questions like the ones presented by our project at E-Z, or to obtain empirically-based answers to any other questions which might stem from your own particular interests. The tools of the computer and SPSS^x, and the means of using them have been introduced here—it remains for you to take advantage of them.

Appendix A: Coding the Survey Questionnaire

In this appendix we discuss:

- how to pre-code a questionnaire
- how to construct a codebook
- techniques for "cleaning" the data of errors

A.1 Introduction

Survey research is very likely the best method available to the social scientist wishing to collect data from a population too large to observe directly. Surveys may be used for several purposes—to describe a population, to explore new topics of research, and to explain relationships through the testing of hypotheses. While surveys are most often used with individual persons as the units of analysis, they may also be employed to study other units of analysis such as groups, divorces, marriages, etc. Surveys are also well suited for the measurement of attitudes within a large population. Careful probability sampling results in the selection of respondents whose characteristics may be considered representative of those in the larger population.

There are two basic methods for the administration of questionnaires to respondents: (1) self administered questionnaires which are mailed or handed to respondents who then proceed to complete them on their own and (2) interviews administered by specially trained people who contact respondents, read the questions to them, and record the respondents' answers on the spot.

With either method of survey research, it is advisable to construct the research instrument so that a computer can be used for analysis of data. Survey samples are usually large, and the research instruments may be long and complex. Hand analysis of such research results is extremely time-consuming and error-prone. Both for economy and accuracy, surveys should be designed for computer analysis whenever possible.

This appendix will cover four aspects of preparing questionnaires for computerized analysis: (1) pre-coding the questionnaires, (2) constructing the codebook, (3) options for data processing, and (4) techniques for "cleaning" the data of errors.

A.2   Guidelines for Pre-Coding Questionnaires

We do not attempt to discuss the rules governing the substantive content of questionnaires. Information on writing questions for questionnaires can be found in any textbook on methods of research in the social sciences. Rather, we will discuss techniques that simplify the use of computer analysis in survey research.

A.2a   *The Nature of Survey Instruments*

Survey instruments commonly contain both **statements** and **questions**. Let's begin by examining survey "statements." A researcher may be able to summarize an attitude in a fairly brief statement which s/he then presents to the respondents and asks whether they "agree" or "disagree" with it. Often the researcher will create a "Likert scale," a format in which respondents are asked to mark whether they "strongly agree," "agree," "are undecided," "disagree," or "strongly disagree" with the statement. For computer purposes, it is necessary to assign numbers as symbols for each response: for example, "5 = strongly agrees," "4 = agrees," "3 = undecided," "2 = disagrees," "1 = strongly disagrees." If the responses provided are "yes" and "no," one could assign "1 = yes" and "0 = no." The only caution required is that the researcher be consistent in his/her selection of numerical assignments. Later we will demonstrate how the construction of a codebook can provide the required consistency.

"Questions" in survey research present more complications than most statements. The researcher has two options in the realm of questions. S/he may ask "closed-ended" questions which provide the respondent with a list of answers from which to select his/her choice:

What were you doing last week?
□ keeping house
□ going to school

☐ on vacation
☐ retired
☐ disabled
☐ other _____

As with statements, the researcher can, again, assign numbers to the above choices to represent each response selection. However, the researcher may prefer to ask "open-ended" questions in which case the respondent is asked to provide his/her own answer to a question such as "What do you feel is the most important issue in the upcoming Presidential election?"

Here the researcher most likely has little idea of the answers likely to be given. Answers may be few in number, or they may be many in number. The researcher's best recourse is to assign a numerical code of at least two digits on the basis of a review of part or all of the collected data. Such responses can often be combined into a relatively small number of logical categories with the RECODE function, but this cannot usually be done before all the data have been collected.

In writing questions and statements, the researcher need not feel restricted to choosing items easily coded for computer analysis, but being aware of the techniques involved should prevent most nasty surprises after the data have been collected.

A.2b   Making the Responses Computer Readable

Ultimately, most survey data will be transformed into a machine readable form and entered into a computer system. For most purposes numerical data are easier to enter and more efficient to use than alphanumeric data (data which contain letters as well as or instead of numbers). Many variables are easily represented as numbers. Age is one obvious variable that needs no transformation. Sex, for example, can be coded as "1" for male and "2" for female. Most closed-ended questions can also be coded very easily as we have seen. Moreover, this process can be made even more efficient if the numbers to be assigned and the columns in which they are to be recorded are printed on the left-hand side of the items on the questionnaire. This is referred to as "pre-coding" and an example appears below:

(16-5)   14. How would you rate the physical appearance of your fiance(e)?
            ☐ very good looking
            ☐ good looking
            ☐ average looking
            ☐ plain looking
            ☐ very plain looking

The number "16" in parentheses directs the researcher to record this subject's response to question number 14 in column 16 of her/his data file. The "5" tells the researcher to record in column 16 of the data cards a "5" if the first response—"very good looking" was selected; a "4" if "good looking" was selected; a "3" if "average looking" was selected; etc.

While such pre-coding requires additional preparation time, it is of great help if very lengthy questionnaires are constructed and/or several individuals will be involved in the actual recording of the information.

A.3   The Codebook

A codebook is a device that describes the location of variables in the research data file. It also provides instructions for assigning values to the respondents' answers and statements. In addition to serving as a guide to the researchers as they prepare the responses for machine analysis, the codebook also serves as a guide to the location of variables during analysis of the data. Inspect Table A.1 to view a sample of a survey codebook.

Notice that in the example in Table A.1 the codebook is divided into three columns: these are labeled "Column," "Variable Name," and "Item Description." Let's begin by focusing on the meaning of the numbers

Table A.1   Sample Survey Codebook

Column	Variable Name	Item Description
1–3	ID	Respondent Identification Number
4	RECNO	Record Identification Number
5	SEX	Sex: 1 = Male
		2 = Female
		9 = No answer (missing value)
6–7	AGE	Actual age coded in years
		00 = No answer (missing value)
8	MARSTAT	Current marital status
		1 = Single, never married
		2 = Presently married
		3 = Widowed, divorced, or separated
		9 = No answer (missing value)
9	VAR01	What this country needs is a good nickel cigar.
		1 = strongly agree
		2 = agree
		3 = no opinion
		4 = disagree
		5 = strongly disagree
		9 = no answer (missing value)

listed in the first column (labeled "Column") in the table. Numbers in this first column are used to locate each variable on the data records. Also in this column we specify the number of columns assigned to each variable. For example, the first line (1–3) indicates that the first three positions (or Columns 1, 2, and 3) of the data record will contain the identification number of each questionnaire—001, 002, 003 . . . . 112 . . . . . N of respondents. Obviously, three columns are sufficient for up to 999 respondents. If one were to survey only 60 respondents as in the Leadership Data File (Chapter 5), then two digits would be sufficient for their identification numbers.

The second line under the first column in the sample codebook is a "4." Thus, whatever number appears in the fourth position or column on the data record specifies the record identification number for each line of data. Consider the following: for purposes of clarity it is usually desirable to restrict the length of data lines to about 80 columns (the length of the now-extinct IBM cards). If only 80 columns or less of information are to be collected for each respondent, then only one record ("card" in the old days) would be used per subject and this "record number" column would be unnecessary. If, however, 210 columns of information were collected for each subject, then three records would be required for each subject. That is, coding the information from each subject would then require three records (with 80 columns available on each) and column 4 would contain "1" for the first record of each subject (the first 80 columns of information); and "2" in column 4 of the second record (columns 81 through 160 of information); and "3" in column 4 of the third record (columns 161 through 210 of information).

As we continue down the first column of Table A.1, we see that the sixth and seventh columns of the data record will contain the age of the respondent, measured in years. It should be apparent that for samples of the total population of the United States the careful researcher should provide three columns for age. For most student surveys of college-age samples, two columns will be sufficient—there are few college-enrolled students over ninety-nine years of age!

Let's now turn our attention to the second major column of Table A.1—titled "Variable Name." If the researcher expects to use computer analysis, s/he is very likely to be restricted in the length and format of the names s/he can assign to the variables. With SPSS[x] for example, one can use no more than eight characters for a variable name, and no blank spaces can be included in the variable name. Therefore, the researcher might use "MARSTAT" as the variable name for marital status of the respondent, SES for socioeconomic status, etc. Some variables will be difficult to name and may be conveniently referred to as VAR02, VAR24, etc. It is likely that for these cases the researcher would need additional information about the coding procedures. Such additional information is provided in the third column of the sample codebook in Table A.1.

The third column—titled "Item Descriptions"—presents the questionnaire item and specifies the actual numerical values assigned to the responses for each question or statement. For example, the respondent's marital status is to be recorded as a number in column 8 of a record of the data file. The codebook informs the researcher to code all single respondents as "1," all married respondents as "2," and widowed respondents as "3." Notice also that for each variable the researcher has provided a numerical value for those cases in which a respondent failed to provide her/his choice. There is nothing magical about the number "9," but it is convenient to assign the same values for missing data wherever practical. If a researcher were to find missing values for age, s/he might encounter some confusion if "99" were used. A better choice is to use "00" as in the sample, since one is very unlikely to find a respondent with that actual age.

The codebook for each survey will be unique. Each researcher will provide more or less information than in the example in Table A.1. The actual form of the codebook is unimportant; what is important is (1) that the codebook specify enough columns to adequately code responses to each item and (2) that it provide sufficient information to assign a unique number to each possible response. Once the codebook is complete, the researcher is ready to consider the actual process of transferring collected data into a computer readable format.

A.4 Options for Data Processing

There are many data processing options now available to the researcher. Optical scanning has been available for some time and is an efficient technique for processing surveys consisting primarily of closed-ended items. There are also software programs that permit one to input data directly from the research instrument into SSPS[x] (or other software packages) formatted data files. However, probably the most commonly used technique is the transferring of coding assignments to a code sheet. Here, data from the questionnaires is transferred to code sheets similar to the one shown in Figure A.1 before being entered into the computer.

Data can fill all eighty columns of each line of the code sheet, and each line may be thought of as the equivalent of one record (or line) of data. The use of code sheets, while appearing to create an extra step in the research process, provides an easy way to follow an outline for entering the data either onto those ancient IBM cards or, more commonly, into an

Figure A-1   Sample Code Sheet Used to Facilitate Data Entry

STATEMENT NUMBER																																												
1	2	3	4	5	6	7	8	9	10	11	12	13	14	15	16	17	18	19	20	21	22	23	24	25	26	27	28	29	30	31	32	33	34	35	36	37	38	39	40	41	42	43	44	45

SPSS^x data file which follows the specifications listed in the DATA LIST statement. It is highly recommended that students follow this method in preparing their survey data for computer analysis.

A.5 "Cleaning" the Data

We must emphasize that the techniques for "cleaning" the data as discussed in this appendix are no substitute for care in the mechanical tasks of coding each questionnaire and entering the data into the computer. One of the best techniques to use at this stage is to have more than one trained assistant code the same data and verify that the data have been entered correctly. Assuming that due care has been exercised up to this point, you should proceed to make use of SPSS^x's ability to quickly scan the data.

Even the most highly skilled data-entry person is likely to make some mistakes. To be confident about the data analysis, one tries to eliminate as many of these errors as possible. Luckily some mistakes will be easy to detect and correct. The first step is to run a FREQUENCIES procedure for every variable in the file. While this may result in a lengthy output file and bring mumbles of disbelief from "computer jockeys," it is an excellent way to take a first look at the data (see Chapter 6). One of the things you want to look for is evidence of coding errors. For example, some mistakes will result in responses out of the range specified by the codebook (e.g., in the sample codebook discussed above, if "4" appeared in column 5 where only "1" (for male), "2" (for female), or "9" (for missing data) were expected, we have located a data entry error. Similarly, we might have also located two "7's" for the variable VAR01—where only "1" through "5" and "9" are expected values.

Other ways can be used to detect data entry errors. The researcher can use the LIST procedure to obtain a printout of any number of variables in the data file. Using a series of "SELECT IF" statements and the "LIST" procedure (refer to Chapter 7), one can let the computer do the "dirty work" and search through the file for the out-of-range values, and print them and the identification number of the subject (named "ID" in our sample codebook above) for which each was recorded. To do this one need only remove any existing procedures request (FREQUENCIES, CROSSTABS, etc.) and add the following several records (or lines) immediately after the "END DATA" line in the file. An example of how you might go about setting up such a program is listed below. Following END DATA, add:

```
TEMPORARY
SELECT IF (SEX EQ 4)
```

```
LIST VARIABLES= ID SEX
TEMPORARY
SELECT IF (VAR01 EQ 7)
LIST VARIABLES= ID VAR01
```

The output of this run will result in a *temporary* transformation of the data. By designating "temporary" in the run, we ensure that the SELECT IF statements are in effect only for the LIST VARIABLES operation shown above, i.e., no other data analysis or manipulation within this particular run will be affected by these particular SELECT IF statements. The above run will generate two separate lists, with each list providing the identification number of the subject and the out-of-range scores for the variables on the list request. To be specific, wherever SEX was given a value of "4," and wherever VAR01 was given a value of "7," will be listed in the output.

The next step in the process would be to examine the actual questionnaires for these subjects to verify the correct value. This correct value should then be inserted into the data file at the correct location. It is a good idea to carefully check the entire line in which an error has been located to determine that the error was an isolated one and not a case of missing a column or more of data—thereby creating a systematic error that could affect a large number of variables.

Unfortunately, not all types of errors can be located and corrected as conveniently as those representing out-of-range values. For example, it would be impossible to detect the case where a female respondent ("2" in our sample codebook above) had been entered instead as a male ("1"). However, if there were few out-of-range values in the data set, the researcher can be fairly confident about the overall quality of the data-entry process. If a large number of such errors were found, a systematic spot check of entered cases with the actual questionnaires should be conducted.

Once all known errors have been corrected, the researcher is ready to commence the actual data analysis with confidence. The analysis can become addictive, for it is here that the excitement of research is at its highest.

Exercises

Below is a sample survey questionnaire. It will be sent to 100 graduates of Millard Fillmore College. You are to construct a complete codebook for this questionnaire and illustrate how you would suggest pre-coding this questionnaire.

1. Year you graduated from Millard Fillmore College?
2. How many years did you attend Millard Filmore College?
3. What was your major?
   □ Business and Industrial Management
   □ Engineering
   □ Liberal Arts
   □ Music or Fine Arts
   □ Nursing
   □ Science
   □ Other
4. What is your present opinion of the education you received at Millard Fillmore College?
   □ Excellent
   □ Above average
   □ About average
   □ Below average
   □ Poor
5. What changes do you think should be made at Millard Fillmore College to improve the quality of education its students receive?

   _____

   _____

   _____

6. How much were your financial contributions to Millard Fillmore College during the last year?

Appendix B: Scale Construction with the SPSS^x Reliability Procedure

In this appendix we will discuss:

- how to construct a Likert scale
- scale construction and the Leadership Data File
- the SPSS^x RELIABILITY program
- the output from RELIABILITY

B.1 Introduction

Social scientists, particularly those engaged in attitudinal research, have found it necessary to develop composite measures of variables that are created by combining two or more empirical indicators into a single scale or index. These composite measures are useful when no single indicator adequately measures a complex variable, where the measurable range of variation in the variable needs to be increased, or where working with a single measure is more efficient than analyzing a number of empirical indicators separately.

We shall discuss the steps involved in constructing the most frequently used type of scale in social research—the Likert scale. In the process, we will demonstrate that the use of SPSS^x routines will greatly simplify the task of constructing adequate scales.

B.2 Constructing the Likert Scale

The Likert scale consists of a series of questionnaire items (usually statements rather than questions) with a uniformly scored set of fixed responses indicating differing degrees of agreement and disagreement with the statements. These responses may be as few in number as two (e.g., "agree" and "disagree") although five is the more common number of responses ("strongly agree", "agree", "undecided", "disagree", "strongly disagree"). Composite measures are created by adding together scores on the separate items that compose the scale. Before the composite measure is determined, however, the researcher must first select the items to be included in the composite, and the adequacy of the scale that is being constructed must be assessed. The SPSS^x subprogram RELIABILITY can greatly simplify this task.

B.2a   Steps in Constructing the Scale

The first step in constructing a Likert scale is to select items on the basis of their "face validity," i.e., all items should appear to measure the same attitude, belief, or action orientation. Furthermore, all items selected should have some range of variation although they need not all have the same range (i.e., each item must have a non-zero standard deviation and ideally all items should have nearly equal standard deviation scores). Use of the five common categories adds considerably to the probability of obtaining an adequate range of variation.

These selected items must then be administered to a sample of respondents (ideally this would be a "pre-test," but in some survey research it is necessary to submit these items to the actual research sample and refine the scales after the data are collected). For reliable pre-testing, there should be a ratio of at least five (and preferably ten) subjects to each item in the scales being tested.

The second step can occur only after the scale has been administered to a number of subjects. This step requires the researcher to examine the correlations between each of the items. If the correlation between one item and many others in the scale is nearly zero, it is an indication that this item is not measuring the same thing as most of the others and should be deleted from the scale. Likewise, if two items are perfectly correlated (r nearly equals $+1.00$), one of them should be deleted as it is redundant and is adding no information to the scale. A negative correlation between one item and many others suggest that the scoring of that item needs to be reversed (this could be accomplished using the RECODE procedure discussed in Chapter 7).

The third step is to analyze the correlations of each item with the total scale score in which that item is included (this is accomplished by reviewing the "Item-Total correlation," which is typically provided in the printout from computerized scale construction). Any items whose correlation with the total scale score is less than 0.20 should be eliminated, although exceptions can be made if the number of items in a scale is very large—approaching 80.

The final step is to compute a reliability coefficient for the scale. While there are many estimates of reliability, the one that should be obtained first, and is sufficient in most cases, is the "Coefficient Alpha." Coefficient Alpha is a statistic based on the internal consistency of the scale, but it also includes a number of other sources of error that are reflected in the sampling of content. After the first three steps outlined above have been completed, Coefficient Alpha (or simply Alpha) can be computed as an estimate for the "cleaned" scale. The minimum Alpha for an acceptable scale is 0.70.

Fortunately, the SPSS^x program RELIABILITY makes the construction of acceptable Likert scales a simple task; but it must be realized that the entire process of scale construction is ultimately dependent upon the researcher's initial selection of items. You cannot take short cuts during the selection process. It should include careful review of the literature, search for preexisting scales, and consultation with other, perhaps more experienced researchers.

B.3   Scale Construction and the Leadership Data File

Although there is no critical need to construct individual scales on the data collected for the project at E-Z Manufacturing, an instance does arise in which scale construction could have led to a savings in the time and energy for both the employees at E-Z and researchers who are conducting the project. Recall that we have collected data on each subject's responses to the Bem Sex Role Inventory (BSRI). The score for the BSRI was calculated by adding the responses to sixty individual items, each of which was scored from a "1" to a "7". Rather than using all 60 items, it would have been far more efficient to select only a handful of BSRI items and determine if they constituted a simpler, yet adequately reliable, measure of sex role identity. If so, the need to collect responses to all 60 items would be eliminated.

Let's assume that we decide to see if we could construct a reliable "mini-BSRI" from six items chosen from the original survey instrument. We ask forty employees to complete our six item test. Once we have the responses of these forty employees on these six items, we can proceed with the next steps involved in scale construction (discussed in Section B.2a): inter-item correlation, comparison of each item with the total scale score, and determination of the reliability coefficient. These steps, however, may be accomplished using a program such as the RELIABIL-ITY procedure available on SPSS[x].

B.4   Using the SPSS[x] Program RELIABILITY for Likert Scale Construction

The RELIABILITY program is designed specifically for scale construction in social science research. This program is very versatile in that it can be adapted to situations involving a variety of assumptions about the data, and for this reason, the program can be rather complex. However, we will limit our application to a simple example involving the data collected at E-Z Manufacturing; and from this, you should obtain an idea as to how the program can be used.

In essence, the RELIABILITY program carries out three of the four steps discussed above in the construction of Likert scales. It computes correlations among potential items for inclusion in the composite measure, it enables a comparison of each item with a total scale score, and it computes reliability coefficients. A brief description of the records required to run the RELIABILITY program are given in the ensuing paragraphs.

B.4a   *The RELIABILITY Statement*

The RELIABILITY record calls up the program necessary for scale construction. The specification field of this record contains several subcommands, and as noted previously, each of these must be separated with a "/". The first of these is the "VARIABLES=" subcommand, where all the variables or items that are likely to be considered for the Likert scale are listed. Each variable so listed must, of course, have been previously defined in the DATA LIST statement or by COMPUTE, RECODE, or IF statements. In our example of creating a "mini-BSRI," the variables listed after the VARIABLES= subcommand would include at least the six items (to which we have assigned variable names) selected from the BSRI, since it is from these items that we are constructing our new composite measure (mini-BSRI). For example:

```
RELIABILITY   VARIABLES = ITEM1   ITEM2   ITEM3   ITEM4
           ITEM5   ITEM6
```

The "SCALE=" subcommand, separated from the "VARIABLES=" subcommand by a slash, instructs SPSS[x] to construct the particular scale that is to be tested. Here we list the variables to be included in the scale that we are interested in constructing. Although in our example on the mini-BSRI we would use *all* six items in our SCALE subcommand, it is not always necessary to use all the variables in the "VARIABLES=" list. One may choose to work with subgroups of variables so as to construct several different possible scales which are made up of a slightly different group of items. Also note that it is not necessary to list each variable by name if we intend to use an inclusive list; rather we could simply indicate the first and last variables in the list, joined by the keyword TO. For example, we could set up our statement as follows:

```
RELIABILITY   VARIABLES= ITEM1 TO ITEM6/
SCALE (MINIBSRI)= ITEM1 TO ITEM6
```

Note that within parentheses, after the subcommand SCALE and before the "=", the author may, at her/his discretion, insert a name for the scale being tested for reliability. However, this name is only used to identify this one set of items on the printed output. The name is not automatically entered into the file's variable list, and therefore, it cannot yet be used to represent a composite score made up of the individual scores from the six items of the BSRI. This task can be achieved later with the use of a COMPUTE statement (as is discussed in Section B.7).

B.4b   The STATISTICS Record

RELIABILITY automatically calculates and displays Alpha, the reliability coefficient. By including the STATISTICS record, one can obtain a great deal of other statistical information for the scale that has been created. These include such numbers as the item means and standard deviations, scale means, inter-item correlations, and item total statistics, to name a few.

B.5   A Sample RELIABILITY Program for Likert Scale Construction

Below is an example of how the RELIABILITY program would be set up to construct a scale (which we call MINIBSRI) from six items selected from the BSRI. Several important points need to be made. The program listed below could not be used in conjunction with the Leadership Data File. Remember, in that data file we entered a single score that represented all sixty items from the BSRI; we did not enter the responses to each individual item, and therefore, those items do not exist as variables in the Leadership Data File. In other words, the BSRI score entered for each subject in the Leadership Data File already represents a composite score.

Our task in the example presented here is to analyze some of the items that were used in determining that composite score; therefore we would first have to create a data file comprised of individual responses to six items drawn from the BSRI. For the sake of ease, let's assume that we create such a data file. The complete SPSS^x program might appear as:

```
DATA LIST   RECORDS=1/1 ITEM1 1   ITEM2 2   ITEM3 3   ITEM4 4
   ITEM5 5   ITEM6 6
RELIABILITY   VARIABLES=ITEM1 TO ITEM6/
   SCALE (MINIBSRI) = ITEM1 TO ITEM6
STATISTICS   ALL
BEGIN DATA

data records

END DATA
```

B.6   Explanation of RELIABILITY Output

Table B.1 contains a sample output from the above RELIABILITY procedure in which we determined reliability coefficients from six items selected from the BSRI. You might note that in the above run the OPTIONS record has been omitted. As a result, the subprogram is directed to use the default options—it will use the covariance matrix method, assume raw data input rather than matrix input, use listwise deletion of missing data, and print out extended variable labels where present. This set of default options represents the most common mode for student research.

B.6a   *Descriptive Statistics*

Reading the output follows the logical pattern initially outlined in Section B.2a. First, take a brief look at the descriptive statistics that are provided by the RELIABILITY program. Normally, all standard deviations should be of approximately the same magnitude. Any variables with unusually small standard deviations should be recorded and deleted from the scale before its final application. For the six items included in our analysis, all have standard deviations on the order of 2.0, so based upon this criterion all six may remain in the analysis.

B.6b   *Intercorrelations*

The next important information is contained in the "Correlation Matrix." All intercorrelations between the variables to be included in the scale are computed. One needs to look at entire rows (and columns) to determine if any item is consistently uncorrelated with the others (i.e., a row of "r" values equaling around 0.00). If such an item is found, it should be noted as one that must be eliminated from the scale. If any row (or column) is found to contain all negative "r" values, the scores for that item should be reversed with a RECODE statement. Again, the researcher must make note of this information for subsequent computer runs. Finally, any extremely large correlation coefficients (any with values approaching 1.00) suggest that one of the variables in the pair should be eliminated as it is redundant and contributing nothing to the scale.

The printout in Table B.1 reveals that ITEM6 is correlated only weakly with the other items, and therefore is a candidate for omission from the scale. However, there are no negatively related items, and there are none which approach perfect correlations, so the remaining five items appear to be potential variables for inclusion in our scale.

B.6c   Item-Total Statistics

The next step is to inspect the ITEM-TOTAL STATISTICS in order to assess the extent to which each item is related to the total score on the scale. As before, any negative correlations suggest a need to reverse the scale for that particular item with the RECODE statement. Any item-total correlations of less than 0.20 call for eliminating that item or variable from the final scale. In Table B.1, ITEM6 is just below the 0.20 limit at 0.1941, so once again, we might seriously consider dropping this item from the scale. Furthermore, the last column of the ITEM-TOTAL STA-TISTICS (with the heading "ALPHA IF ITEM DELETED") indicates that the scale would be much more reliable if this item were deleted.

B.6d   The Reliability Coefficients

Here the Alpha coefficient for the items included in the run is presented. If it is at least 0.70, the scale is acceptable and may be used in subsequent data analyses with other variables in the file. If the coefficient of reliability (Alpha) is below 0.70, or if the researcher has noted items with very small standard deviations, negative inter-item or item-total correlations, then the RELIABILITY program should be run again with any suspicious items deleted. Note that our sample program in Table B.1 has produced an Alpha of 0.8337 for the six-item scale drawn from the BSRI, and therefore, we have an acceptable scale. Yet we also know from the "Item-Total Statistics" that the Alpha would improve to 0.8811 *if ITEM6 were removed from the scale.* Thus, the best strategy would be to eliminate this item from the final scale.

Table B.1   Sample Output from RELIABILITY Run

R E L I A B I L I T Y   A N A L Y S I S – S C A L E (M I N I B R S I)

1. ITEM1
2. ITEM2
3. ITEM3
4. ITEM4
5. ITEM5
6. ITEM6

	MEAN	STD DEV	CASES
1. ITEM1	3.2000	2.1862	40.0
2. ITEM2	3.6000	2.2509	40.0
3. ITEM3	4.1000	1.9189	40.0
4. ITEM4	3.5000	1.5525	40.0
5. ITEM5	4.3000	1.7276	40.0
6. ITEM6	3.7500	1.8640	40.0

COVARIANCE MATRIX

	ITEM1	ITEM2	ITEM3	ITEM4	ITEM5	ITEM6
ITEM1	4.7795					
ITEM2	3.9795	5.0667				
ITEM3	2.2872	2.1436	3.6821			
ITEM4	1.8462	2.5641	2.1538	2.4103		
ITEM5	1.8872	2.2769	1.5590	1.8974	2.9846	
ITEM6	.1538	.6667	.3846	.6410	1.0513	3.4744

CORRELATION MATRIX

	ITEM1	ITEM2	ITEM3	ITEM4	ITEM5	ITEM6
ITEM1	1.0000					
ITEM2	.8087	1.0000				

ITEM3	.5452	.4963	1.0000			
ITEM4	.5439	.7337	.7230	1.0000		
ITEM5	.4997	.5855	.4703	.7074	1.0000	
ITEM6	.0378	.1589	.1075	.2215	.3265	1.0000

OF CASES =   40.0

STATISTICS FOR SCALE	MEAN	VARIANCE	STD DEV	# OF VARIABLES
	22.4500	73.3821	8.5663	6

	MEAN	MINIMUM	MAXIMUM	RANGE	MAX/MIN	VARIANCE
ITEM MEANS	3.7417	3.2000	4.3000	1.1000	1.3437	.1624
ITEM VARIANCES	3.7329	2.4103	5.0667	2.6564	2.1021	1.0506
INTER-ITEM COVARIANCES	1.6995	.1538	3.9795	3.8256	25.8667	.9565
INTER-ITEM CORRELATIONS	.4644	.0378	.8087	.7709	21.4199	.0571

ITEM-TOTAL STATISTICS

	SCALE MEAN IF ITEM DELETED	SCALE VARIANCE IF ITEM DELETED	CORRECTED ITEM-TOTAL CORRELATION	SQUARED MULTIPLE CORRELATION	ALPHA IF ITEM DELETED
ITEM1	19.2500	48.2949	.6683	.7470	.7940
ITEM2	18.8500	45.0538	.7698	.8132	.7692
ITEM3	18.3500	52.6436	.6125	.6322	.8056
ITEM4	18.9500	52.7667	.8071	.8114	.7765
ITEM5	18.1500	53.0538	.6891	.5662	.7926
ITEM6	18.7000	64.1128	.1941	.1382	.8811

continued

Table B.1   *Continued*

R E L I A B I L I T Y   A N A L Y S I S   –   S C A L E   (M I N I B R S I)

ANALYSIS OF VARIANCE

SOURCE OF VARIATION	SUM OF SQ.	DF	MEAN SQUARE	F	PROB.
BETWEEN PEOPLE	476.9833	39	12.2303		
WITHIN PEOPLE	429.0000	200	2.1450		
BETWEEN MEASURES	32.4833	5	6.4967	3.1949	.0085
RESIDUAL	396.5167	195	2.0334		
NONADDITIVITY	3.4621	1	3.4621	1.7088	.1927
BALANCE	393.0546	194	2.0261		
TOTAL	905.9833	239	3.7907		

GRAND MEAN = 3.7417
TUKEY ESTIMATE OF POWER TO WHICH OBSERVATIONS
MUST BE RAISED TO ACHIEVE ADDITIVITY   =   1.8665

HOTELLINGS T-SQUARED =   48.7722   F =   8.7540   PROB. =   .0000
DEGREES OF FREEDOM: NUMERATOR =   5   DENOMINATOR =   35

RELIABILITY COEFFICIENTS   6 ITEMS

ALPHA =   .8337   STANDARDIZED ITEM ALPHA =   .8388

Typically, a researcher will run through the above process several times, shortening the scale with each run. When the number of items remaining is ten or less, the most efficient course of action is to scan the column headed "ALPHA IF ITEM DELETED." This column will indicate what effect eliminating each item would have on the reliability coefficient of the scale. Of course, there is a rapidly reached point of no return such that the coefficient of reliability may begin to decrease simply because of the decreasing number of items. Usually, the "cleaning" of scales may be stopped when an Alpha of at least 0.70 is reached. If it is not obtained, then the scale should not be used.

B.7   Making the Composite Score a Part of the Data File

Once the scale has attained an acceptable level of reliability, the researcher may use the COMPUTE program to actually create a new variable based upon the composite score of the items in the scale. This new variable may then be used for further data analysis. In the example given above, we found it helpful to eliminate ITEM6 so as to achieve the high Alpha level of 0.8811. Operating on this procedure, we could compute a new variable which represents the sum of the five items from the BSRI. We could create this variable (which we might call MINIBSRI) by including a COMPUTE statement in our run, as shown below:

```
DATA LIST    RECORDS=1/1    ITEM1 1    ITEM2 2. . . .
COMPUTE    MINIBSRI=SUM(ITEM1, ITEM2, ITEM3, ITEM4, ITEM5)
FREQUENCIES    VARIABLES=MINIBSRI/FORMAT=ONEPAGE/
    STATISTIC=ALL
```

By inserting the COMPUTE record after the DATA LIST statement, we have now created a new variable which is based upon the sum of each individual's responses to five BSRI items. This new variable, designated MINIBSRI in the COMPUTE statement, is added to the data file and is subject to all the rules applying to variables in the SPSS* software system. An appropriate strategy would include obtaining a frequency distribution and descriptive statistics on this new variable, as we have done by inserting the FREQUENCIES statement in the above example.

Exercises in Scale Construction with SPSS*

1. Data (1=agrees; 0=disagrees) on ten variables have been collected from 25 respondents and are presented below:

Respondent	V1	V2	V3	V4	V5	V6	V7	V8	V9	V10
1	1	1	0	0	1	1	0	1	1	0
2	1	1	0	0	0	1	0	0	0	0
3	1	1	1	1	1	1	1	1	0	1
4	0	0	1	1	1	0	0	1	0	0
5	0	1	1	1	1	0	1	0	0	0
6	1	0	0	0	0	0	0	0	0	0
7	1	1	1	1	1	0	1	1	0	0
8	1	0	0	1	1	1	1	0	0	0
9	1	0	0	1	0	0	0	0	0	0
10	1	1	1	1	1	1	1	1	1	1
11	1	1	0	1	1	0	0	1	0	1
12	1	1	1	1	1	1	0	0	1	1
13	0	0	0	0	0	0	0	0	0	0
14	1	0	1	1	0	1	1	1	0	1
15	1	1	1	1	1	1	1	1	1	0
16	1	1	1	1	0	1	0	1	0	1
17	1	1	1	1	1	0	0	0	0	0
18	1	1	0	0	0	1	1	0	0	0
19	1	1	0	0	0	0	0	0	1	0
20	0	1	0	0	0	0	0	0	0	0
21	1	1	1	1	0	1	1	0	1	0
22	1	1	1	1	0	1	0	0	0	0
23	0	1	1	0	0	0	0	0	0	0
24	1	1	1	0	0	1	0	0	1	1
25	0	0	1	1	0	0	1	0	0	1

   a. Run the RELIABILITY program to determine whether these ten items constitute an adequate Likert scale. Using the information from the output (including the overall coefficient of reliability), decide if any items should be deleted.

   b. From the information obtained from above, recode these Likert scale scores into three categories—low, medium, and high—so there are approximately equal number of respondents in each category. This process will require creating a new variable with RECODE, COMPUTE, or IF statements (hint: review Chapter 7, Section 2).

2. In an attempt to find a less complex way to measure sex role orientation, researchers at the E-Z Manufacturing Company have selected a sample of forty respondents and given them a shortened version of the Bem Sex Role Inventory. This version consists of only six items. Below are the values for these six variables. Construct an SPSS^x file and use the RELIABILITY procedure to see if these six items constitute an adequate scale. Is there anything further you could do to improve this six-item scale?

Respondent	Item 1	Item 2	Item 3	Item 4	Item 5	Item 6
1	6	3	6	5	6	1
2	1	2	3	4	5	6
3	7	7	5	4	6	5
4	2	4	3	4	4	5
5	1	1	1	1	2	2
6	5	7	7	6	5	4
7	3	5	5	5	5	2
8	2	2	4	2	2	6
9	1	1	5	2	4	3
10	5	5	2	3	7	6
11	6	5	4	3	2	1
12	1	2	3	4	5	6
13	7	7	5	4	6	5
14	2	4	3	4	4	5
15	1	1	1	1	2	2
16	3	5	5	5	7	2
17	5	7	7	6	5	4
18	1	1	5	2	4	3
19	1	1	1	1	1	1
20	4	2	7	4	4	6
21	6	3	6	5	6	1
22	1	2	3	4	5	6
23	7	7	5	4	6	5
24	2	4	3	4	4	5
25	1	1	1	1	2	2
26	5	7	7	6	5	4
27	3	5	5	5	5	2
28	2	2	4	2	2	6
29	1	1	5	2	4	3
30	5	5	2	3	7	6
31	6	5	4	3	2	1
32	1	2	3	4	5	6
33	7	6	5	4	6	5
34	2	4	3	4	4	5
35	1	1	1	1	2	2
36	5	7	7	6	5	4
37	3	5	5	5	7	2
38	1	1	5	2	4	3
39	1	1	1	1	1	1
40	4	2	7	4	4	6

Index